CONTENTS

PREFACE

The emergence of post-structuralism and postmodernism within social theory has challenged many of the fundamentals of modernist social science. The emphasis which these approaches place on language, firstly as the unavoidable mediator between an object of study and a description of that object, and secondly as something which is profoundly unstable, marks the broadest of these challenges – to the possibility that sociology and the other human sciences might achieve rational knowledge of the world.

I became interested in what this might mean for the efforts which sociology has made to involve itself with issues arising from health and healing. Over the past three decades, the alliance between sociology and health professions has been remarkably successful, and, as I shall suggest in this book, has led to the construction of an entirely new model of medical practice – the so-called 'biopsychosocial' model, which has benefited both medicine and social theory in different ways.

While the 'big' challenge of postmodernism is undoubtedly central to the future of this relationship, it is often in the less dramatic consequences of this challenge that some of the most interesting new possibilities for a social theory of health derive. This book is devoted to exploring some of these new readings of health and illness. For example, postmodern positions are well known for 'decentring the subject': refusing to accept a human subject as interior, an 'essence' of a human, and replacing this idea of subjectivity with one fabricated by knowledge, expertise and power, including the professional knowledge of medicine. What does that mean for the experience of pain and suffering, apparently the most personal of experiences? What does it mean to be the subject of 'care'?

Although I decided eventually to make the phrase 'the politics of health-talk' the slogan for what I wrote, I was also attracted to the idea of 'a politics of care', because this latter phrase has (at least) a double association.

Firstly, it places 'care' at the centre of the discussions which arise from the postmodern social theory of health, and which suggest that care is to be read as a political process: that is, one concerned with power and with the achievement of power through expertise. Two versions of care will emerge in this book – a modern form which I see as negative, concerned with control and possession of its subject, and a positive generosity, which enables its subject to cast off its very subjectivity, to become something else.

The second association is with an ethical-political engagement with practice which takes a responsibility to be 'caring' in one's engagement as an ethical principle for action, over and above a responsibility for action *per se* (the 'disinterested' practice which flows from modernist 'explanations' of the world). I do not have room in this preface to explain in any detail what this means for the ethics and politics of postmodern social theory. The argument is addressed in the final part of the book in terms of a notion of 'grieving delight', which draws together both a celebration of difference (in place of sameness or identity) and a shared sorrow in human finitude. I see the necessity of an *ethical* engagement as one of the positive benefits of the reflexivity which postmodern positions force upon social theory. I hope this will help to challenge a commonly held position that postmodernism is ethically and politically unengaged, although at the same time demonstrating that this engagement is far from straightforward.

One of the buzz-words of postmodernism is 'intertextuality', by which is meant the play of one text on another. Every reading is a new writing, and every writing entails new readings. Writing this book has involved me in many readings of other authors, some from post-structuralism, some from modernist social science, some from social theory, others from philosophy and literary criticism. In this mass of texts I have found some positions which I had not expected, and recognized some difficulties which previously I had glossed over. The three-way dialogue between my themes (postmodernism, sociology and health) has hopefully thrown out perspectives which will enhance all three: that, at least, is the intention. In places I am very conscious that my reading merely scratches the surface of difficult issues, and that my reading is only one among many that may be made in the future. But this is not a book in which to explore the minute detail of the philosophical developments in postmodernism: there are other books which do that already, and probably much more successfully than anything I could produce. For this reason, I have generally kept to the major texts of the post-structuralist canon, rather than delving into the more obscure material which the specialist reader can pursue elsewhere.

Although the discussions in this book concentrate upon health-related topics, I hope that the exploration of some positions, and in particular the examination of the possibility of resistance to discourse through intertextual practice, and my efforts to explore Deleuze and Guattari's model of desire and the Body-without-Organs, will interest social theorists not directly concerned with health and care. The examples which I have drawn upon freely throughout are almost all concerned with health and welfare, and these will, I hope, situate the abstractions for those specifically concerned with this field. Others can skim these if they wish. That, as Barthes said, is the pleasure of the text!

While many people have unknowingly influenced what I have written (and many of these might be quite horrified to realize the consequences of their influence), some deserve particular mention. Helen Nicholson was a continual supporter and supplied my original introduction to literary criticism and post-structuralism. Jane Naish first made me aware of postmodernism as pertinent to social theory. Gillie Bolton and Phil Levy made helpful comments on parts of the manuscript. Wendy Stainton Rogers's comments on the original proposal had a crucial influence upon the final theoretical positon which I think she will recognize. My thanks to all those who have heard and made suggestions on parts of the book at various conferences and seminars. Jacinta Evans, Joan Malherbe and Frances White at the Open University Press, and Richard Baggaley who has now moved on, have been very supportive of the project, and I am grateful to them for their encouragement and efficiency. Finally, to friends, colleagues and students who had to put up with me while I wrote this, thanks.

LIST OF ABBREVIATIONS

BwO	Body-without-Organs
CC	community care
CHD	coronary heart disease
FPS	feminist post-structuralism
HCS	health-care system
NHS	National Health Service
PSTH	postmodern social theory of health
SHH	sociology of health and healing
SP	strong programme in the sociology of science

1

INTRODUCTION

On my bookshelf I can see a novel – *Foucault's Pendulum* by Umberto Eco (1988). The title refers not to the philosopher Michel Foucault (who will feature in the coming pages), but to an earlier bearer of the name, an Enlightenment physicist, the inventor of the pendulum with which he demonstrated the rotation of the Earth.

In Eco's fiction, the protagonists – three publishers, Casaubon, Belbo and Diotallevi – become intrigued by the genre of conspiracy theory which dominated the 1970s and 1980s, the esoterica which drew together myths of Atlantis, early Christianity, dope cultures, the French and American revolutions, Nazism, Masonry, and so on, to constitute 'explanations' of history which apparently provide a way of 'understanding' some grand movement which has been hidden by those 'behind' the plot. The publishers set out to devise just such a plan, using random associations generated by computer – on the basis that the more unlikely the connections made, the more convincing the plot which ensues. They achieve their objective, beyond their wildest dreams, inasmuch as they fabricate so compelling, so inclusive and so promising a plan (one which explains 600 years of history, and offers the power of the philosopher's stone as its reward), that their fabrication is taken to be true by an esoteric group constituted and hierarchically sustained by a shared commitment to a conspiracy-theory explanation of history. One publisher suffers a grisly death, suspended by his neck from Foucault's Pendulum, because he is unable (unwilling) to disclose the ultimate secret he is thought to possess.

My reading of this tale is that knowledge is powerful in ways which may not be immediately obvious to those who fabricate it, that knowledge which 'explains' reality is dangerous, and must be treated with caution, lest it overwhelms those who create it, and those who are its subject.

But in particular, and this is the reason I start this book with Eco's story, I also take the fiction to be a salutary lesson for those in the social sciences whose analytical objectives have been the development of explanatory 'grand designs'. In particular, I read the 'plan' as an allegory for the grand designs which structuralist perspectives have constituted. Seeking structures and systems, strategies and grand narratives, structuralism has fabricated the world, to the extent that it *is* the world. If only the jigsaw can be constructed from the pieces of data strewn about, structuralism argues, we can have the big picture. Once we have the big picture, we can control it, change it, we will be empowered.

These kinds of ideas, of course, pervade not just the human sciences, but the natural sciences as well. As I write, we have been told that cosmologists have solved the mysteries of the universe, and it is now empirically proven that time started with a big bang. No doubt this fabrication of nature will continue to be espoused until some other scientist comes up with some new answer. I am fairly agnostic about the rightness or wrongness of such theories, and am hardly qualified to make any assessment. In the human sciences, theorizing can have a more direct impact on people's lives. The subjects of the 'human sciences', unlike atoms, can read the texts which claim to explain the structures by which our lives are organized. Football hooligans have read the sociological accounts of their activities which have explained that life on the terraces is not anarchic, but highly structured as part of a 'sub-culture' with rules and roles as rigid as those of 'respectable' groups (Marsh 1981). Working-class mothers learn that they smoke cigarettes not as a consequence of socialization, or of self-destructiveness (two prior 'explanations'), but because it provides the only part of their lives over which they have control.

Sociology is not the only discipline which can be criticized for this tendency: psychology and most notably anthropology can both be implicated. And, of course, the humanities – history, philosophy and literary criticism – have been at the core of generating a reflexive culture in the modern era. The impact of the human sciences in fabricating modernity was explored by the other, more recent Foucault (1970) in *The Order of Things*.

This broad canvas of the critique of modernism provides the backcloth for a more modest picture, concerned with the impact of the grand designs of sociology, in particular in relation to health and illness. With Eco as my inspiration, I would show how sociology, a discipline created and developed in the era of modernity, has fabricated – alongside other disciplines which it has often criticized for the same tendency – modern understandings of health, disease, illness and healing. Regardless of its direct impact on popular notions of these entities, it has generated a wealth of discourse which can be reread by those who would speak authoritatively about health and illness.

Is this anything more than an interesting academic critique, to be read as a useful caution for those who are doing the sociology of health and illness? It is the intention of this book to suggest that this argument goes beyond academicism, to touch upon the concern which motivates many who work in this field of social science: the suffering of the sick, and the protection of those who like themselves possess vulnerable human bodies.

Firstly, were I to fabricate my own grand design, I would echo Susan Sontag (1978): why cannot *illness be just illness*? By this, Sontag means, do not encircle illness with metaphors, things which make it something other than what it 'really' is. Cancer, AIDS and other diseases are transformed in discourse, from biological patternings of DNA, protein, and so on, affecting other patternings which we call our bodies, into deviations with cultural significances. AIDS is a 'plague', cancer an 'enemy' to be battled against.

Who are the authors of these discourses? To take AIDS as an example, one obvious grouping that has caused the infection and resultant syndrome to be metaphorically transformed is the popular press and media. Ann Karpf (1988: 143) reports a typical media reconstitution, in a newspaper headline and story describing the 'gay plague' and its effects on 'terrified citizens', and the vocabulary used in the media to describe the AIDS 'attack' on people 'under threat'. To what extent such reporting generates the metaphors, or whether the media are merely reiterating ideas already in the population, is an issue researched by public health and media specialists (Meyer 1990; Wallack 1990). Clearly, however, lay representations of disease utilize such metaphors, in an attempt to explain or constrain what is perceived as a deviation, a challenge or source of uncertainty in the environment. The sociology of health has volumes of such lay perceptions in its archives. Examples from a collection edited by Caroline Currer and Margaret Stacey (1986) include an exploration of the models of colds and fevers held by British people, complete with concepts of aetiology, course and treatment (Helman 1986). Herzlich and Pierret (1986) conclude that diseases are poorly grasped by medical ideas of contagion, and are conceptualized as within the body, integral with the sense of self. For another review, see Calnan 1987; Kleinman's book, *The Illness Narratives* (1988), will be discussed further in Chapter 5.

The absence of congruence between lay and medical definitions of disease has also been a favourite topic of the sociology of health. Hannay's (1980) discovery of an 'iceberg' of symptoms going untreated in the community, and a related mass of 'trivia' presented to family doctors by patients, provided a quantitative estimate of this discrepancy, while Strong's (1978) study of paediatric clinics, the explorations of 'meetings between experts' (Tuckett *et al.* 1985), the differing perspectives on the consultation among family doctors and their opiate-abusing patients (McKeganey 1989) and those with Parkinson's disease (Pinder 1992), and Kleinman's (1980) theoretical exposition of explanatory models have contributed to a corpus which has perceived professional and lay models of disease as equally valid, situated and 'rational' discourses. Calnan's (1987: 7) study of lay perspectives on health ratifies this 'pluralism' of approaches, granting medical and lay theories as of equal status in understanding the world. Stacey (1986: 9–11) tells us that:

> for purposes of investigation I take all value, belief and knowledge systems to be of equal importance and validity; initially they should be judged on their own terms and within their own logic ... all concepts of health and illness, like all healing systems, are social constructions which relate to their historically specific time or period. Powerful and pervasive systems such as biomedicine I include in this just as much as more fragmentary and localised ones.

This position has led to strong condemnation of medical and professional discourses as uncaring, stigmatizing, disempowering or individualizing. The ethnographic excerpt of a male doctor querying a female patient's statement concerning the sex of her two children has become a classic example of disempowerment (Graham and Oakley 1986). In a study of patients with chronic renal failure, Waissman (1990: 448) concluded: 'The choices about where to conduct dialysis were mainly determined by the doctor's criteria – even if they were not always meaningful to the families – and their *opinions* about the families' (emphasis added). In other words (and this extract follows a long review of the social processes involved in agreeing home dialysis), the professional discourse is not value-free scientific reasoning, but prejudiced and socially constructed.

Despite this relativizing of biomedicine into just another discourse, the sociology of health has also been inclined to a distinction between discourses (predominantly biomedical) which concern themselves with 'disease', and others – lay or non-medical – which speak of 'illness'. This dichotomy was elaborated by Frankenberg (1980) so that disease is defined through physiology, while illness is subjective or experiential, and 'sickness' is the social response which surrounds disease and illness. Sickness is consequently the realm within which the sociological holds sway, able to generate its concepts of a sick role, stigma, moral panics, and so on.

However, a simple equation of lay discourse with 'the social' cannot go unchallenged. Fisher's (1991) study of doctor and nurse-practitioner interactions with female patients demonstrates how 'the social' is a discourse also available to professionals, and may be used to disempower alongside biomedical discourse. The production of the arena of 'the social' supplies additional ways of categorizing, and does not necessarily lead to a 'patient-centred' discourse.

> While there is little doubt that the language of medicine has entered our accounts of ourselves, in both ... consultations, a social/cultural discourse about women, work and the nuclear family interrupts and interpenetrates a presumable medical discourse. In one case the doctor incorporates the talk into his diagnosis and recommendation

without either providing a space for the patient to speak about her life, or inciting her to do so. In the other case, the nurse practitioner encourages/incites the patient to speak about the social (Fisher 1991: 176).

Fisher's study offers an appropriate return to the main thrust of my commentary upon Sontag's plea, with the assertion that, in addition to the medical and lay discourses whose interactions have provided so much material for modernist sociologists of health, sociology has *itself* contributed to making disease more than *just* disease. While it has reflected upon constitutions of diseases in popular media or medical discourse, it has failed to recognize that it has itself meanwhile fabricated discourses which (while being explicitly or implicitly claimed to be somehow 'better' than biomedical discourse or lay prejudice) still contributes to making disease a culturally defined phenomenon. Later in this book I will reflect upon the widespread co-opting of sociological-sounding theorizing into medical discourse, and the generation of the 'biopsychosocial' model (Engel 1977). Once again using the example of HIV/AIDS, consider a recent sociological discourse setting out a model of 'epidemic psychology'

when a disease is new and there are no routine collective ways of handling it, a thousand different converts may spring up drawn from every part of society, each possibly with their own plan of action, their own strategy for containing and controlling the disease (Strong 1990: 254).

From a phenomenological perspective, the author argues that diseases act not only in biology but also in language, creating a severe challenge to social order. Later he suggests:

Fatal epidemics have the potential . . . to create a medical version of the Hobbesian nightmare: the war of all against all. Moreover, not only does contagious disease strike directly at the microprocesses through which society is constructed, but the human possession of language means that the fear of such disease can be rapidly, even instantly transmitted (as through television) across millions of people and from one society to another (1990: 258).

The use of the metaphoric in this article, and its general tone of doom – 'the assault on public order is in part moulded by the other ravages made by the epidemic' (1990: 249); 'epidemic psychology is unusual, powerful and extremely disturbing' (1990: 255) – generates a new, sociological, version of HIV/AIDS, questionably less coloured than the 'gay plague' tag.

My point is that sociology cannot claim to be whiter than white when it comes to explanation. As Dingwall (1976) points out, science, magic, religions and politics are all folk systems for explaining the world, but so too is sociology. While generally professing to be on the side of rationality, empowerment, democracy, and so on, sociology still fabricates a reality, and when it comes to issues so close to pain and suffering, life and death, when it concerns itself with health and illness, sociology must accept that it is treading a very difficult line indeed. The critic of this position might reply that this is a trivial argument: we all know that reality is socially constructed. However, sociology has developed tools which provide it with resources to protect it from generating false pictures of reality. Furthermore, most sociology of health and illness discourse is dedicated to mitigating the worst excesses of a non-social biomedical discourse; and this will mean that it is unlikely to be causing more harm than good.

Throughout this book I shall devote space to examining these kinds of argument, and shall challenge the modernist claims of sociology to progress, rationality and truth. This, however, is not intended as a nihilist project, but as part of a formulation of an entirely different position from the modernist sociology of health and healing (SHH), a postmodern position. Despite the criticism of Strong's vocabulary above, I actually share (although from a different perspective) his view of the importance of language in constituting the world. The reason for a postmodern social theory of health (PSTH) derives from the conclusion that, in spite of Sontag's aspiration, illness cannot be *just* illness, for the simple reason that human culture is constituted in language, that there is *nothing knowable outside language*, and that health and illness, being things which fundamentally concern humans, and hence need to be 'explained', enter into language and are constituted in language, regardless of whether or not they have some independent reality in nature. What the PSTH does is to start from this position, and having done so, takes as its subject not 'health' or 'illness' but the *politics of health-talk or illness-talk*. I will explore the implications of this movement later in this introductory chapter, but before that I need to consider briefly the fundamentals of the opposition modern–postmodern, which I have already used too freely without proper examination.

Modernism and postmodernism

Fortunately, there are now a number of texts available which both provide a secondary literature on the theorists of post-structuralism and post-modernism, and consider in some detail the implications of the postmodern position for social research. While in no sense providing an uncontested programme for postmodern social theory (could there be such a thing anyway?) these texts supply a far more substantial discussion than could ever be offered here. I shall therefore confine myself to a fairly brief outline of a number of central features of the postmodern positioning. For those readers who feel they need further background, Sarup (1988) offers a helpful comparison of modernism and postmodernism, while an excellent introduction to Foucault and Derrida is available in Boyne (1992). Moi (1985) and Hutcheon (1989) are both accessible discussions, while for a complex and stimulating exploration of postmodernism and sociology, Game's (1991) book is recommended. Various discourses on postmodernism and the social sciences, positive and negative, which might be referred to include Bauman (1988), Kellner (1988), Flax (1990), Lemert (1992) and Rosenau (1992).

In this book, *modernity* is taken to refer to the historical period which is supposed to have begun in the West with the 'Age of Enlightenment' towards the end of the eighteenth century, with the secularization of societies and the rise of scientific and philosophical rationalism (Giddens 1987). Foucault (1970) identifies this period with birth of the modern scientific disciplines of labour, life and language (economics, biology and philology) and the human 'sciences' which built on them (sociology, psychology and the study of literature and myth). In my reading, modernity and modernism are thought of as coinciding with philosophical commitments, to 'truth', 'rationality' and rationalization, 'progress', with the belief that scientific analysis is the means by which the world will come to be known, and with 'humanism' – the centring of the human subject as the wellspring of knowledge and good. Derrida does not identify a distinct 'modern' era (Silverman 1987), merely a change in the foundation for 'truth' from predominantly religious to predominantly secular and humanistic discourse.

For some writers, including Baudrillard and Lyotard, we have now entered into an era of postmodernity, where these values have been subverted in philosophy and in art and culture. Reality has been replaced with simulation, rationality by multivocality, monolithic organization by fragmentation, theory by play. In this book I am less concerned with such a *periodization* (which, as Kumar (1978) has written, is remarkably difficult to evaluate when one is still within the period one is trying to analyse), than with some of these subversions of the 'modern way of doing things' as applied to social theory. I shall not be writing a 'sociology of postmodernity' or a sociology of health in the postmodern era, but a postmodern social theory of health and illness.

For a position which values fragmentation, openness, multivocality, there is clearly an attraction in a fairly eclectic approach, and indeed 'postmodernism' is, by its very nature, impossible to delimit and define. But lest this indeterminancy leads to undue confusion, I shall set out at this stage two elements of the post-structuralist critique which I shall use throughout this book, deriving from the work of Jacques Derrida. They are directly related, and I think show the extent to which the postmodern position on health which I wish to develop makes a distinct break with modernist sociological perspectives. The first element concerns Derrida's analysis of *différance* (for detailed analyses, see Boyne 1992; Lemert 1992). Briefly, *différance* concerns the fundamental *undecidability* which resides in language and its continual *deferral* of meaning, the slippage of meaning which occurs as soon as one tries to pin a concept down. *Différance* is unavoidable once one enters into a language or other symbolic mode of representation, in which signifiers can refer not to referents (the 'underlying reality'), but only to other signifiers. While trying to represent the real, one finds that the meaning which one is trying to communicate slips from one's grasp. We are left not with the reality, but with an approximation which, however much we try to make it 'more real', is always already deferred and irrecoverable.

This theory of *différance* builds on the discovery in semiotic theory that language constitutes meanings not in terms of the *essence* of a thing but in its *difference* from other things (Lemert 1992). Derrida argues that the recognition of *différance* forces us to abandon any essentialism or foundationalism in our search for the real, to see instead the movements of difference which constitute the world. This subversion of essentialism takes us to the second element which I wish to examine: *logocentrism*.

Logocentrism (for Derrida) is the claim to be able to achieve the *logos*, an *unmediated* knowledge of the world; a claim, which in Derrida's (1976) view, has informed philosophy since Socrates, and is a theme replicated in the variety of discourses which have sought to explain the world, be they philosophical, religious or scientific. 'Presence' – this unmediated knowledge – is an indicator of authenticity, of experience of reality, of – simply put – being able to speak 'the truth' about something or other. This idea of 'presence' will crop up throughout this book.

In scientific discourse, logocentrism inheres in the claim that scientific method makes reality accessible, without the intervention of any mediating process which might distort our perception. Natural science fought its battles to claim *presence* in the classical era, against a rival theological logocentrism, a struggle which continues in the debates between science and fundamentalist religions today. With the Enlightenment, humans became an object of study in the empirical sciences of economics, biology and linguistics, and in the human and social sciences (Foucault 1970; Hamilton 1992). To put it another way, since then, empirical and human sciences have been able to legitimate (although not uncontestably) their claims to presence.

Part of this claim within the human sciences has been mediated through debates on methodology. For sociology, the decline of positivism has meant a crisis of confidence in its claims to presence (Gouldner 1970). In terms of the critique of logocentrism, the rival attractions of Marxist sociology grounded in realism, of structuralism, with its model of the human mind as structured according to rules, and of phenomenology, which offers a rationale for intersubjectivity, can all be understood as consisting in their (partial) ability to offer a logic for a claim to presence. In all but the most deterministic theory, despite its focus upon 'the social', modernist sociology places the human being centre-stage as the constructor of 'the social': through her thought able to rationalize and take control of the world around her. This logocentrism offers an attractive but spurious validity to sociological knowledge: it is the product of the reflexivity of the human mind, therefore it must be true.

So the critique of logocentrism opens up a new focus for a postmodern social theory; precisely an interest in *how claims to presence are constituted in discourse*. It rejects the possibility – epitomized by modernist obsessions with representation (Hutcheon 1989; Flax 1990) – of a transparent mediation of knowledge of the world by the human observer. With regard to a PSTH, this is important for two reasons. Firstly, the postmodern position on health asks some questions which focus upon the creation of knowledgeability about illness and health. How do discourses on health and illness, be they medical, lay or from other groupings, claim authenticity, how do they claim authority, and how is it that we are willing to accept their 'knowledge' of the character of health and illness?

It would be wrong to claim that a PSTH breaks entirely new ground in asking such questions. In the UK, medical sociology has been strongly influenced by ethnomethodological perspectives (Atkinson and Heath 1976; Dingwall 1976; Silverman and Perakyla 1990), which focused on the ways actors in medical settings routinely achieved certain outcomes. To take an example: Bloor's (1977) study identified various strategies adopted in a medical clinic by doctors to exclude parents from decisions over the treatment of their children, such as the use of technical information or language to support the doctor's case. These artful practices were understood as constitutive of the interactions and their outcomes (doctors usually get their way, parents usually don't).

What enhances the postmodern position is the theorizing of the character of authority as relating to both power (ability to claim presence) and knowledge (the presence which is claimed), and this adds a new incisiveness to studies in SHH which took ethnomethodological approaches to the exploration of health settings. With the understanding of the mutually constitutive character of knowledge and power provided by the postmodern position, such strategies gain new significance. In the Bloor study above, one might wish to explore the limits to these claims to knowledgeability, for example the use of a technical exclusionary language as opposed to the validation of the 'scientific' character of tests. One might explore the possibilities of resistance by parents based on rival claims to truth about their children based in turn on a discourse on parenthood. The importance of rival 'stories' is taken up in discussions of 'intertextuality' in Part 2 of this book.

The second reason why the critique of logocentrism is a focus concerns the paradox that, if it is the case that discourses on health are constituted around claims to knowledgeability, the same also applies to sociological texts, including of course, this one. The postmodern position requires sociology to be reflexive about its own production as a discipline claiming knowledge of the social. These claims to authenticity are complex, and are grounded in the millions of words which have been written upon sociological

method since the discipline began. Statistical analysis and the method of
the survey make claims on the basis of empiricism and an approximation
to natural scientific methods. In Britain, a tradition within the SHH of
ethnographic as opposed to survey methodology might be understood as
a claim to authenticity grounded in 'telling it like it was'. The techniques
of ethnography have been subjected to a devastating analysis by Atkinson
(1990), who has demonstrated how they constitute a discourse on its
object, which, by the use of stylistic and rhetorical devices, makes claims
of presence as to the reality it is describing. For example, Tyler (1986)
documents how the crisis of ethnographic description in anthropology
forced a reappraisal of the methodology as inherently ethnocentric and
damaging to the subject-matter of which it would speak: sociology has as
yet failed to follow suit. For the postmodernist, the sociology of representation is replaced with the representation of sociology.

So logocentrism, in this perspective, pervades all those discourses, be
they political texts, professional codes or systems of thought, biographical
or autobiographical accounts, or fashion notes: in short, any textual construction which seeks to persuade or denote knowledge, 'the truth', reality
or authentic experience or feelings. In the era of modernity, the urge to
represent has become so obsessional (Finlay 1989) that rival claims to
presence, and the methodology for valid presence, have become commodified. Information, and information goods, have become the most
valuable commodities (Douglas and Isherwood 1979) as we seek to know
the world a little better than those with whom we compete. The human
sciences have become popularized, and are extremely popular as subjects
in higher education, offering the promise to 'know oneself' and to know
the social world.

With the claim to presence, or unmediated knowledgeability, as the
sustaining movement within modern social theory, it is possible to situate
a number of other 'centrisms' constitutive of logocentrism (Silverman 1987:
281, 286). These, and the modernist and postmodern readings, are sum-
marized in Table 1. The postmodern project is to deconstruct these
'centrisms', to show how they constitute 'reality' and, importantly, the
distortions they create in the process. For the PSTH, deconstruction of
these 'centrisms' has practical implications for the project of reformulating
the sociological study of health.

Phonocentrism: we would wish to examine critically any claims of
authenticity or authority deriving from a 'speaking subject'. Biographical
approaches which claim to present 'real' patients' or professionals'
thoughts or feelings are to be treated with extreme caution, as are
reports which use extracts of talk to 'prove' structural schemata generated to explain the patterning of health settings.

Egocentrism: we would be suspicious of discourses which constitute
essentialist human actors, or privilege an immanent or prior human

Table 1 Logocentrism and its related 'centrisms'

Centrism	Modern reading	Postmodern response
Logocentrism	Authority grounded in access to knowledge of reality.	Knowledge is an effect of power, and constituted in language not in access to reality.
Phonocentrism	Privileging of authorial voice, speaking 'from the heart'.	Speech is not privileged over writing; both show the traces of their production as means of persuasion.
Ethnocentrism	Knowledge is transcultural and transhistorical.	Knowledge is only applicable in context. Valucs and commitments should be exposed.
Phallocentrism	Privileging of the masculine voice, possession and dominance.	Masculine values have been privileged in claiming knowledgeability.
Egocentrism	Privileging the human subject as prior, an essence, foundation or point of reference.	Subjectivity is fabricated through the accretion of acts of power. The human subject is a modernist concept.

subjectivity as the foundation for claims to presence. This would include discourses which distinguish a particular variety of experience, for example based upon being female or of a particular ethnic origin.

Ethnocentrism: claims to provide a transcultural or transhistorical explanation would be treated with caution. Discourses would be assumed to be quite local to a situation (for a discussion, see Gubrium 1989).

Phallocentrism: an emphasis on possessing or having control of knowledge or power, of the value of active or competitive transformation of the environment as opposed to a co-operative position, of the conscious over the unconscious, of sublimation over desire, of being over becoming, would all be questioned.

The body: biological or social?

I said earlier that the postmodern interest in logocentrism and its sub-'centrisms' in the SHH lies in identifying the distortions of health and illness which arise in discourse, be it lay, professional or sociological. This should not, of course, be taken as implying that there can be some way of being 'distortion-free' (presumably through my new improved postmodern discourse). That would be merely to constitute another version of the 'let illness be just illness' paradox, and indeed can also be seen as a classic example of a claim to presence. What I intend is to indicate that, while there can be no knowledge beyond discourse, nothing outside the text, no discourse can avoid implication in the process of constituting authority, a claim to be able to speak authentically about the world, a claim which can be contested, and should be contested. The significance of this with regard to health should be obvious: if one is constituting relations involving the human body, its continuity or impairment, distortions resulting from discursive strategies of claiming truth are extremely important, particularly if it is your body which is being constituted. This critique, when applied to women's bodies, is, of course, already well developed (Ehrenreich and English 1979; Oakley 1980; Dworkin 1981; Gallop 1982; Hanmer 1990).

Everything which has been said so far concerning logocentrism and the claim to presence applies equally to all sociological discourse. However, some topics in sociology face an added complication inasmuch as they address directly a subject-matter which inheres in both domains which have been constituted in the modern era as the 'social' and the 'natural'. I wish to look now, in some detail, at the distortions in the SHH arising from its particular subject-area. I have suggested elsewhere that sociology has difficulties with topics which are overly 'natural' – for example, 'the environment' (Fox 1991b) – and that this is because sociology as a discipline became possible through a privileging of cultural over natural explanations. The sociology of health is another obvious example, given that the object at the centre of its discourses – although surprisingly absent in many accounts (Turner 1987) – the human body, is similarly both 'natural' and 'cultural'. Recently, principally as a consequence of the growing influence of Michel Foucault (or at least of the 'sociological Foucault'), Bryan Turner (1984; 1992) has sought to remind the SHH of the body. So far this project has not really moved beyond the Foucauldian insight that the body is a site for the exercise of power. In my own view this enterprise requires a far wider theoretical input from post-structuralism, and indeed this book is an effort to provide such an input.

There is perhaps no more dramatic an illustration of the contested and problematic character of the human body than that to be found in the opening pages of Foucault's *Birth of the Clinic* (1976: ix–xii), in which are described the great changes between the mid-eighteenth and mid-nineteenth centuries in what could be seen by those who explored the interior of the human body (also discussed in Armstrong 1983). Something which at any one point in history has been constituted (by a 'gaze' of power), might seem quite different at another time, even when the observers came from the same discipline. Over this same time period, medicine, as informed by a new empirical biology, was rivalled as the only legitimate discipline to study the human body by the 'human sciences'. The rise of psychology, anthropology and sociology offered different ways of describing the body and its functions.

Just as it is possible to conduct a genealogy of medical discourses on the body, so the same may be done for human science discourses, and one of the things this book tries to do is examine the representation in 'the social' of health and illness. For now, I want to focus on one aspect of that genealogy: the constitution in sociological discourse of 'the natural', and in particular how the sociology of health has constituted the 'natural body'. The intention is to demonstrate the peculiar distortions into which sociological discourse forces its subject, when it seeks to articulate with the 'natural', and to substantiate in this way the need for a PSTH reflexive about the problems of representation generated in a modernist arrticulation with health. I would suggest that we can discern five distinct ways in which the sociology of health has dealt with nature, each entailing a distortion which serves to constitute its own claim to authority as a discipline with something valid to say.

Outright rejection of natural influences

The first position might be regarded as the least sophisticated, or the most radical, depending on one's point of view. The classic example is the debate over intelligence and the IQ test which is supposed to measure this biological individual difference (for a flavour of the debate, see Eysenck and Kamin 1981), and became most heated when racial difference was implicated in intelligence. In response to the proposals that phenotypical differences were manifestations of genetic difference, it was argued that the differences reflected cultural bias in the instruments, and that the suggested biological differences were artefacts of measurement.

In support of this rival hypothesis, the roots of the eugenics movement and statistical analysis have been discredited as based upon prejudice and vested interests (Manier 1980). The methodology of experiments which claim to demonstrate genetic differences are subjected to exhaustive analysis to disclose social or cultural explanations (Kamin 1981).

Introducing its own terms for biological factors – gender in place of sex, ethnicity in place of race – helped sociology construct an alternative, social, discursive framework for exploring differences. Thus the sociology of gender demonstrated how the gendering of discourse rather than any biological difference led to an ideological privileging of male biology and the exploitation of women in human societies. Marxism claimed that humanity should be defined not by biological difference, but by its unique ability to produce the means of subsistence (Seidman 1992: 57).

In this perspective, the natural is simply *denied* to ensure the ascendancy of the social/political position.

Nature is important only in manifesting culture

This perspective encompasses a number of differing approaches, depending upon the theoretical framework adopted. Drawing upon anthropological and structuralist approaches, the dichotomization of culture/nature is identified as fundamental to other cultures (Levi-Strauss 1963; Bloor 1976), and aspects of Western culture, for instance concepts of infection (Fox 1988). Food, gardening, hair and sexual organs are used in various cultures to represent something more than aspects of the natural: they are texts, tropes for the social relations pertaining within that group (Douglas 1970). For a medical example, see Katz's (1984) discussion of the symbolic significances of blood and other body fluids in the operating room.

Approaches which recognize that there *is* a nature, but that what is interesting about it is the way that culture uses it to create social relations, are well represented in the SHH. Here, nature is conceptualized as basically ineffectual and able to be bracketed out of the equation. Hence food taboos are seen as a consequence of cultural systems whereby nature is classified, rather than being explicatory of any 'real' danger associated with the foods themselves (Douglas 1984). Durkheim's claim that variations in suicide rates were due to social rather than biological explanations undercut biologism (Benton 1991: 12), yet this analysis depends on the ideological belief that different nationalities and groups were not more or less prone to suicide as a consequence of biological or genetic differences, or for that matter something affecting the physical body in the environment – an invisible, odourless but dangerous gas such as radon, for example. Baszanger (1992) examined the treatment of chronic pain at two clinics. Within an interactionist perspective, her finding that the 'deciphering' of patients' pain differed between the two clinics was not put down to any underlying biological difference in the pain suffered (after all 'pain is a private sensation' (1992: 181)), but rather down to the fact that

> physicians are constructing chronic pain as an original medical entity that opens up a new field of clinical practice, which in turn, justifies the entity's existence . . . Crucial to this debate is the question of how to draw up an authoritative definition of chronic pain for delimiting the specialty and organizing practice (1992: 182).

Progress has subjected nature to human mastery

Unlike the previous discourse, the third way of speaking about nature in the sociology of health recognizes that natural factors can have an effect upon the human body. However, the natural world is reconstituted as a consequence of human activity. This discourse is fundamental to the critique of capitalism as the cause of morbidity and mortality. Pollution, road traffic accidents, industrial diseases, despite being physical causes of physical illnesses, are regarded as having an importance primarily as implicating industrialism or capitalism in human suffering. For example, Paul (1978: 274) writes that:

Recent US-sponsored wars, counter-revolutions and pacification programs have spread death and havoc ... Widespread hunger and starvation have resulted from the operations of American agribusiness, which removes land from local food production ... Famines now sweeping Africa and Asia are largely due to this diversion of local resources and the accompanying soil-depletion of one crop farming ... Clearly imperialism is not a healthful social arrangement.

On the other hand, this position can be used to demonstrate human ingenuity – for example in conquering famine, infertility or infectious diseases. The biological processes involved are downgraded, with the sociological issues becoming the important aspects of the technological change. For example, reproductive technology has been subjected to scrutiny as having profound social and ethical implications (Strickler 1992).

In this perspective nature does change, but the important thing is not in the physical world, but in the social relations of human activity, and it is upon these relations that attention is to be focused. Human bodies are reconstituted within sociological discourses of place and community, organized according to sociological principles. The metanarrative of sociology shapes the natural body in its own image, representing it as no longer 'natural' at all!

The impossibility of knowing the world

A somewhat different discourse is grounded in the philosophical debate which arose in modern social theory over what really is 'out there', in that tricky region beyond culture, and, more importantly, how precisely we might gain knowledge of it. Drawing on debates in the sociology of science (Bloor 1976; Laudan 1977; Collins 1981), some studies in the sociology of health and illness have articulated a 'strong programme', which equates 'incorrect' knowledge and 'science' as similarly ideological. Scientific theorizing is shown to be a social process, consequent upon interests or non-scientific beliefs: which, of course, are amenable only to sociological exploration. Foucault (1970: 345–6) commented upon the perpetual controversy between the sciences and the human sciences in the era of modernity, the latter constantly claiming to be the foundation of the former, the former continually having to justify their methods and history in the face of 'psychologism' and 'sociologism'.

To take a recent example from the SHH, Nicolson and McLaughlin (1988) examined rival theories of the causes of multiple sclerosis (MS). One group of scientists interpreted evidence as supportive of an etiology due to failure of the microcirculation of blood in the nervous system. This opposed the received knowledge that the nervous deterioration in MS was due to an autoimmune response. Nicolson and McLaughlin (1988: 246) chart the course of the debate in the medical journals, finding that the controversy cannot be resolved on rational grounds, but reflects 'competition between a large and powerful social group and a weak and marginal one'. Orthodoxy is a powerful weapon against any innovative theory; scientific knowledge is subjected to a calculation in a social and professional rather than a scientific arena (1988: 248–9, 257). They conclude that extra-scientific factors such as prestige, power, authority and rivalry demonstrate medical research to be a *human activity* (1988: 254), and that 'in principle, the form of analysis presented here ought to be applicable not only to the specific details of individual theories but to the totality of modern medical knowledge' (1988: 253).

While sharing the position that science as knowledge is fabricated rather than discovered, the postmodern critique of logocentrism forces us to see a discontinuity in this discourse. Somehow, sociology's analysis of the historical or social factors are the only ones to be free of their own social determination; we are supposed to believe that the sociological analysis is 'methodologically sound' (1988: 255). In retaining its own claim to (social) scientific status, the strong programme fails to subject its own discourse to the analysis which it demands of other sciences, to acknowledge that its own truth-claims are representations constituted – in the case of sociology – by a privileging of the social, and the denial of the natural.

(Despite the sophistication of the argument in Nicolson and McLaughlin's discourse, their difficulty lies in a wish to be both realist and relativist: is there a reality or isn't there? They see their relativizing of scientific knowledge as methodological. The trouble is that the process is not neutral, it generates a sociological representation of their subject (scientific discourses) which enables the social to be privileged at the expense of the natural. One cannot then simply pretend this rewriting has not happened, and claim that one has elucidated the underlying 'reality'. The 'strong programme' became the subject of a debate in papers by Bury (1986), Nicolson and McLaughlin (1987) and Bury (1987). Unfortunately, a failure to distinguish adequately between the differing concerns of the sociology of knowledge theorists and post-structuralism mars the discussion. For a more informed analysis as relating to health and illness, see Bartley (1990), and see also the discussion in Chapter 7 of the present volume.)

Romanticism in medical sociological discourse

It is a characteristic of the human body that its physical form changes – it grows and it senesces, it is attacked by other organisms, and may or may not come off the best. It interacts with the rest of the natural world, and is damaged by it both acutely and chronically. It eventually disintegrates and is gone for ever. In focusing upon the processes of degeneration associated with health/illness, the specialty articulates with a nature which is changing, unstable and ephemeral. Much of the application of sociological theory in this area has concerned the transitory nature of the underlying body. For example, studies of old people, those with different abilities or with chronic or non-reversible impairments have shown that the stigma associated with their deviances derives from a 'premature social death' (Bellaby 1988), a mismatch of their situation with notions of what it is to be human (Goffman 1970), or the inappropriateness of their dependency at an early stage in the 'natural' life course (de Swaan 1990). Analysis depends upon recognizing the discontinuity between the natural and the ascription of social attributes. Another example is the sociological analysis of medical uncertainty. The sociological task is to identify how, for instance, uncertain prognoses of malignant tumours in the natural body are regularized by social definitions and social practice by doctors and epidemiologists.

In such studies, to ignore or to bracket as a social epiphenomenon the reality of variability and unpredictability of natural outcomes would be a nonsense; it is precisely this variability – and the social responses to it – which is the topic. Nor would it be appropriate to adopt a sociology of knowledge approach, given the sub-text in many SHH studies of some possibility of practical intervention. Sometimes, in these circumstances, a romanticist discourse may be identified.

Romanticism is best known in 'fictional' texts, but may be identified as a theme in philosophical writings in which humans are seen as possessing some essential character (Letwin 1987), and even in the *Communist Manifesto* (Eagleton 1983) in which humanity is perceived as debased by social forms which deny it its 'true' character of Reason and of Grace. In sociology it offers a model for a discourse in which the underlying nature is not something to be bracketed as unchanging, but a variable which is unstable and liable to affect social processes, and be affected by them. By exposing these social forms, there is the possibility for humanity to achieve some better state of being. This theme may be discerned in sociological texts which point up explicitly or implicitly the righteousness, rationality or the inherent 'goodness' of the debased or downtrodden (for discussions, see Silverman 1989; Strong and Dingwall 1989).

The patient is a typically romantic subject, vulnerable, ground down by inhuman forces and sometimes equally inhuman institutions, and a representative for us all. Nature, in the twin forms of disease and the finite life span of the individual, is an adversary to be fought and kept at bay (Bertholet 1991: 392). Bureaucratic and authoritarian regimes put these victims at double disadvantage (Gerson 1976; Davis and Horobin 1977). The criticism sometimes levelled at medical sociologists – that they have lost their critical separateness from the medics and scientists they should be studying – fails to recognize fully the romantic character of much of the writing generated by the specialty. The narrative form, which in the form of the ethnographic account is often used in SHH writing, is peculiarly suited to romanticism (Brooks 1984). Sometimes in SHH accounts the romanticism is ascribed to the subject's own perspective, and one is left unclear whether the author actually shares it. So, for example, in the

Graham and Oakley (1986) study of obstetric encounters, mothers' views of childbirth are described as deriving from 'life', 'biography', 'knowledge of the body and its sensations'. Although it remains unclear whether the authors see these as legitimate claims for authenticity, one is left in little doubt as to which side of the obstetrician–mother interaction they favour.

In Pinder's (1992: 13) study of Parkinson's disease patients, she writes that:

> For most patients in the study, diagnosis not only marked a significant turning point in their lives. It was also often a life crisis ... Nothing could ever be quite the same again ... it marked a transition from a past that might have been perceived as 'normal' to a future over which there now hung an ominous shadow.

Concerning one patient:

> Both Mr D's mother and grandmother had had PD, yet his own identity was suddenly transformed by the news. He had, all of a sudden, become a 'Shaky Bill' ... He was experiencing what it was like at first hand. Acquaintance was raw (1992: 14).

Summing up her findings, Pinder (1992: 19) concludes that 'patients found their lives splintered in a thousand pieces'. This imagery is powerful, and the romantic perspective contributes a lot to the story. We can see clearly the essentialism of the account, and (referring back to the discussion earlier in this chapter) the implicit egocentrism by which subjectivity is conceived as prior and privileged. The 'romantic subject' may be enticing, a way of imagining one is sharing the suffering while still doing 'sociology', yet it is only a representation, and a distorted one at that.

The objective of this discussion of the sociology of health's discourses on 'the natural' has been to show how in each case the outcome is a reduction of nature to caricature. The last of the five strategies is particularly interesting in that what is distorted is the modernist social scientific model of the rational human actor itself. Where the natural cannot be bracketed or reduced to the social, the romantic subject supplies an essentialist *rapprochement*. Essentialism, of course, is just the kind of sleight of hand that the postmodernist will pounce upon (Flax 1990: 37).

The politics of health-talk

This introductory chapter has dwelt at some length upon the problems which the postmodern critique identifies in a modernist project for a sociology of health and healing. This has been necessary to situate the perspective which is to be developed in this book, to demonstrate the need for a PSTH and to counterpose the positions which are to be developed to the modernist SHH. It is probably already clear to the reader that I have two separate, though related objectives in writing this text. The first is to develop a distinct postmodern perspective on health. The second is to supply a critique of the modernist position. To attempt to set out any kind of a programme for a postmodern enterprise is distinctly questionable, given the kinds of commitment to open-endedness, difference and fragmentation which postmodern writers espouse (Baudrillard 1988: 185; Hutcheon 1989). The perspective which I shall develop in the coming pages can be neatly expressed, all the same, in the phrase *the politics of health-talk*. This phrase, adapted from Nancy Fraser's (1989) discussion of the politics of needs-talk, implies an interest in discourse and its consequences for power, control and knowledgeability. The following are themes within this interest:

1 A concern to explore discourse and discursive formations in terms not of the grand designs which they are supposed to constitute (in modern social theory), but with the 'small designs': the movements of difference and deferral which enable them to serve their authors. Exploration of these small designs involves the activity of *deconstruction.*
2 A concern with the constitution of subjectivity through discourse, knowledge and power. In place of the unitary, prior, essential subject, there is a fragmented subject, constituted in difference. Power is evaluated not as a negative constrained action, but as a positive, constitutive activity, contested and resisted.
3 A scepticism about the commonsensical notions of social structuring, organization and continuity of the world.
4 A concern with the repressed and the unconscious, and with the relationship between desire and discourse.
5 A concern with intertextuality (the 'play of texts' upon each other), and a reflexiveness over the production of my own text.

I will now briefly outline the form which the coming chapters will take. The greater part of the book is devoted to developing a PSTH around the themes of the politics of health-talk. In the final two chapters, which are less discursive and more programmatic, I will address the differing perspectives of the modernist SHH and the PSTH in terms of ethics, politics and engagement with health care. My two objectives, as I have said, are intertwining, and in this opening chapter I have already become involved in a dialogue, generating the postmodern position and critiquing its modernist counterpart. This dialogue will continue to play a part in the body of the text, particularly where I utilize studies written in a modernist vein to develop the postmodern position, rereading material in the new perspective.

I have already touched on the supression of the human body in much of modernist SHH, and the first part of the book (Chapters 2 and 3) explores a postmodern theorization of embodiment, looking first at the work of Foucault and his followers in developing the study of the disciplining of the body through techniques of power/knowledge. Foucault's notion of surveillance of bodies and conception of desire in the work of Deleuze and Guattari are brought together to explore the 'writing of the body': the inscription of bodies in discourses on beauty, gesture, fashion, fitness, pathology, culture, and so on. The body, it is suggested, has become – along with its 'health' or 'illness' – a text, to be read, written and rewritten by 'body-experts', be they doctors, beauticians, sports instructors or lovers.

Chapter 3 concerns itself with the writing of healthy and sick bodies in the rationalist discourses of the organization of health and health care. The reader is introduced in this chapter to the postmodern theory of organization. This position rejects structuralist sociologies of 'organizations', seeing these as consequences of the search for system, rather than reflections of real entities. The review of the postmodern position is set out through the use of a case study – of a hospital ward round – to show how organization is a discursive strategy, developed in response to challenges to power interests. Organization favours those who are empowered, but power is never absolutely held – it is constantly the object of resistance. Two new directions are developed. First the potential for deconstruction theory to explore these discourses, to demonstrate their commitments, and hence to offer the possibility of emancipation. Second, the implication of the modernist SHH in organizing health and health care.

Part 2 (Chapters 4 and 5) introduces the counterpoint to the earlier discussion of inscription. Now the interest is with *resistance* to discourse. This theme, which subsequently sets the tone of the book, is addressed through the conscious–unconscious, rational–irrational oppositions in modernist sociology, and in particular the character of *desire*.

Notions of health, in both modernist medical and sociological discourses, have largely ignored or denied any role for desire, its repression and the consequences of repression. Where it has been used, psychoanalytic theories have argued the importance of unconscious symbolic representations, for example in motivating the Parsonian sick role. I subject this theorizing of health care to a critical reading, taking a perspective on desire as a positive investment rather than a lack, deriving from the writing of Deleuze and Guattari. Trust, responsibility, vulnerability and guilt are topics opened up in this reading, which explores the sick role and care as repetitions of familial relations.

In Chapter 5, I continue this discussion, introducing the idea of a 'Gift of care' deriving from the writing of feminist post-structuralism. But the chapter also marks a turn back to Derridean ideas of *différance* and of intertextuality. From these positions I attempt a reading on the politics of resistance, and show how this can be applied in care settings.

In Part 3 (Chapters 6 and 7) I address the practical politics and ethics of a postmodern social theory of health. I seek to show that, contrary to positions which argue that postmodernism is apolitical or reactionary, modernism's claims to be progressive are deeply flawed. Postmodernity implies a 'responsibility to otherness', and while this raises difficulties for a straightforward engagement with the world, an ethics and politics of action can be developed which addresses the delight in difference and a certain grieving mood towards human finitude. The last chapter looks at a few specific positions where there is a marked divergence between modern and postmodern perspectives.

PART 1

POWER AND INSCRIPTION

What does it mean to inscribe a body? Postmodernism has replaced the modernist conception of a body, possessed of an interiority containing a mind or a soul – the motivating force of agency – and an exterior upon which the mind or soul forges a public face. It has replaced it with the idea of a surface, without depth. Subjectivity is no longer understood as a phenomenon of the essential, interior self, but as an *effect* of power which has been inscribed upon this surface (Butler 1990: 139).

Chapter 2 examines this perspective in detail, looking at this so-called *decentring of the human subject*. The objective is to explore what it means to inscribe a body with power, how that power is mediated in discourses of expertise, and what it might mean to inscribe 'health' and 'illness' on the body. I hope that, as this book continues, the alternative 'postmodern self' will emerge as an alternative to the Cartesian self which has been at the root of modernist social science.

In Chapter 3, the concern is with the postmodern perspectives on organization. Health care often gives the impression of being oddly unsuited organizationally to its enterprise. Vulnerable sick humans are drawn into monolithic organizational arrangements by which they are to be cured or cared for. Why should this be, and what is the impact of organization upon the inscription of health and illness? The chapter addresses the possibilities of resisting organization, exploring a number of case studies of health-care settings.

The gaze

In the conception of the 'gaze of power', Foucault provided post-structuralism with a fundamental position concerning the way that power is to be conceptualized. In making a connection between knowledge and power,

Foucault broke with the position which – deriving from Marxism – viewed power as unitary, imposed from above, and manipulated through a state apparatus of coercion mingled with practices of ideological legitimation, including democratic government and an emphasis on individual choice and freedom.

The gaze (which, as its name implies, entails the making visible of a person or a population) is a technology of power, by which the object of the gaze becomes known to the observer. This knowledge, codified and organized, becomes a resource by which the observer develops both an expertise, and a control over those s/he observes. Foucault suggested that – in relation to medicine – the knowledge of the medical profession about the human body, about illness and its prevalence in a population, supplies the basis for medical dominance. Those who have identified the source of this power in the trappings of a high-status group, have mistaken the epiphenomena of power for the means of gaining and sustaining that power, which rests in the knowledge which has been accrued and which is legitimized in every interaction between patient and health 'professional'. Medicine stands alongside education, the law and penology, psychiatry and social work, as one of the *disciplines* of the modern era, both a realm of expertise and a way of literally disciplining the bodies of those who are the subjects of these experts (Foucault 1976; 1979; 1980; 1984).

The Body-without-Organs (BwO)

The notion of a body which is not the anatomical body of medical discourse, but a Body-without-Organs, derives from the writing of post-structuralists Deleuze and Guattari (1984; 1988). It is a central idea in this book, and will be explored at length in Chapter 4, although it is first mentioned at the end of the next chapter.

The BwO is a political surface, upon which are inscribed the discourses which have just been mentioned in connection with the gaze of power. A person's BwO is *territorialized* by these discourses of knowledge – which may derive not only from expertise, but also from lovers, parents, friends, and so on. But the surface of this BwO, which is totally inscribed, is also the place where resistance to discourse can occur. The BwO can be *de-territorialized*, enabling it to become something other than that which it was as a consequence of its inscription. The continual play of discourses, and the deferral of meanings (discussed in Chapter 1) which prevent any discourse from having a single reading, supply this potential for *becoming*.

It is this political body which is the locus for the politics of health-talk, not the anatomical body which medicine and its adjunct disciplines have fabricated. The BwO is not passive, but active, continuously subjected to inscription, continually resisting. The politics and ethics of the postmodern social theory of health which I develop in this book concern this contested surface, and the ways in which health care territorializes the BwO of those who are the subjects of care.

2

INSCRIBING THE BODY

The modern body and its experts

Take a walk down the main street of any city in the Western world to discover some of the significances associated with modern bodies. The surface of the body is surely the most discussed, imagined, prescribed and proscribed, disfigured, disguised and disciplined surface in the physical world. On our outing, we can be clothed and shod, we can adorn ourselves with jewellery or other body ornaments. We can purchase scent to disguise the body's usual smell, tan to change its usual colour, make-up to disguise its ageing. We can sign up for diets. We can process the films we have taken of each other's bodies. Above some of the shops are health clinics, solaria, fitness centres. Hairdressers, beauty salons and manicurists offer their services. Posters on hoardings teach us how to look, how to be fashionable. There is a disco where we can dance and display, attract and be attracted. A little way back from the main street there is a tattooist and piercer. The massage parlour offers a range of relaxation techniques. Strip joints and magazines provide displays of naked skin, while sex is sold on the street and in cheap hotels. In the church, we are told to avoid the sins of the flesh, while in the police station, transgressors are photographed, fingerprinted and restrained. And all about, in the bedroom and on the street, we gaze upon each other, spying beauty or repulsion, distinction or drabness, inspiring pleasure, disdain or fear.

Behind closed doors, professionals gaze upon the surface of the body for indications of what is happening beneath that surface. Once, phrenologists sought the personality in the bumps on the scalp, criminologists scrutinized the facial features for deviance. Now therapists look in the eyes or explore the feet for clues to disease, acupuncturists stimulate the skin far from the site of pathology, while fortune-tellers find the future in the palms of our hands. In doctors' surgeries, clinical signs – a rash, swelling or tenderness – suggest pathology or senescence. Thermometer, stethoscope and sphygmomanometer help the doctor see below the surface. Electrodes strapped to the skin feed back signs of the heart and brain. X-rays and ultrasound see through the skin to reveal the inner functions. The most adventurous of the profession cut us open to find their objective. The memory of their enterprise is inscribed in the scars that remain. For others the skin is still the locus of activity – lifting faces, stretching wrinkles, sucking away fat, disguising age. In the main street, in the clinics, and in private rooms experts inscribe the body, be they doctors, sports instructors or lovers.

In Chapter 1, I explored the problems of representing objects – such as the human body – which are both in biology and in culture. The purpose there was to identify the difficulties for explicitly *sociological* representation. But those arguments also provide the starting point for a more general exploration of the interplay of the two realms. In this chapter I wish to challenge the very facticity of the human body, its very character as constituted in modernist biology and modernist social theory; and to fabricate a different, postmodern body, constituted through the collision of those realms, between 'desire' (which might be seen as belonging to the realm of the physical world) and 'the social' (which is the cultural, meaningful discourse on that world). Upon this postmodern body, inscribed by the social yet motivated in its desire, we will examine the inscription of one set of discourses known as 'health and illness', to challenge these concepts too, to see them not as attributes of the biological body, or even as experienced psychosocial states, but as relations of power positively constituting a body, but at odds with it and its desire.

Our shopping trip along the main street has suggested how important the surface of the body has become in the West, how *visible* it has become, how much *expertise* has been generated to achieve this visibility. Postmodern social theory has focused attention on issues of embodiment (see, for example, Kroker and Kroker 1988; Boyne 1991; Sawicki 1991) after its neglect in sociological (though not anthropological) discourse (Turner 1992). In the postmodern position, the interest is in how beauty, fitness, couture and coiffure, diet, gesture and posture and sexual arousal *inscribe* bodies, marking them and enabling them to serve as markers. By this, I mean how bodies serve as signifiers, just as a text in a book or a piece of film. They have been attributed meaning, and they can be read by others, and rewritten, they *are* texts, carrying knowledgeability and power.

If fitness and beauty are powerful markers of the body, then surely the same must be said of health and illness. Health – or at least its promotion and protection – is a commodity (Busfield 1990; Cant and Calnan 1992), consumed and ascribed value, its marks are visible, so it can be displayed and, up to a point, dissembled. Indeed, health as a notion partly depends on notions of fitness, beauty, slimness, youthfulness and so on, just as these notions depend on ideas of health (Glassner 1989). The post-structuralist understanding of the chaining of signifiers, and the slippage of meaning (*différance*) in language supply our understanding of how this may be. Consequently we may begin by recognizing a politics of health and illness, or, as one might say, of how health and illness become attached to bodies.

Although I am indeed concerned with the character of these politics, a postmodern social theory of health (PSTH) must also concern itself primarily with the object of the politics, the body, and with the body's inscription by these relations of power. What precisely does it mean to say that the body is inscribed? What exactly is inscribed? Clearly, I am not speaking here simply of physical marks on a physical entity: so *how* does this inscription actually take place, upon what kind of 'body' does it occur? These questions must be explored carefully if our intention, ultimately, is to develop an understanding of what it means to speak about a 'sick body', what it means to have a 'sick body'.

Power, knowledge and the body

The greatest theorist of the history of the body – how it became what it became, not biologically but in relation to power – has been Michel Foucault. Hence it is appropriate in this exploration of inscription of health to begin with his studies of medicine and the other disciplines of the body, and to the Foucauldian canon. Before this, it is perhaps worth flagging the subsequent discussion of desire, which will turn to the work of Deleuze and Guattari for inspiration. Despite the centrality of the Foucauldian position in exploring bodily inscription, Foucault has been criticised (Butler 1990: 130) for his model of the body as totally transfigured by relentless cultural inscription, yet somehow prior to that inscription. By focusing upon 'the body' as the concern of genealogy, Lash (1991: 261) argues, it becomes passive, no more than a vehicle for the inscription of history, incapable of resistance.

This – what I call the sociological Foucault – seems to possess little to commend it in relation to much structuralist sociology. Other postmodernists have concerned themselves more explicitly with the possibility of resistance to discourse, and for this reason, the development of a PSTH in this book will move beyond Foucault, to seek some conceptualization of bodily desire. The full impact of this will become clear later. But, with this criticism in mind, perhaps while exploring the Foucauldian position we need to seek not only the character of the social which constitutes bodies in 'health' and 'illness', inscribes the body with these manifestations of power and knowledgeability, but also the sources of bodily resistance and the positive investment in bodies of powers (of some sort) which might challenge the discourses of these social 'healths' and 'illnesses'.

In exploring the politics of the body, we might start with its *visibility*.

Foucault's interests in the micro-politics of bodily regulation and the macro-politics of surveillance of populations (Turner 1992) turn on his notion of *le regard*, commonly translated as the gaze of power. And they come together in his notion of *governmentality*, which has not been fully explored in relationship to health and illness. Finally, in the later works, Foucault's (1984; 1986; 1988) interests come to lie in the techniques of *self-surveillance* and self-confessing, by which subjectivity comes to be acquired. Can these themes illuminate the inscription of the body, and, in particular, the inscription of health and illness upon the body?

The exemplar of modern surveillance which inspired Foucault's study of the birth of the prison was Bentham's *panopticon*, an architectural design which permitted the permanent surveillance of prison inmates by hidden observers. Cells are open only towards the observers, not to other cells:

> All that is needed then is to place a supervisor in a central tower, and place in each cell a madman, a patient, a condemned man, a worker or a schoolboy ... they are like so many cages, so many small theatres, in which each actor is alone, perfectly individualised, and constantly visible ... Full lighting and the eye of a supervisor capture better than darkness, which ultimately protected. Visibility is a trap (Foucault 1979: 200).

The principles of panopticism are thus the exercise of power through relations of observer–observed, a permanence and totality of that power mediated by its subjects (the observed) themselves, not in its actual exercising by the supervisor (who may not always be observing), a deindividualizing of the wielder of power – anyone can take on the supervision (Foucault 1979: 202) and the creation of a subjectivity in the observed as 'prisoner', 'patient' or whatever. A panoptic penitentiary in Stateville, USA, is illustrated in Foucault's book, while a prison chapel built on the principle that prisoners should all be observable by the preacher, but unable to see each other, can be visited at Lincoln Castle in the UK. Visitors can try the pulpit and also sit in the compartments where the prisoners were enclosed during the service. But non-custodial settings offer more widespread examples of panopticism. The modern factory generated techniques of surveillance of the workforce (Sewell and Wilkinson 1992), while the hospital ward design of the nineteenth century, with its light airy spaces, beds arranged around the walls and a central nursing station were explicitly designed to achieve 'watchfulness'. Some circular wards were built in the last century, but the design was unpopular with staff, who themselves felt surveyed by management.

Panopticism, Foucault suggested, enabled the observation and classification of individuals: in a medical setting, to make comparisons between patients, to monitor the effects of different medicines (Foucault 1979: 203). Regardless of the architecture, the medical gaze allowed the exercise of an institutionalized disciplinary power by doctors (Foucault 1976: 89).

In the form of the clinic, in the technique of the medical examination, the disseminated power of the gaze permitted the constitution of a knowledgeability about disease, observable in symptoms and signs. The symptoms 'allow the invariable form of the disease ... visible and invisible, to *show through*' (1976: 92, emphasis in original).

The relationship between symptom and clinical sign, as analysed in Foucault's consideration of the medical gaze, provides insight into the character of the inscription of the body in this setting. Whereas a symptom *is*, a sign *says* (1976: 93). The clinical sign (which is elicited, not observed) is constituted in language, achieved through consciousness:

> the sign is the symptom itself, but in its original truth ... for a doctor whose skills would be carried 'to the highest degree of perfection, all symptoms would become signs', all pathological manifestations would speak a clear ordered language (1976: 94).

This emphasis affects the power balance between professional and patient, dissolving a patient's claims to authenticity. Kleinman (1988: 16) suggests that

> clinicians sleuth for pathognomonic signs – the observable, telltale clues to secret pathology ... the patient–physician interaction is organized as an interrogation. What is important is not what a patient thinks, but what he or she says.

The gaze thus offers the prospect, through the exercise of its power to achieve knowledge and expertise, of knowing the body. The inscription of the body which medicine deciphers in its examinations, is not straightforward, it cannot be 'read' 'correctly' by just anyone: the reader must be an *expert*. And consequently, this expertise is achieved at the expense of those who must be subjected to the power of the gaze. Body-expertise is a relation of power, as well as of knowledge. The constitution of subjectivity – in this case of patienthood, is an important aspect of Foucault's (1980) notion of the gaze.

The political anatomy of the body

A number of studies have utilized the concepts outlined here to construct Foucauldian genealogies of elements of medicine. Arney and Neill (1982) studied the history of obstetrics, while Arney and Bergen (1983) explored the transformation of disability from a notion of anomaly during the twentieth century. A genealogy of dentistry (Nettleton 1988; 1992) similarly identifies the significance of prevention in constituting the professional concern of the dentist and the processes by which the mouth came to be separated from the rest of the body as an arena within which social relations of power and knowledgeability are played out. A study of mortuary practices suggests that even in death we are the subjects of discipline (Prior 1987).

Armstrong's studies of paediatrics (1979), geriatrics (1981) and chronic illness (1990), elements of which are also constituted in his book *The Political Anatomy of the Body* (1983) contribute a history of modern medicine (developing Foucault's genealogy of 'the clinic') unlike that commonly written, in which the past is seen as an imperfect present, but one sowing the seeds of our present good practice. In place of this, the genealogical method uncovers discontinuity, and the fabrication of medical realities, in which knowledge has been used to rewrite human bodies, and to constitute medical expertise and authority, which in turn gave legitimacy to the knowledge.

Reading modern medicine in this way tells a tale in which the themes of rational development and progress are replaced with an unpredictable and discontinuous unfolding of discourses on 'the medical'. While Foucault identified within the 'clinic' a new perspective on the object of the medical gaze, Armstrong's genealogy of UK medicine in the twentieth century focused on the rise of the survey in medical discourse, and the move of the clinical gaze into the community and the social space, suggesting how the study of populations, public health and more recently discourses on prevention and health promotion have come to be paradigms in medicine alongside clinical specialties. Armstrong (1983: 7) calls this move into the community 'the dispensary'. For example, in the development of psychiatry:

> The Dispensary provided a new technology to ensure that 'square pegs are fitted into square holes'. A system based on ascription or achievement could be replaced by one based on observations, tests, interviews, questionnaires, analyses, selection and follow-up. During World War II . . . new techniques of personnel selection were applied rigorously to the officer class . . . The adoption of this vision of mental health provided a means of controlling a population – without repression – through constant mapping and surveillance (1983: 29).

One of the most powerful techniques of both public health medicine and social science, the survey, began to be used in the era of the Dispensary.

> The survey was not just a mechanical technique, but a technology through which power operated as a positive force: the survey created a discourse, a practice, a reality. In this sense, the survey was not just an aspect of 'natural history' but a means of constituting and sustaining the very conception of 'natural history' as applied to illness (1983: 86).

Armstrong (1983: 115–16) elaborates this parallel between medicine and social science in his postscript, where he argues that both are engaged in the same enterprise: 'the production of a discourse on the individual which corresponds to an extended disciplinary power'. Changes in medical discourse on the patient often preceded those in medical sociology, while at other times they have diverged to produce independent gazes on the patient body, based in differing models of subjectivity.

The discontinuity in medical practice identified by the genealogical method may be seen in the rewriting of the 'model' of medicine deemed 'most appropriate' for practice in the light of current knowledgeability. Hence, the biomedical model of medicine was challenged in the 1970s, partly as a consequence of the changing face of illness in the West from primarily acute to principally chronic, by a 'biopsychosocial' model (Engel 1977; Fisher 1991), supposedly incorporating a patient-centred perspective (see also Armstrong 1987). More recently, it is claimed, a 'psychoneuroimmunological' model has superseded this, providing a medical gaze which is universal and holistic (Levin and Solomon 1990). The constitution of the 'social' in medical discourse, and the rise of medical sociology, is, of course, one of the topics of this book.

One principle of the Foucauldian approach is to concern oneself always with the effects of power at the sites of its action, rather than at some conjectured sovereign point (the state, the law, or wherever). In common with the technique of deconstruction, the method 'seeks the small design'. This localization of power, Foucault argued, is through its actions on bodies. The outcome, it may be concluded, is the inscription of those bodies by that power. To examine such an inscription of bodies, their deciphering, and the creation of a subjectivity in the owners of those bodies, I shall take a study whose author offered a very different theoretical framework to explain his data, but which can also supply a postmodern rereading. It is a well-known study by Roger Jeffrey (1979) of an accident and emergency department of a UK hospital and the categorization of patients by its medical and nursing staff (similar US studies have been undertaken by Lorber 1975; Leiderman and Grisso 1985).

Jeffrey's ethnography of this setting identified a classification of patients into 'good' and 'bad' categories, depending upon their characteristics. Good patients were acute cases, preferably urgent or emergencies, requiring some expertise on the part of the medical staff, and some need for an exercise of judgement. Bad patients, also known as 'rubbish', were non-urgent, and often had disagreeable personal characteristics – they were drunk, smelt or were dirty, were 'tramps', or had inflicted the injury on themselves in suicide attempts. They provided little opportunity for clinical expertise.

In the original article, the concern was principally with the criteria used by the staff to make this dichotomy and the apparent discovery that the staff used a model of sickness remarkably like that of Parsons' (1951) sick role! Here I am more concerned with the exercise of power, and the ways in which, in turning the patients' symptoms into signs (of disease, malingering, time-wasting or non-medical problems, staff read off messages inscribed on the bodies which could only be read with expertise, rewrote these patients as legitimate cases or rubbish, and constituted them into subjectivities (as deserving or undeserving). In this reading of the study, both with good and bad patients, expertise was brought to bear, and the clinical gaze generated effects of power upon both sets of patients. The staff complaints about bad patients derive from the failure to be able to apply medical power through knowledge, being restricted to more overt forms of power entailing punishments (roughness, being kept waiting or being discharged untreated). While the good patient is a docile body, inscribed in the gaze of the doctor, made a subject through the doctor's power and knowledge, the creation of the bad patient as subject of power is problematic as a consequence of her/his resistance to discourses (on what a good patient or a good citizen should be like).

This study offers some understanding of what is entailed in inscription, and, in addition, makes the connection between inscription and what is called 'stigma' in the modernist SHH. Because of the interest in inscription of the body, many of the studies to which I shall refer in these pages concern aspects of stigmatization. Kleinman (1988: 22) has called stigma an 'exoskeleton' of culturally marked illness which radically spoils identity. In the postmodern perspective, this inside/outside metaphor is dissolved (Butler 1990: 135). There is no longer a prior, inner 'identity' to be encased; instead 'stigma' *is* the identity or the subjectivity of the person thus inscribed. I think this reading throws some light upon the impact of stigma and labelling, which for people with 'stigmatizing social identities' are often not felt as imposed, but as *integral* to their person.

Governmentality

I want to turn now to two further elements of Foucault's position which can assist this exploration of inscription: first, the notion of *governmentality*, and in particular the liberal mode of governance characterizing the modern period; and second, the *self-surveillance* or the care of the self.

Foucault (1988: 18) addressed domination in terms of four realms: production; signs and communication; conduct of individuals; and the self. Governmentality is the interlinking of the latter two realms of technology, of the domination of others and of the self (1988: 19). Panopticism could be interpreted as a governmentality, inasmuch as the disciplining of the others is ultimately a self-disciplining by the prisoner or the patient caught up in the relations of power constituted in visibility. Further, the panopticon is 'democratic'; in it the exercise of power may be supervised by a society as a whole (Foucault 1979: 207). In many ways we live in a society in which the technologies of surveillance have achieved the Benthamite intention of a society disciplined according to panoptic principles. However, the panopticon is not the best example of governmentality, which is conceived as a subtle, comprehensive management of life deriving both from a top-down exercise of power over conduct – see, for example, Foucault's (1988: 156–8) discussion of French political philosophy and the 'administrative police' of the eighteenth century – with a subjectivity constituted in a sense of personal responsibility, rights, freedoms and dependencies (Dean 1991). The latter, Foucault considered, were achieved through the technologies of the self.

Governmentality entails two apparently conflicting effects: the reinforcement of the 'community' and increasing individualization (Foucault 1988: 162). To take an aspect of governmentality with regard to health, Nettleton's (1991) study of the recruitment of mothers in the disciplining of oral hygiene demonstrates such a regime of governance, in which the care of the self is elevated to a moral virtue which creates a subjectivity of motherhood in the subjects of its discourse, while formulating a liberal 'welfare mentality' of surveillance of the population of children's mouths and teeth. The mouths of the children are inscribed in this exercise of governmentality, but so, too, are the bodies of the 'mothers', through the diligence with which they approach the task of sustaining oral hygiene.

Turning to the final element of Foucauldian theory, 'self-surveillance' or the 'care of the self' became the principal interest of the later Foucault. I will interject briefly here that I find some problems with this notion, which, if taken to its limits, would implicate all behaviours as self-surveillance, discourses of subjectivity, leaving little or no room for resistance. I will return to this point in a moment.

To illustrate the care of the self, Foucault chose a somewhat arcane example from early Christian monastic life. He documents a number of 'technologies of the self', including the practices of public admission of sin by a penitent (known as *exomologesis* in the monastic rule), and self-examination and obedient confession to the master (known as *exagoreusis*). Foucault (1988: 48–9) traces this latter technology of self-disclosure through into the human sciences of the modern era, though now entailing not renunciation of the self but instead the constitution of a new self. Hutton (1988) follows this practice of self-disclosure into psychoanalytic theory, while Nicolson (1993) argues that women's 'confessions' of their sexuality in letters to magazines or in therapy constitute them in a patriarchal and heterosexist subjectivity. Rose (1989: 240) identifies the double movement entailed in the confessional form

> In confessing, one is subjectified by another, for one confesses in the actual or imagined presence of a figure who prescribes the form of the confession ... But in confessing, one also constitutes oneself. In the act of speaking, through the obligation to produce words that are true to an inner reality, through the self examination that precedes and accompanies speech, one becomes a subject for oneself. Confession, then, is the diagram of a certain form of subjectification that binds us to others at the very moment we affirm our identity.

The technology of the confessional has been refined in modern societies, Foucault argued, into an incitement continually to reflect upon and regulate one's own conduct as an 'ethical subject' – monitoring, testing and improving the self, according to self-imposed moral goals (1989: 241).

A study which illustrates another 'technology of the care of the self' may be found in Glassner's (1989) exploration of 'fitness' discourses in the modern United States. These discourses (which often are closely associated with notions of health) explicitly construct a subjectivity and a self-image which goes way beyond physical exercise.

> By becoming fit, persons are said to achieve a degree of independence from medical professionals and medical technology. They also achieve protection against temptations to alienated or marginalized forms of deviancy such as obesity, drug abuse, and psychological depression, and a set of frames within which information from and about the body can be effectively reduced and catalogued (Glassner 1989: 187).

The inscription of 'fitness' upon the bodies of those who exercise is therefore not simply concerned with muscle tone, heart rate, or anything in the physical domain. It entails a discipline of the self, and a necessary self-reflexivity about being a particular kind of person who 'does fitness'. This suggests that we need, when considering the body inscribed by health, to resist the notion that we are here talking about about the medical, anatomical, body-with-organs at all. The possibility of the *Body-without-Organs* is something to which we will turn in a moment.

To illustrate the various elements of the Foucauldian genealogical approach, I want to look in some detail at a study which pursues this theme of the care of the self, within a perspective of 'liberal governance' or 'governmentality' in which there is no discernible State behind a policy, but a much more disseminated set of discursive agents. The study (once again subject to my rereading) offers a perspective on the growth of self-help groups among the chronically ill. These groups can be seen as a feature of a pluralistic, liberal society, in which it is recognized that professional discourses on disease can be augmented by sufferers' discourses, to supply support which is not provided by formal medical institutions. Williams (1989) describes one such grouping in Britain, the National Ankylosing Spondylitis Society (NASS), which caters for chronic sufferers from this arthritic disease of the spine. The group, Williams (1989: 145) concludes, was set up with an emphasis on self-care and mutual support, and a focus upon exercise rather than drugs or general discussion. An ambivalence towards welfare-orientated activities reinforced this message of self-reliance (1989: 146), while an analysis of the NASS newsletter found this theme to dominate the publication alongside an emphasis on orthodox medical treatment, and reports of medical advances (1989: 148–9). These two themes were recapitulated in responses to readers' letters, even when these letters suggested distress (1989: 151).

One feature of NASS thus seems to be, as Williams points out, the extension of therapeutic activities of health professionals into the lives of patients. Despite the doubts expressed by the author as to the ethos behind the group, it appears to reflect the characteristics identified in Foucauldian analysis of governmentality, incorporating both top-down welfare practices, and a self-care constitution of subjectivity – perhaps in this case – of survivors of disease, stoical in the face of pain, rational about medical progress and trusting of clinical expertise. The bodies of NASS members are inscribed through their practices as part of the group, and their relationships with the knowledgeability which the group constitutes in its themes of science and self-help.

In this study, too, we see not only the physical bodies of the people diagnosed as having ankylosing spondylitis (AS), but also their embodiment within a subjectivity of what it is to be a 'sufferer' of AS. This is in part constituted in medical discourse, but as much in the governmental regime of self-help by which they are expected to discipline *both physical body and self.*

This case provides a useful summary of the main components of Foucault's perspective, as regarding inscription of the body: the relationship of knowledgeability and power, the centrality of the human body in disciplines (in both senses of the term) and expertise, the construction of selfhood and subjectivity by power/knowledge and the significance of self-care within regimes of governance. While illuminating these positions, the study introduces a further element – the apparent *resistance* by NASS members to the totalizing perspectives of the group. Resistance to discourse is not dealt with particularly well in Foucault's genealogies, as it remains unclear from where, if not from discourse, such resistance might derive. The issue of resistance has major implications for the postmodern reading of social theory, and must be addressed in the exploration of the character of the inscription and of the 'body' which is inscribed. This will become particularly clear as I develop a position on the inscription of 'health' and 'illness'.

The Body-without-Organs

With the benefit of the Foucauldian positions on power, knowledge and the disciplining of the body, it is now possible to set out in greater detail what it means to speak of inscription of the human body in discourse, and in particular in discourses on health and illness. What has become absolutely clear is that we are not speaking simply of some physical inscription on the surface of the physical body. On the other hand, it is fair to speak of this inscription as material, in the sense that it is capable of being 'read' on to the body, and from the body, 'rewritten' endlessly by further disciplining by the social and in the technologies of the self.

In the dualism of mind–body differentiation, the explanation of inscription would be constituted through a double process of discipline, on the one hand the behaviours and demeanour of the physical body, on the other hand the ideal representations of belief, taste, judgements and choice, codes of morality, and knowledge. It is this duality, of the rational human actor, affected by truth and by false consciousness and ideology, which is swept away in the postmodern position, to be replaced by some other figure of embodiment, in which the ego is no longer prior. The inscription is not 'read' by the self, the inscription *is* the self, subjectivity. To give an example, one reaction to a diagnosis of a chronic incurable illness is a sense of great loss. The diagnosis inscribes the body, cutting across patternings of desire which have constituted the subjectivity of the person previously. Her/his whole sense of self is challenged, s/he responds with grief and sadness, fabricating cognitions, emotions and patterns of behaviour to inform and pad out this new subjectivity. Her/his sadness may be read (and misread) by others in demeanour and in interaction, reinforcing or refining the subject. The subject adopts new bodily strategies (self-care, risk reduction or perhaps abandonment), through which s/he in turn is reconstituted and reread (see Kleinman 1988; de Swaan 1990). Butler (1990: 139) emphasizes the active character of this process, referring to the 'performative acts' by which identity is constructed.

The body of inscription in such a figure is not the organic body of medicine. In place of the anatomical body, the body of interest here is a non-organic, political surface: a *Body-without-Organs*. This terminology derives from the work of Deleuze and Guattari (1984; 1988), who use it to explore the constitution of the self in the collision between the social world and desire. This concept is central to the PSTH and will be explored in great detail in Part 2. The failure adequately to address this political body is, in my view, a fundamental shortcoming of the so-called 'sociology of the body'.

This idea of the Body-without-Organs (BwO) sums up the different conception of the body in the PSTH, and reminds us that we are not speaking of the representation of the body-with-organs which has constituted the medical body of the modern era. Nor are we speaking of the body as it is vaguely conceptualized in modernist SHH. The body, we are reminded (Giddens 1984) takes up space and cannot be superimposed on other physical entities. It moves through a 'life course', and the 'biographical body conception' is both subjective and constrained by this unidirectional and finite temporality (Bury 1991: 453).

The Body-without-Organs is not constrained in space and time: not because it is imaginary or symbolic, but because it cannot 'know' these concepts in some privileged way. Of course it becomes subject to spatial and temporal constraint, but this is the outcome of inscription. The BwO has been variously imagined in space, as a 'sort of hollow sphere' (Lash 1991: 269), or as an egg (Deleuze and Guattari 1984) – there is even a drawing of an egg in Deleuze and Guattari's *A Thousand Plateaux* (1988)! However, I regard these metaphors as playful, and prefer not to represent it as other than a surface for inscription.

So what is inscribed upon the BwO, we might conclude from the discussion thus far, is nothing more nor less than the power/knowledge of discourse, or, to put it another way, *the social*. This, however, seems inadequate: implicating a realm of docile, determined bodies, passive subjects of discourse. At the end of the last section I raised the issue of resistance to discourse. While the possibility of resistance to discourses of power/knowledge is fundamental to Foucault's position (see, for example, Martin's (1988: 14) interview with Foucault), liberation from discourse seemed to him to entail a further totalizing system of power relations (Ostrander 1988: 176), for example Marxism or utopian socialism. In his view the body was passive, totally imprinted by history. Civilization as the project of history relentlessly writes the body, seeking its total destruction and transfiguring in the realm of the social, in order that cultural values may emerge (Butler 1990: 129–30). Whether or not Butler (1990) is correct in asserting that Foucault saw the body as 'a blank page' to be inscribed, he was unable epistemologically to develop a perspective in which this inscription might be seen as a contested process. For example, sexual 'liberation' from 'repression of desires' was not liberation at all, but the domination and subjection of the body in a normalizing discourse on sexuality and desire. Any theory of resistance was merely further discourses on power and knowledge, creating a new subjectivity. The outcome, in Lash's (1991: 260) view, was a delibidinized actor incapable of resistance or of mobilizing resources.

Deleuze and Guattari are conscious of this problem of the passive agent, and they consider the BwO as a contested realm, between the social world and desire. For them, desire is a positive force, and not (as in psychoanalysis) an absence or lack, but a material and positive investment of libido in a person or thing: the body's *will-to-power*. They see the BwO as the site of inscription not only by the social but also by desire. The self and subjectivity are the outcome of the patterning of inscription of the BwO by the Foucauldian disciplines, by the body's own will-to-power, and by a third element: the positive investments of libido by others in the body. Needless to say, this is a never-ending contest of discipline and resistance to discipline, in which the inscription is never static, always in flux.

I will have much more to say about this contestation in Part 2, and in particular about the familial or 'oedipal' symbolism of the medical. Deleuze and Guattari see familial metaphors (the boss as father-figure, and so on) as central to the inscription of the BwO in modern capitalist society. Because of this, it cannot be straightforward to speak of positive investments of libido in another person: for as we saw in Chapter 1, that which is intended to empower may in fact close down possibilities rather than open them. To give an example: in a therapeutic setting, a person undergoing treatment may invest trust in the therapist, based on an investment on the part of the therapist in a wish genuinely to empower the patient. These investments of desire inscribe and contest the BwO of both parties. If the flows of desire become codified – as I will argue in Chapter 4 is often the case in caring settings – within a parent–child transference of dependency, then what was an empowering relationship becomes disempowerment.

A methodology for exploring inscription

Because of this problem of codification, which I think Deleuze and Guattari seek to avoid by their emphasis upon a single kind of symbolizing – that of Oedipus – we are denied the possibility of deciphering the flows of desire which pattern the surface of the BwO, without doing great damage to them. The exploration of the patternings on the BwO must adopt the same kind of open, playful, fragmented and reflexive attitude as might enhance the flow of desire itself. One might indeed call for a method which *is* a flow of desire. So that the PSTH does not simply recapitulate a modernist endeavour, seeking truth and enlightenment, knowledge which can give expertise over the Other, we cannot reify the Body-without-Organs, replacing the medical body in discourse as the true body. The BwO is a *political surface*, with real properties which must be explored, and a trajectory in the material which has effects which can be traced. But it is not knowable in the sense that the medical body is 'knowable'. I touched a moment ago upon 'trust', a virtually unexplored topic in the SHH. As will be seen, 'health' and 'illness' inhere in topics such as trust and responsibility which are constituted not only in the social, but also in desire. We are faced with patternings on the BwO which can at best be inferred, and which cannot be simply decoded.

To exemplify the approach which must be taken, and to introduce the method of deconstruction, I want to look in detail at a study which will enable us to explore the issues which have been raised in this chapter concerning the inscription of health. This study is a very well-known documentation of women's experiences of gynaecological examinations (Emerson 1970). Emerson took a perspective based in phenomenology; here I shall consider what can be brought to it by the postmodern position.

The topic which is explored in this study is the construction and sustaining of a reality during internal vaginal examinations in gynaecological settings. Emerson suggests that this requires an ongoing and minute-to-minute effort on the part of the participants: the woman, the doctor, the nurse. This is partly grounded in background knowledge:

> What happens in a gynecological examination is part of the common stock of knowledge. Most people know that a gynecological examination is when a doctor examines a woman's genitals in a medical setting . . . Besides knowing what equipment to provide for the doctor, the nurse has in mind a typology of responses patients have to the situation, and a typology of doctors' styles of performance. The doctor has technical knowledge about the examining procedures . . . (Emerson 1970: 77).

Despite this, Emerson says, the reality is still precarious, and not only must people be convinced that what is happening is 'a gynecological examination', but that it is one which is 'going right'. But alongside this, there is also an element of what Goffman would see as self-presentation: staff adopt a nonchalance, implying both that they are doing something which is medical, not sexual or cruel, and that they wish the patient similarly to take the examination in a matter-of-fact way. The scene, says Emerson (1990: 78), works 'precisely because staff act as if they have the right to do what they are doing. Any hint of doubt would compromise the medical definition'. However, as Emerson adds, the nonchalance of the patient is dispensable, as it only serves to *validate* staff behaviour. Here we may discern something of the power relations of the setting, a discontinuity and asymmetry in the shared construction of meaning, privileging staff interpretations, and making patient meanings less significant.

The aspect which Emerson wishes to develop, however, is more subtle. It is that a medical reality alone is apparently insufficient. Staff do not treat gynaecological examinations like other examinations; they continually behave so as to indicate that there is something 'special' about this part of the body, and also to flag that they are treating the patient as a person. Doctors continually shift between the medical definition of the situation, and general community definitions of such bodily contact. They 'show deference to general community meanings [while] at the same time . . . disregarding them' (Emerson 1970: 80). The paper goes on to describe this shifting between medical and community definitions. Patients are examined in medical space, but draped so as to be exposed only at the examinations site (despite this being the area which is normally least likely to be unclothed), while medical talk retains a delicacy about mentioning genitals or associated bodily functions, sometimes using euphemisms or referring to 'it'. Patients are expected to be nonchalant, alert, dispassionate, the doctor soothing but not intimate.

Breakdowns in the definition of the situation occur when participants hesitate over their 'lines', blush, or if patients become sexually aroused, display themselves excessively, refer to their body's unappealing characteristics, or talk too openly about what is happening to them. These breakdowns are neutralized by staff through reasserting the medical definition, discounting sexual arousal as a different kind of response, or, if all else fails, by labelling the patient as emotionally unstable.

This study is of so much interest because of its detailed documentation of a 'slice of life'. The author is concerned with how such a precarious activity holds together, how it is carried off from moment to moment, despite the continually fluctuating balance of definitions.

> Sometimes even before one issue is completed, another may impose itself as taking priority. Further, each balance contains the seeds of its own demise, in that a temporary emphasis on one theme may

disturb the long-run balance unless subsequent emphasis on the counter-theme negates it (Emerson 1970: 92).

This is indeed a very postmodern way of talking about organization, as will be seen in Chapter 3. Within the postmodern position there are a number of further questions which might be asked. First, what is the politics of the truth-claims about what is happening in this setting? Whom do they benefit? How do these beneficiaries try to ensure that they are not subverted by other truth claims? Second, what kinds of subjectivity are constituted in the participants by the discursive practices of the gynaeco-logical examination? What is inscribed upon the bodies of participants? Third, and importantly, what are the conditions of possibility of resis-tance to these discourses? What investments would be entailed in such resistance?

The deconstructive strategy looks within texts, not trying to locate them in relation to structure, but seeking out claims to know the way things should be, claims about the essential character of people or settings. It subverts privileged positions, examining how things look the other way round. This is what I mean by 'seeking the small design'. Of course, what I shall be exploring is not the field setting itself, but Emerson's account of it. But what is of interest is precisely this *intertextuality*, the play of signification between the field, Emerson's and my accounts. I am not sug-gesting my account is truer, or more complete: indeed, it is partial and fragmentary.

We might begin by looking at the two discourses which Emerson iden-tifies: a medical discourse on the setting, in which staff definitions are privileged through claims to expertise, technical knowledge and access to resources. Emerson opposes this to the commonsensical definition of what is happening, and makes the shifting balance the topic of her analysis. Is there an alternative way of seeing this: not as an opposition between these discourses, but within both? The medical discourse, as we have seen, is structured to privilege the medical: claiming a facticity to the anatomy and functions, and to the technologies and procedures of the medical. As Emerson (1970: 79) suggests, 'the medical definition grants the staff the right to carry out their task [which otherwise] could be defined as [*sic*] unconscionable assaults on the dignity of individuals ... [or] taken as offenses against propriety'. Such assaults and impropriety are the negated aspect of the polarity upon which the medical definition in fact depends.

What, however, of the other 'general community' discourse on the set-ting? Emerson (1970: 79) tells us that 'gestures acknowledge the pelvic area as special; other gestures acknowledge the patient as a person ... A physician may gain a patient's cooperation by acknowledging her as a person ... He can offer her attention and acknowledgement'. The reduction in exposure of nakedness by the use of sheets or towels constitutes a 'general community' notion of modesty. Doctors hint at intimacy, radiate concern in their demeanour, offer extra assistance, and may sacrifice their task requirements for the sake of gentleness (1970: 85). Yet these activities seem to be little more than *parodies* of life outside the clinic. People do not normally wait to be acknowledged as people, or expect others to clothe them. Here we have a discourse which, in adopting the rhetoric of every-day life, adapts it so that the patient is passive, and the staff active. If the patient's demeanour of modesty, non-arousal and nonchalance slips, it is the staff who cover the gaffe. So the discourse serves to render patients passive. Further, and the 'chivalrous' gentleness and concern support this, it is a gendered discourse, associating femininity and passivity.

The discourses, then, are not in opposition, but in tandem: both privileging staff activity, disempowering patient activity. We would then see the balancing act not as a skilful shared performance of 'doing examination', but as a skilful – and desperate – effort by staff at sustaining control over a situation which is contested and threatening to the successful displaying of gynaecological expertise. Indeed, as Emerson (1970: 86) reports, resist-ance does occur, when patients refuse to accept the staff's enterprise:

> Intractable patients may complain about the pain, discomfort and indignities of submitting to medical treatment and care . . . Even if they are complying, they may indirectly challenge the expert status of the staff, as by 'asking too many questions'.

No doubt I could continue with this deconstructive activity, but this is, after all, something that the reader may pursue herself/himself in exploring the text. But I want to devote some time to examining the processes of inscription of the Bodies-without-Organs in this study, the investments of desire, and the conditions of resistance. As a first approximation we may draw four conclusions.

1 The medical discourse and the 'general community' discourse collabo-rate to inscribe patient *and* staff BwOs with a knowledge of the gynae-cological examination, constituted in relation to other kinds of genital contact (child–parent, lover–lover, sexual abuse, and so on). The BwOs are inscribed in these differences, by which are constructed knowl-edgeability – 'this is gynecology' – and a power – 'this is a legitimate activity, conducted within patternings of what may be imposed in the name of gynecology, and the authority by which it may be conducted by certain individuals'.

2 A wider politics of power, based in activity/passivity, gender relations, sexuality, morality, and so on, is inscribed on the BwO of both parties. These inscriptions are relational between patients and staff: they may be reciprocal, mirroring, or sometimes equivalent (for instance, the gendering of sex roles on patients and female staff).

3 These inscriptions pattern an active, not a passive BwO. Alongside the inscription of power/knowledge, fluxes of desire affect the patterning,

as do prior inscriptions of power/knowledge. Positive investments of desire may be made in the other participants, in their sexual, emotional and cognitive attributes. They may have strong flows of desire for life, health, curing or caring, a particular sexuality or subjectivity.

4 Participants may also invest desire not in the real other, but in symbolic others. The doctor may be cathected as the father or as the child, or even as the Lacanian transcendental phallus! These inscribe the BwO 'oedipally'.

The outcome for participants in terms of their constitution as subjects within the discipline of the gynaecological examination (a subjectivity which is, of course, carried to other settings, perhaps affecting the sexuality of gynaecologists as well as their patients), is the intermingling of all four elements of inscription. While the discourses of power/knowledge in points 1 and 2 above discipline the BwOs and contribute a subjectivity in terms of power, the investment of desire in point 3 offers the possibility of resistance and empowerment (I will save discussion of oedipal investment to Chapter 4).

Earlier in this chapter I mentioned investment of trust, and we might expect that such a positive investment is significant in the gynaecological examination. Patients trust staff not to hurt them unduly, to treat them with compassion and as fellow humans, not to exploit them for sexual fantasy or actual use, not to breach confidentiality. Staff trust patients to cooperate and submit to the technologies and competences claimed by the discipline. Both parties may invest the other with a degree of responsibility. Patients, we might expect, would invest staff with caring and curing capabilities, or with more general human attributes as comforters or advisers.

It is to these investments of desire that we need to look for the possibilities of resistance to discourses of power/knowledge. If we were to situate Emerson's study within the wider discussions of the medical discourse on women's bodies (Graham 1979; Nathanson 1975; Oakley 1980; Boston Women's Health Book Collective 1978), we might constitute gynaecological examinations as patriarchal, demeaning and disempowering. The postmodern position which I have developed in this chapter suggests that while tinkering with the ways power/knowledge of health and illness is discursively produced, the route to resistance rests not with somehow making the discourse 'nice', for example by injecting medical sociological discourses into the equation. This merely changes the power/knowledge which creates the subject and the subjectivity. But because inscription of power/knowledge is not an uncontested process on the BwO, the desiring-production by the BwO, and the investments of desire in others, can be used to resist discourse. This is the point which I wish to address in the concluding section of this chapter.

Against 'health', towards desire

The reading of inscription has thus returned the discussion to the idea of 'the politics of health-talk' as the topic of the PSTH. The discursive character of health-talk, and in particular the expertise by which 'health' and 'illness' become inscribed on bodies, is available for analysis in deconstruction in terms of how it can make its claims to truth. But we are now faced with the position that the facticity of 'health' and 'illness' must be questioned: rather they are *highly contested, fragmented and fluctuating struggles for the body*, constituted in the social, and resisted by desire. The PSTH turns out to have a completely different conception of these entities to the modernist sociology of 'health' and 'illness'.

In the example of the gynaecological clinic described above, we saw two separate discourses used by medical staff to achieve a particular subjectivity in their patient. To make the point about the contestation and the struggle for the Body-without-Organs, I want to make brief reference to a situation in which two conflicting discourses on a patient are played out within a medical setting. In a piece of research which I conducted upon in-patient surgery (Fox 1992), I found that surgeons and anaesthetists used different and potentially opposing discourses on their patients while undergoing surgical procedures. Surgeons constituted their patient within a framework of her/his disease, while the anaesthetist was concerned with the patient's 'fitness', that is, her/his capacity to undergo the rigours of surgery and recover. Both specialists depend upon the other for their work, yet their perspectives on the patient mean that, while surgeons want to do as radical as job as possible to ensure that the disease is removed or reduced, anaesthetists want surgeons to exercise caution, so as to avoid placing too much physiological stress upon the patient's resource of fitness.

These opposing views are played out in the actual practices of the surgical operation, in what one anaesthetist described as a 'love–hate' relationship, a symbiosis, but one in which the surgeon has greater control. An anaesthetist complains that:

> The surgeons don't consider the anaesthesia to be anything other than time wasted ... We have to have a patient ready when they want it [sic] (Fox 1992: 59).

When an elderly patient was inadequately anaesthetized to enable surgery to proceed, the anaesthetist was 'put in the wrong' and had to compromise the fitness further than he wished. But when a neurosurgical patient suffered a haemorrhage as a consequence of the surgical procedure, it was the anaesthetist who took command, organizing a second emergency operation to remove the haematoma. With an anaesthetized patient, unable to add a third rival discourse or take sides, the two specialties enact a struggle in which the inscription of health on the patient is particularly extreme, and is played out post-operatively once the patient is recovering (see Fox

1993). But we might see in this internecine contestation the desires of surgeon and anaesthetist vying with each other: wills-to-power investing their definitions upon the third party (the patient) in a continuing struggle to control the operating theatre.

If the PSTH has identified the contestation of the Body-without-Organs and the politics of that contestation as its interest, then it suggests that its concern is twofold: first, with the processes of representational transformation within discourses of power/knowledge on 'health' and 'illness'; and second, with the possibility that 'things could be otherwise'. With a model of a contested Body-without-Organs, and the strategic role of desire in the struggle for the body, the postmodern project becomes political. As Boyne and Lash (1984: 156) suggest:

> the reclaiming of the body, desire, the subject, from the Oedipal operations of the social machine is just a first step against the prevailing forms of domination. And further steps are possible as soon as it is understood that the social order of capitalism is only one of a myriad possibilities, and that its cohesive force is present everywhere as the manifestations of constrained and twisted desiring machines.

So the perspective of the PSTH is no longer to try (as in the modernist SHH) to enhance 'health', or limit 'illness'. Health and illness turn out to be aspects of power/knowledge inscribed on the Body-without-Organs, and – in the era of ultra-oedipalization (Kroker and Kroker 1988: 27) – the symbolic familializing of health care. Against these various 'healths' – constituted in biomedical, biopsychosocial or psychoneuroimmunological models, be they 'absence of illness', 'total physical and mental well-being' (WHO 1985) or the medical sociological discourses such as Oleson's (1989) definition in relation to gender and the division of labour, de Swaan's (1990: 22) reading of ill health as a 'notion of increasing dependency', Canguilhem's (1989) negative and positive biological values, or Kleinman's (1988: 206) exploration of lived experience – the object of a PSTH is an 'arche-health' and an 'arche-illness'. The PSTH, in its political sense, is to do with the will-to-power of the BwO, the investment of real bodies with a positive desire. Arche-health is a *fragmented, multivocal and disseminated manifestation of desire.* (Arche-health is explored in detail in Chapter 6.)

That does not mean that the PSTH becomes a theoretical activity, and that we abandon efforts to involve ourselves in the practicalities of health care. On the contrary, the PSTH is not relativistic. *Against* the moral relativism of modernity, here is an unequivocable commitment to an ethics and politics of action.

We seem to have travelled a long way from the main street with its boutiques, hairdressers and beautifiers. But we are right back there, in the world of inscription and of desire. Just as we are the subjects of fashion discourses, while using clothes to channel our desire, we are – in the realm of health and illness – both subjected and the active investors of our desire, our will-to-power, our arche-health. The rest of this book is an exploration of this arche-health, and its dismal, pathetic fabricated pretender: 'health'. I should make clear that by arche-health, I do not mean some kind of natural, underlying or historically prior health, upon which the other healths are superimposed. However, I do see arche-health as material, based in flows of desire, invested consciously or unconsciously.

Arche-health refuses to be reduced to language and discourse. Perhaps it is easiest to understand as the *play of pure difference*, which, as soon as it becomes a text, ceases to be 'arche-health'. Yet that does not mean that its trace cannot be discerned, and much of the rest of this book will be concerned with tracking arche-health, seeing how it can be encouraged and enhanced in settings of caring. I must, therefore, point out to readers that they will not discover some essential arche-health in the coming pages, or that there is one arche-health. Rather, the objective will be to open up the possibilities for a *politics* of arche-health, through the deconstruction of discourses on health and illness, from wherever they derive, and an *ethics* of arche-health, which offers difference in place of identity, generosity in place of control, desire in place of discourse.

3

ORGANIZING HEALTH

Modernity, power and organization

Try to define modernity and sooner or later one will invoke notions of rational or scientific planning and organization, bureaucracy and administrative structures. And if organization and 'organizations' (it will become clear in this chapter why I put the latter term in inverted commas) are not distinctively the creations of the modern era – one can read of feats of organization in Julius Caesar's journals of his military campaigns – then organization theory certainly is (Clegg 1990: 2). The theory of rational organization has been traced to another military figure, Frederick the Great, who ruled Prussia from 1740 to 1786. He took over an undisciplined army of conscripts and mercenaries, and with inspiration from his interest in mechanical toys, introduced reforms which effectively turned his soldiers into automata. He introduced standarized regulations, specialization, systematic training and drill, and a strong line of command (Morgan 1986: 24).

One can see many of these ideas reflected and mimicked in the factory-based systems of production introduced in the era of industrial capitalism. During the nineteenth century the principles of scientific organization were refined and developed, within this mechanistic image of organization. Taylorism advocated the scientific analysis of organization, based on maximizing efficiency, routinizing work within precise definitions of how it should be undertaken, breaking every task into the smallest possible component parts. Fordism implemented Taylor's principles on the assembly line, forcing workers to work at the speed of the line (Morgan 1986: 30–31). Ford and Taylor's names are synonymous with the deskilled, top-down, routine work which dominated the industrial scene until quite recently, when new ideas of flexible specialization became fashionable (Clegg 1990).

A further feature by which the modernist mode of organization has been characterized was the development, as a consequence of the increased division of labour, of bureaucracy. Dictated by the split between the 'doers' and the 'thinkers' in Taylorist philosophy, a new army of administrators were required to regulate, monitor and refine the organizational machine. At which point: enter the sociologist Max Weber, theorist of capitalist organization, bureaucracy and the 'iron cage'. Weber's discussions of rationality and the rise of the bureaucratic form warrants him a special place in the history of organization theory, and theorists still regularly turn to Weber as a source of inspiration.

Genealogically, the development of organization theory since Weber can be seen as a fragmenting and discontinuous movement to explain and rationalize organization. Morgan (1986) documents these discontinuous perspectives as a series of 'images of organization': machine, organism, brain, culture, psychic prison, and so on. We might perhaps see in these contested perspectives, rhetorics for comprehending and controlling something which, according to modernism, should be rational, but continually fails to achieve this objective. Sociology has contributed very significantly to these images, in its modernist project to understand the modern world.

Morgan's 'images' are interesting in addition because they reflect – in their pluralism and fragmentation – the more recent discourses which have characterized organization theory: concepts of 'flexibility' in place of mechanization, local in place of global, multi-skilling in place of differentiation. Clegg (1990: 180ff.) speaks of these as 'post-modern forms of organization'. However, I intend to take a different tack in this chapter, in keeping with my main definition of postmodernism, concerning myself not with organization in the era of 'post-modernity', but with postmodern perspectives on organization theory. The postmodern critique of organization theory, to adopt Cooper's (1989: 501) neat phrase, entails the substitution of the 'writing of organization', by an exploration of the 'organization of writing'.

My intention, then, is to illustrate the possibilities for exploring health-care systems which are opened up by the postmodern reading. First, I address a continuing theme: the need to resolve the problem of critiquing modernity from within a modernist discourse, and set out the postmodern alternative. Second, I shall illustrate the possibilities of the postmodern position, using a case study of hospital ward rounds as an example of the approach. Finally, I will identify some issues faced by modernist sociologies of health-care organization which need detailed consideration in a post-modern reading.

Sociological contributions to organization

Sociologists of health and illness have tapped a rich seam of material in their commentaries upon modern health-care organization. Patients await treatment as if they were components on an assembly line (although this line often seems to move very slowly indeed), are subjected to depersonalizing indignities (Davis and Horobin 1977), and are categorized and their records filed in antiquated systems or on computers which can summon patients to suit the clinician (Pope 1991). They are processed ever more rapidly, to increase the efficiency of the use of hospital beds (Fox 1992), while the hospital is run on strictly defined, regulated and interlocking patterns of time management (Zerubavel 1981).

In many sociological discourses on health-care organization, however, there seems little sign of the characteristics of recent organizations identified by Clegg. If the flexible firm has become a motif for current industrial activity in the West, when it comes to health-care organization, the shades of these pioneers of scientific management, Ford and Taylor, seem still to haunt the poorly lit, pastel-painted corridors. They are overseen by domineering consultants, or, more recently, by efficiency-obsessed managers (Cox 1991; Elston 1991; Hugman 1991). Health-care organizations exemplify (in these discourses) modernist features of bureaucratic, rigidly hierarchical, impersonal and unresponsive machine-images of organization.

These 'traditional' sociological readings intentionally or unintentionally contribute to a continuing modernist discourse on health-care organization. This is hardly surprising, given that these readings constitute their 'problems' within the same realm of discourse in which the 'organizations' themselves were constituted. In what amounts to reification, descriptions of the models or methods used in organizing are seen to create a thing: an 'organization'. 'Organizations' can be subjected to scientific analysis, manipulated and used as a signifier of the power and control which the organizers would wield over the organized. While often strongly critical, each critique of the 'organization', whether from sociological, economic, humanistic or psychological perspectives, recapitulates and serves the continuity of this modernist conception. (For a review of the range of these perspectives, see Silverman 1970.)

Where the modernist SHH has concerned itself with organization, this tendency may take the form of an effort to address the 'problem' of the anti-humanist principles of efficiency and effectiveness motivating modern health-care organization: for example, Gerson's (1976) analysis of the organizational principles which arrange the routines of hospital life for the benefit of staff rather than of patients. Alternatively, the approach is an evaluation of the 'problem' of the extent to which this efficiency/effectiveness falls short of perfection, followed in many cases by a proposal of somewhat different forms of organization which might possibly resolve these 'problems'. For example, Pope's (1991) study of the organization of waiting lists demonstrated how *ad hoc* arrangements in the system destroyed any semblance of rational planning of hospital admissions for elective surgery.

Despite the critical motivation of these studies, such modernist sociological theorizing, so long as it takes the 'organization' as a given, cannot but contribute to the sense of continuity and the reality of the 'modern organization'. Even when documenting such recent developments as 'flexible specialization', these discourses do not question the assumption of an underlying rationalist project to maximize certain ends (Clegg 1990: 184). In a sentence, modernist sociological commentaries on organization help to make 'organizations' real.

A postmodern perspective

In place of this modernist sociological theorizing of organization, I offer a radical alternative: in another single sentence, a postmodern perspective on organization. Simply put, *all organizations are mythologies constituted discursively to serve particular interests of power, and contested by other interests of power.*

To enlarge upon this rather bald statement and to clarify the extent to which this entails a rereading of modern organization theory, I will now set out five elements of a postmodern study of organization (not all of which are necessarily exclusive to this position), drawing on the writings of Cooper and Burrell (1988), Mumby and Stohl (1991) and Parker (1990). If these in turn seem over-abstracted, they will be explored fully in the case study which follows.

1 Organization is to be seen as a verb not a noun, as process rather than structure. Whereas 'the organization' is seen as a bounded social system, with specific structures and goals, acting more or less rationally and coherently, to further actively the aims of people like a machine or a prosthesis, organization as process is *reactive* or *remedial*, existing only in relation to dis-organization.

2 Modern organization continually privileges unity, identity and immediacy, denying discontinuity, contradiction and contestation. That which is undecidable is organized so that its undecidability is obscured. Consequently, there is always the possibility of discontinuity re-emerging: organization must constantly guard against this, by further organization.

3 Organization acts in the realm of the social, constituting discourses which are *self-referential*, in themselves independent of reason, purpose or meanings which may be claimed for them by their creators or detractors. As coherent texts, organizational discourses may be read, and they may also act on other texts, writing them, rewriting them. In this sense, we can understand the *inscription* of humans by organization.

But (referring back to point 2), they are also vulnerable to rewriting: organizational discourse may be – and continually is – subverted. This subversion (in the play of intertextuality, we might say), is final. There is no such thing as 'the dysfunctional organization', only contested, fragmented, subverted discourses.

4 Organization is to be seen not as oppressing or alienating of some prior

human subject captured by an iron cage of bureaucracy, but as constitutive of that subjectivity, enabling actions to become meaningful.
5 Organization may act in the unconscious. (This point is so contradictory
to the modernist conception of organization as rational activity to achieve
some end or other, that unconscious organization is likely to be redefined as something else: paranoia, oedipal fixation, sociopathic activity.
The unconscious is seen as a barrier to effective organization (Morgan
1986: 229). This is one of the ways the unconscious is suppressed in
modernism, and in modernist social science.)

The reader may identify in this overview positions familiar from earlier
in this book: rejections of logocentrism and its associated centrisms (adopted
in much organizational writing to claim a privileged position on 'effective
organization'), an emphasis on difference in place of essence, an antipathy
to the metanarratives of social structure, and interests in intertextuality,
power and knowledge. There is also a continuity of concerns between
these interpretations of organization and the positions which were set out
in Chapter 2 on inscription of health, and the resistance to discourse
located in desire. Too often in the SHH, discussions at the level of 'the
organization' have appeared distinct from the 'micro level' of interactions
(Silverman 1985). For the PSTH, the organization of health care is also the
discursive and hence inscriptive organization of bodies. Resistance to discourse is that which organization seeks to suppress through its technologies of subjectification. Desire (that which is beyond discourse), where it
challenges discourses of power, is the most feared and oppressively dealt
with object of organizational discourse. These elements of a PSTH are
explored in the case study which follows.

Organizing the ward round

The purpose of this case study – of the organization of post-operative
ward interactions between surgeons and patients – is to illustrate the elements of postmodern theory of organization. It is drawn from an ethnographic study of surgery which I undertook in UK hospitals during the late
1980s. While many episodes of co-presence between surgeons and their
patients occur with the latter as silent, docile bodies during operative
procedures – unresisting subjects of the surgical discourse – when they
meet pre- and post-operatively on the ward, there is the possibility of
interaction. In such situations, patients possess the potential to challenge
the surgical discourse on their treatment directly. In the extracts of the
ethnography which I represent below, I want to show, firstly, how surgeons organize these interactions *reactively*, to minimize these challenges.
Secondly, it will be clear that patients regularly *do* seize the initiative.
Thirdly, I intend to indicate how these interactions serve to create a

subjectivity on the patient, inscribed in a number of surgeon-inspired discourses. Fourthly, I will show that these discourses are continually rewritten, as organization is refined. Fifthly, I will argue that organization can serve unconscious as well as conscious ends, and that these reflect the desire (or will-to-power) of the participants. Finally, I will suggest that together these positions dissolve the mythical 'ward round' which is claimed as a shorthand for these organizational discourses.

(Methodologically, I am less concerned here with a formal 'deconstruction', although I have undertaken such an exercise with these data (Fox 1993). I explored the opposition of surgical healing with the injury which surgery causes, and the efforts surgeons used to privilege the first and dismiss the latter. The reader can see this deconstruction as underpinning the following discussion of the case study.)

What are the objectives of the post-operative surgical ward round? We might identify a number, as seen from the surgeon's point of view. To begin with, it provides an opportunity for a consultant with overall responsibility for a patient to assess the progress of that patient, even though the day-to-day care has been carried out by nursing and junior surgical staff. It enables the consultant to check the notes held on the ward concerning her/his patient, and to make judgements as to the forthcoming management of the case. It also allows the consultant to check up on her/his junior staff. One consultant observed during the fieldwork used the opportunity of a ward round to make derogatory comments about a registrar whom she did not like, imputing surgical and linguistic incompetence and doubtful sexual motivations to him.

The ward round provides the forum within which the patient can be observed, examined and quizzed as to her/his symptoms and clinical signs. In a recapitulation of the original clinic examination, the post-operative ward round enables the elicitation of the signs which the surgeon will use to pursue a clinical management plan. Of course, now the signs will be different, as will their significance. Whereas pre-operatively they signified the *disease*, now they are intended to signify the *cure* achieved by the surgical intervention.

Finally, the round allows – within defined limits – a patient input to the management of the care. Despite the dependency relationship, the patient has a legal autonomy and her/his compliance is required in order to achieve the management of care which the surgeon perceives as appropriate.

The ward round is thus an arena in which a number of conflicting objectives of surgical organization coincide. From the perspectives of the PSTH we might identify these as follows: the authority of the consultant over patient and staff, generated within an arena of a surgical gaze; the continuing exercise of discourses on the skills and expertise of diagnosis and care management; the negotiation with the patient of compliance within this discourse of care, even if this may conflict with patient-centred concerns of discharge, comfort, family life or whatever (a realm of governmentality of self-care). Furthermore, the first of these, the surgeon's authority, depends for its continuation upon the second, the display of expertise, and the third, the compliance of the patient.

From a patient's perspective, on the other hand, there may be different objectives. The ward round is a high point in a tedious regime of hospital life, the consultant is a very significant other, and a patient may have invested very heavily in trust, confidence or respect towards this surgeon. The treatment may have had unexpected side-effects, there may be a doubt in a patient's mind as to whether the outcome was as had been predicted: the ward round is an opportunity to air these doubts and fears, or to reinvest in trust or respect.

Some aspects of ward rounds – the processional form, the white coats, the use of screens and the hierarchical relations between staff – may no doubt contribute to ensuring that the surgeon's perspective is bolstered. These rituals are interesting as rhetorics of control, yet they obscure the more subtle intertextuality of the surgeon–patient encounter, in which power is not a given, but constantly to be reachieved, and is consequently vulnerable to challenge. Processions and white coats, of themselves, count for little when surgical discourse is seriously subjected to alternative interpretation.

If it is the case that organization is to be seen as reactive, a response to a threat, then it is possible that the subtlety of this organizational strategy ('the ward round') will be greatest when there is also the greatest challenge to surgical discourse of authority. Take, for example, those instances so often reported in humanistic medical sociology, of doctors talking across a patient, using technical language and discussing her/him in the third person (Roberts 1985; Graham and Oakley 1986). This, it would be hypothesized, would occur not when the surgeon perceives a challenge, but instead when *no* challenge can feasibly be mounted – perhaps because the patient is very poorly or is highly dependent. This proposition counters the view that such behaviour is a way of dealing with difficult patients; rather, it is behaviour indulged when there is no threat at all.

The fieldwork revealed some such situation with minimal contact with the patient, or contact which did not seriously include the patient in discussions of care management. I called these examples 'the discourse on physiology', as this was the dominant – surgeon-centred – theme in these interactions (Fox 1993).

Patient B had had surgery to remove a tumour of the gastro-intestinal tract. During surgery, the tumour had been found to be disseminated, and during the extensive operation to remove as much as possible, B had had a cardiac arrest. He was conscious but poorly.

Mr D: (to junior staff and researcher) 'Despite what we've done he seems to be getting better. How is his . . . ' (a long discussion on technical details of the patient's metabolism ensues, including reports on tests and suggestions of further tests and action to stabilize the patient's condition).

The house officer introduced the problem of the surgical wound, which was leaking as a consequence of having been very rapidly closed following the cardiac arrest on the operating table. The discussion now focused upon this problem, and the relative advantages of different forms of skin sutures and staples were debated among the staff. After about five minutes Mr D addresses the patient: 'How are you Mr B? Are you feeling less sick now?'

Patient B: 'Yes, less sick.'

When the patient unexpectedly mounts a challenge, it is summarily dealt with within a discourse on dependency:

Mr D: 'Hallo, Miss F. (sits on edge of bed) Have you passed any wind yet?' (Because he is a gastro-intestinal (GI) surgeon, Mr D has an interest in post-operative flatulence as a clinical sign of GI function.)

Patient F: 'No. Can I take this (oxygen) mask off?'

Nurse: (sharply) 'No, not yet.'

Mr D: 'You can take the mask off when you can breathe, when the bruising on your lungs has gone down. We are going to give you a couple of suppositories which will get you unblocked, because your bowels are bruised too; that will reduce the swelling here, and that'll make your breathing easier. (To researcher) I said she was going to be a difficult patient.'

As with all the examples which will be reported from this study, one can see the surgical discourse as concerned with legitimating the surgeon's right to have intervened to heal the patient – a healing process which as I have discussed elsewhere (Fox 1992) necessarily entails a degree of injury to the patient, making it a strange kind of healing. Surgery which excises part of the 'natural body' faces the danger of an alternative definition as injurious to the patient, which could not possibly assist the achievement of claims to expertise and thus authority. In such situations, the surgeon needs to involve the patient more directly, to head off a challenge which might emerge. The surgeon needs to explain her/his understanding of what has been done, why it was done, and why this is a good thing. Despite this, occasionally the interaction goes in an unexpected direction.

Mrs A: 'Hallo Miss E, we sorted everything out for you, we've taken the [fallopian] tube, but the ovary is still there as usual.'

Patient E: 'You left the ovary?'

Mrs A: 'Oh yes, we *never* take the ovary [1]. So everything's fine [2]; but come and see us when you are trying for a baby, as you only have one tube now ... '

Patient E: 'I don't want a baby.'

Mrs A: (to nurse) 'Fix her up with contraceptives, the sheath' [3].
Miss E: 'I thought I'd use an IUD.'
Mrs A: 'No, I don't want you on IUD or mini-pill, use the sheath and foam' [4].

The surgeon first confirmed that despite having removed a fallopian tube, by leaving the ovary intact she had not interfered with the patient's normal female hormonal balance, and thus her femininity (this was emphasised by Mrs A to the researcher as of great importance during a number of similar operations), and goes on to say that she is 'fine' [1, 2]. A second redefinition occurs when Mrs A suggested that Miss E would fulfil the role of mother in due course. When the patient denied this desire, the surgeon turned away from her, and spoke about her in the third person to the nurse, commenting on a need for future sexual regulation [3]. Finally, there was a return to the discourse on physiology with a comment which referred to the patient's new status as a person with an impaired reproductive system which could be affected by contraception [4].

I suggested earlier that the elicitation of clinical signs supplies an analogy with a diagnostic encounter between doctor and patient. As such, it clearly serves to document the expertise of the doctor. Because surgical patients are often a lot 'less well' after an operation than before it, due to the surgical insult and anaesthesia, the claim to have 'healed' is potentially open to challenge. What I call the 'discourse on the wound' supplies a way in which surgeons organize their discourse to focus on a sign that healing has occurred, regardless of how a patient feels. Patients' concerns are subverted as the wound becomes the marker of progress. A healing wound signifies an underlying successful surgical procedure: it makes the invisible resection visible, and hence a resource for surgeons to use in their discourse on doing successful surgery.

Patient C has undergone surgery to remove an ovarian cyst. The surgeon Mrs A is seeing her the day following.
Mrs A: 'Hallo Mrs C, we have sorted out your problem for you. Let us have a look at your tummy.'
Staff nurse and junior doctor pull curtains around, Mrs C is laid flat, and the dressing is removed.
Mrs A: 'Yes, that's OK. You will not have much of a scar there.'
Patient C: 'Thank you. When can I go home?'
Mrs A: 'We'll see you on Monday.'
The surgeon turns to the nurse and requests a kind of dressing. Consultant and housedoctor dress the wound with gauze and lengths of plaster, with no further interaction with the patient.

Here, an effort to set an agenda for discussing discharge has been side-stepped neatly, first by talking about the satisfactory progress in wound healing, and second by putting the patient into a dependent physical position.

Similarly, where a patient appeared to have a very significant grievance concerning the 'success' of the surgery, the discourse on the wound becomes a way of bargaining: even if the wound is a mess, there is a success under the surface, and the patient's fortitude is to be admired!

Patient S is sitting in an armchair – she is looking quite distraught.

Mr O: 'Hallo, Mrs D; well we were going to send you home yesterday weren't we, thank the God Almighty we didn't.'

Patient S: (quietly) 'No.'

Mr O: 'Well we just don't know why this happened, there's no infection, no haematoma, nothing at all to cause this. You were up and walking ... ?'

Nurse: 'Yes she was walking about, and went to the lavatory and was straining, and then ... '

Mr O: ' ... Yes I hear there was small intestine hanging out. Well, you've had a nasty time, and we'll keep you in for ten days.'

Patient S: (aghast) 'Ten ... days ... ?'

Mr O: 'Yes, but there's absolutely nothing the matter inside, we don't know why this happened, so we'll keep you in for ten days.'

Discharge from hospital is the topic which most surgical patients put at the top of their agendas for the interactions which they spend so much time awaiting. As has been seen, this places patients in the position of challenging surgical authority in situations where discharge cannot be reasonably recommended at that point in the post-operative period. But discharge is, of course, a most potent marker of 'surgical success', and when a surgeon is able to recommend discharge, s/he may make quite a thing of it. In this 'discourse of discharge', the surgeon 'gives' the patient the best thing possible, and the patient is expected to give her/his approbation of the surgeon as a legitimate healer in return. (I will have more to say about these Gift relationships in Chapter 5.)

Patient T has no post-operative problems, but her circumstances are slightly unclear.

Mrs A: 'Hallo, Mrs T, well I think you can go home.'

Patient T: 'Go home today?'

Mrs A: 'Yes I think so, where do you live?'

Patient T: 'In (district) ... '

Mrs A: ' ... near, yes ... have you someone coming?'

Patient T: 'Yes my husband is coming.'

Mrs A: 'Yes ring him to tell him to come this afternoon, and we'll see you in a week for the stitches.'

Even if the operation will have a doubtful long-term outcome, the gift of discharge is made much of. It is used to avoid the issue of whether the surgery has really been 'successful' at all.

Patient W is an old man who has had a major resection for gastric carcinoma. Mr D plans to send him home if he can be looked after.

Researcher: 'Are you sending him home to die?'

Mr D: 'Oh no, I *think* I've cured him. Cancer of the stomach is not that difficult to treat, although in the long term prospects are not good. (Moving over to patient) Who's going to look after you when you get out?'

Patient W: (smiling) 'You tell me when I can go, and I'll arrange to be looked after.'

Mr D: (smiling) 'That's right ... but seriously though ... ?'

Patient W: 'Well my sister. She's older than me of course, but ...'

Mr D: 'Well someone to cook for you?'

Patient W: 'Oh yes, that'll be all right.'

Mr D: 'Make a clinic appointment for next Wednesday and you can go home now.'

Patient W: 'When?'

Mr D: 'As soon as you can arrange it.'

Patient W: (pretends to get out of bed) 'Well I'll give her a ring now ... (very pleased) Thank you.'

Mr D: (joking) 'At least we're not sending you for convalescence, terrible place, worse than here. If you go for convalescence you don't need convalescence.'

Sometimes the challenge to the authority of the surgeon comes from the patient's body, not her/his spoken discourse. The desire of the surgeon for a successful outcome is so great that this rival bodily discourse is silenced.

Mr D: (to patient, looking at chart) 'Hallo Mr Y. Well we want to send you home, but I don't like that raised temperature' [1].

Patient Y: 'No.'

Mr D: 'I don't know what can be causing it. We've cultured the wound and there's no infection there. I just don't know what's causing it ... Are things ready for you to go home?'

Patient Y: 'Yes, my wife can come and collect me today.'

Mr D: 'Can you go to bed, and she can look after you?'

Patient Y: 'Yes.'

Mr D: 'I don't like that raised temperature [2]. Phone your wife and you can go home now.'

Patient Y: 'Thank you very much.'

Mr D uses the phrase 'I don't like that raised temperature' twice in this short interchange, but whereas at [1] the meaning imparted is that the raised temperature is possibly a complication which should be resolved before discharge, at [2] it has changed its meaning, and now the pyrexia is an annoying detail which is preventing the return to home and the categorization of healed. Mr D's dislike of it means he can ignore it and thus allow the patient home!

With these extracts I have tried to show the ways surgeons use the organization of ward-round discourse to sustain their agenda, in the face of possible challenges. It took a really determined patient to mount an effective challenge, but, as the extract below demonstrates, the effect on the surgeon's ability to define herself as a 'healer' was devastating.

Mrs F had had an ectopic pregnancy, and had a fallopian tube removed as a consequence.

Patient F: 'I have a list of questions which I wrote down, because I was a bit hazy when you explained before the operation. (Surgeon Mrs A nods) What exactly have you taken?'

Mrs A: 'We have taken your right tube, that's all.'

Patient F: 'Not the ovary?'

Mrs A: 'We never take the ovary, so you have two good ovaries.'

Patient F: 'So will this make it difficult for me to conceive?' [1]

Mrs A: 'No you can produce an egg every month, same as before.'

Patient F: 'But I will only have a chance every other month?' [2]

Mrs A: 'No, just the same, you have both ovaries.'

Patient F: 'But one is not connected to anything . . . ' [3]

Mrs A: 'No . . . we can't just say which one will produce an egg each month.' [4]

In this sequence, the questions at points [1] [2] and [3] force the surgeon to admit that the operation has not returned the patient to the status of 'normal' fertility, and is forced at [4] to fall back on the randomness of ovulation as a response, thereby at least avoiding being allocated the moral status as potential scapegoat for a future infertility. At this point, Mrs A hurriedly departed, preventing any further questions.

This case study of organization of care can be read as an exercise in logocentrism, in which it is the expertise of the surgeon, her/his claim to speak the truth about how to heal, which is the *logos*. In this perspective, the authority and authenticity as a 'surgeon' is achieved discursively. Power does not derive from coercion of the patient, nor from the surgeon's position in a hierarchy, status or professional closure, but through the practical demonstration of expertise in achieving 'successful' cases of surgical outcome. Status and privilege are consequences of the power achieved through successful claims to expertise.

But the study also suggests ways to resist discourse and power. The postmodern understanding of organization suggests that resistance is primarily achieved not through macro-processes of counterposed authority or regulation (although this will also be effective), but through the use of local everyday narratives. *Resistance is ubiquitous, it is unexceptional and is the reason why there is organization in the first place.*

Organization of the ward round creates subjectivities in its objects – the patients. The 'master-subjectivity' here is 'healed', and, within that position, discourses are ranged to boost that definition. As chance consequences of interaction send the discourses in unexpected directions, new elements of organization are drawn in to sustain the intended direction of subjectivity.

Finally, it is possible to recognize the powerful mix of unconscious as well as conscious desires that motivate the organization of discourse. Where these desires – in the case of the penultimate extract reported, for instance – go against 'rationality', then it may be the unconscious motivation which leads to the outcome of the interaction. Yet we might conjecture that it is only in these exceptional circumstances that we see the play of desire which is a factor in *all* the organizational strategies, in this case the will-to-power of the surgeon.

This case study has supplied some material by which to explore some of the positions generated by the postmodern position. In this reading, the ward round, which in modernist organization theory possesses such facticity, dissolves, and is seen instead as mythic, a fabrication, created to serve particular wills-to-power. Its continuity as an organizational form is a market of the strength of those desires. Its apparent rationality as a way to organize surgeon–patient encounters is part of the logocentrism of surgical power and, in part at least, an outcome of modernist organizational theory as well as surgical tradition. In the postmodern position, it is a further exposition of the politics of health-talk.

In Chapter 2 I discussed at length the inscription of the body (the Body-without-Organs). The case study of ward-round organization is also a study of inscription, and it is clear how what is being inscribed here is 'health' or 'healing' or 'surgical success' or whatever. Organization is often inscribed in written documents: the medical record, the statistics of hospital use or surgical successes. But it is also the inscription of bodies; indeed, without the inscription of bodies, organization would start from scratch in every interaction. Yet, I hope it is also clear from this case study that these definitions of healing or success are not absolutes, but the outcomes of powerful discourses. And also, that these discourses are not necessarily uncontested; they are the consequences of negotiations and intertextual readings of whatever biological, psychological or emotional elements become available during surgeon–patient interactions.

Referring back to the discussion at the end of Chapter 2 of desire and the idea of an 'arche-health', beyond discourse, concerned with the BwO's will-to-power, the exploration of organization in this study of health care demonstrates that what is being inscribed is not an arche-health of positive desire at all, but a fabricated, contingent, partial, local, social, figuration of power/knowledge, constituitive of a particular subjectivity of health or illness. It is precisely this inscription, which can derive as much from sociological discourses as from medical, that the PSTH would expose.

As was mentioned earlier in this chapter, organization claims to base itself in rationalization. Consequently, the unconscious, and the whole issue of desire which I have once again raised, are pushed off the agenda. One might see this as fundamental to the modernist project. In Chapter 4 I return to issues of desire and the unconscious. In the remainder of this chapter I wish to address some of the critical readings of the modernist theory of health-care organization which the PSTH generates, and, in so doing, to critique the modernist texts of sociology which have interpreted and contributed to that modernist enterprise of organizing. We may understand this as a further exercise in intertextuality, exploring the mutual constitution of some texts (organizations) by other texts (sociological knowledge), and their inscription of a further set of texts: the bodies of those organized.

The problem of the monolith

Modernist sociology has supplied a rigorous critique of care organization. Images of modern health care have tended to exemplify rational, bureaucratic organization and the production line and depersonalized mechanisms which epitomize the modern way of life. While this image remains powerful, many efforts have been made to respond to criticisms of this image, from the theorizing of 'care' in the discourses of the nursing process, through policies on replacing institutional care with community-based systems, to instituting appointment systems to replace long waits for medical consultations. In the United Kingdom, where the majority of patients are seen within the state-run NHS, recent competition and discourses on consumerism have contributed to these changes (Elston 1991). In North America, the ever-rising expenditure of a largely insurance-funded health care has achieved quality of both technical and what might loosely be termed humanistic care in the private sector.

We can see here two alternative discourses: first, that of the monolith; and second, that of the flexible, humanistic system which is supposed to have replaced it. The postmodern reading set out here is wary of both images. It *does* recognize flux and flexibility within modern organization (*contra* the monolith), but (against the theorists of care in the postmodern world) it suggests that this fragmentation is *both unintended and inevitable*.

In place of a monolithic organization (and the architecture of the hospital in the modern era has, I suspect, led many to superimpose monolithic notions of social structure on physical structure) we have a fluctuating set of conflicting discourses: political, consumerist, ethical, economic, professional. All vie for control, asserting the advantages of one approach or another. When two coincide (the appointment system suits patients who do not have to wait and family doctors who can have a fixed-length consultation period and a smaller waiting room), there is reorganization, until another challenge from an expertise or wielder of power comes along. Instead of the monolith, we discover that the organization has disappeared, to be replaced by a net of signifying practices, in tension and subject to challenge and resistance.

Having said that, for many who work or are cared for in modern healthcare systems (HCSs) the monolith is an experiential reality. We must not make the error of subsuming the modern discourse of organization within its postmodern critique. The discovery that a fragmenting care system is perceived as monolithic is precisely how we can explore what organization is about. The value of the postmodern perspective is that it stands beyond the discourse it criticizes, to demonstrate the discourses of rationalism and its associated bureaucratic forms as the generative motivation behind modern health care.

Without this distancing we are led either to the attempt to be 'more rational' ('doing ironies'), or into functionalist or Marxist analyses in which the organization is explained as functional for particular goals. The latter analysis might identify (for example) in the dehumanizing processes of stripping (Goffman 1968) which a person undergoes on admission to hospital, the meeting of an organizational 'need' or objective of regimenting the person as patient within the rules of the organization and its staff. It is quite easy to generate a comprehensive functionalist or Marxist 'explanation' of modern health care deriving from an imputed system of social structures which serve the consensual or class-based needs of the social system: in the literature we need look no further than Parsons (1951) and Navarro (1976).

While sociologists have been very circumspect about such models, organizational theory has had no such qualms in formulating discourses which serve the imputed 'needs' of 'the organization'. So we might reasonably expect to find inscribed in organization such discourses upon needs or objectives. Sociological distaste for functionalism is misplaced, and is grounded in the adherence to a notion of social structure within modernist sociology. The postmodernist says not that there is not a functionalist organization with needs, but that there are neither organizations (with or without needs) nor social structures. There are discourses which serve power, and these discourses can be discerned in the fabric of organization.

Thus, in the example of stripping mentioned above, we read in the organization of admission which people undergo, the discourse of organizers (administrators, nurses) whose power is served by processes which are intended, consciously or perhaps unconsciously, as passive, regimented, patient bodies. This is the process documented so brilliantly by Foucault in *Birth of the Clinic* (1976) and *Discipline and Punish* (1979), in which the discipline of panopticism subjects people to a gaze of power. This and the other techniques of rendering people as docile subjects are inscribed in organizational routines, which do indeed, in this sense, contribute to defined objectives.

Gerson (1976) discussed this politics of the care system in his study of patients' experiences of hospitalization. He argued that the organizational imperatives of hospital life derive from the reality of illness as both something undergone by patients and the work of the staff. Without illness, there would be no work, and if illness is not organized in certain ways, work becomes unsatisfactory. Gerson's achievement in this study is to demonstrate how organization is achieved in concrete practices by agents, to meet objectives set by a particular power grouping (in this case the administrators, acting on behalf of the workforce). But his study also suggests how we can understand the monolithic image of some aspects of care, as generated through discourse on organization of the HCS to meet the investments of interest of groups other than patients. To use a postmodern idiom, we would say in the context of Gerson's study, that the patients were inscribed by the staff work, constituted as 'patients' with 'illnesses' which become routine attributes of the business of care. The monolith is mythic, yet has a real impact on people through the practices inscribed upon them according to organizational needs or objectives.

Profession or discipline?

Another classic text, which in many ways has a postmodern edge to it, is the collection of tales by sick sociologists (Davis and Horobin 1977). This volume contains many descriptions of the 'monolithic feel' of HCSs, and the processes by which patients learn to fit into implicit and explicit organizing practices. The 'disciplinary' character of health care is demonstrated time and time again in these cameos, generating discourses and governmentalities within which people transform themselves into patients. The volume also indicates the possibilities of resistance to this governmentality and the sanctions which discourage it. A favourite is Roth's tale of the governmental discipline which transformed his son, during a visit to the UK, from a studious adolescent with a lack of knowledge of English sport into a psychiatric case with a phobia of physical exercise. Teachers, family doctors and specialists contributed to this process of subjectification, required in order to achieve a dispensation from school sports lessons. A legitimate knowledgeability was needed to permit this relaxation of a school rule: and in the absence of any physical health reason, it fell to the profession of psychiatry to supply one (Roth 1977).

Modernist sociology has traditionally separated the analysis of knowledge and power in its studies of profession. The former has been seen as one necessary, but not in itself sufficient, attribute of the professional, contributing to the sociologically interesting issue of the use (or, more often in these texts, misuse) of power. Professional dominance has been achieved through strategies of closure, self-regulation, recruitment, and so on (for a review, see Freidson 1983). Traits of the professional have served to create in sociological discourse either an ever-expanding professional grouping – Wilensky's (1964) professionalization of everybody – or a deprofessionalization (Haug 1973).

The postmodern perspective on profession requires us to reintroduce knowledge as central to the imposition of power. Foucault's genealogies of medicine, law, learning, the workplace can clearly be seen as supplying an alternative framework for the analysis of professional power (Goldstein 1984). But Foucault does not concentrate upon occupational grouping, but upon the recipients of professionalism, the masses. Disciplines are both bodies of knowledge and strategies of power – meticulous methods by which docile bodies are manipulated and controlled.

In my study of surgery (Fox 1992), I attempted the detailed analysis of the power relations of an HCS. Within the enterprise of surgery, different professional groupings constantly sought to inscribe their discursive practices upon each other, and most significantly, patients. It was clear that these groups – surgeons or anaesthetists, for example – held power, but on a fairly tenuous basis, contingent upon continuing demonstrations of the ability of their knowledgeability to be instrumentally valuable, and capable of legitimately defining patients. So, for example, surgeons were able to operate upon patients according to their emphasis on the need to remove disease until the anaesthetic counter-definition of a patient as having only finite resources to cope with the stress of surgery (fitness) came into play. When a surgeon made a mistake, compromising this fitness, s/he lost the authority to continue the surgical initiative, and her/his power over inscription.

Of course, it would take more than a single mistake to destroy a surgeon's authority, and very many to challenge surgery as a specialty. Millman (1977) has documented the strategies adopted to control the impact of such errors. The point, however, is the recognition of the interdependence of power and knowledge, each reinforcing the other. In the study of the professionalization of a group, we would look not at macro-social phenomena such as state registration, but at the ways that knowledgeability legitimates actions, which in turn legitimate the knowledge base. Tattersall (1992) identified such a process in the growth of nursing discourses on accident and emergency unit triage. Triage by nurses concerning patient disposal potentially enhances the professional power and control of nurses in relation to physicians. Tattersall's genealogy of triage noted a counter-discourse emanating from the medical profession, which similarly recognized the attractiveness of triage as a means of organizing work, but with doctors as the agents making the triage decisions! It is in these micro-processes of discourse that we can unearth the sources of power of health professionals.

If the dual meaning of the English word 'discipline' reminds us of the relationship between power and knowledge, it is perhaps interesting at this point to examine what postmodern theory of organization makes of situations where there is coercive power. In modern sociology, Goffman's notion of the 'total institution' has been influential in studies of HCSs, in particular psychiatric hospitals, in which the coercive character of the moral regime has been most clearly opposed to humanistic discourse. In many ways the warders of such institutions are viewed as anti-professional, tarred by their failure to live up to a model of care which includes the facilitation of freedom.

In the previous chapter I dealt with the processes by which docile bodies are achieved, including the technology of panopticism, and the creation of a positive subjectivity in the recipients of disciplinary power. It will be clear that the theoretical framework of this approach would be hard to reconcile with Goffman's positions on subjectivity and social structure. Goffman's human agents are a strange mixture, deriving from his efforts to intermingle interactionist and structuralist models (Gonos 1977; Strong 1978). They dwell in worlds constituted through shared meanings, yet these worlds are deterministically framed by social structures. Actors play out more or less appropriate roles, and despite apparently possessing some inherent subjectivity, are more or less determined by these roles. The total institution is Goffman's extreme frame, in which the role is absolutely determined, allowing no possibility for resistance, and policed ultimately by threats of violence or violence itself.

And yet it is not necessary to reread Goffman through post-structuralism to be able to ask 'how total are total institutions?'. Goffman (1968) describes throughout his book *Asylums* how the total institutional regime leaves room for a sub-culture, an under-life, ways of making out.

We need to make this resistance to organization central, and interrogate modernist organizational texts with the following questions. Do they not focus upon the positivities of power and control, so there is a corresponding failure to recognize the full extent of resistance to organizational discourse – even in institutions which are at the totalizing end of the spectrum such as the psychiatric hospital? Is it not the case that there is a contestation of power, between discursive strategies which seek to control not through violence, but through the *inscription upon the body* of a *subjectivity* as patient, lunatic or prisoner, and the resistances to those discourses? Recall Genet's writings from his prison cell: his resistance to power in the sustaining of a rival subjectivity constituted in a body invested with a will-to-power, a desire. Does the model of the total institution explain only its own modernist discourse of totalization?

Welfare, governmentality and the problem of good intentions

The discussion of 'total institutions' leads neatly on to another issue. In many writings in the sociology of HCSs, there is an apparent paradox. This paradox runs as follows. A study investigates a care system – say, an out-patient clinic. It opposes (ironicizes) the intended rationality of the system, either with its actual irrational functioning, or its anti-humanistic reality. The study uses this irony then to promote a policy intervention that will 'make it better', by fine-tuning, major revision or even (in the case of Marxist studies) by overturning social relations. Sociologists are, along the way, shown to be cleverer than the people running the system (doctors, managers). This scenario is clearly attractive to the sociologist. As the editors of a recent text in this tradition (Gabe *et al.* 1991: 5–6) assert, a rigorous, reflexive sociological analysis of health policy issues

> is highly desirable, especially at a time when health and health policy have come to occupy a more central place in debates about the future of the welfare state and the impact of consumerism, and as the social consensus over the NHS is undergoing severe strain. The issues addressed ... relate to the emergence of a crisis over the development of health care in Britain [which] provides an opportunity for rethinking the relevance of sociological propositions in the health field and thus for sociology to be more policy relevant.

Welfare, and its rationalization in HCSs, is not problematized *per se*, nor is the rationality by which sociology produces its policy interventions. In the last part of this chapter I want to problematize these assumptions by examining this liberal discourse on welfare from the perspective of governmentality. In Chapter 2 I referred to Nettleton's study of the discourse on prevention which developed in dentistry, creating the mouth as an arena for hygienic practices which make children and mothers active subjects. Oral welfare extends its gaze into a population involved in self-regulation (Nettleton 1992), or as Rose (1989: 9) has it, the government of the soul. Rose's recent genealogy of child welfare identifies in the development of discourses on the welfare of children not an obvious value of a modern society, but a nexus of exhortations, expectations, strivings and dreams refined (often discontinuously, rather than incrementally) over the past decades. Philanthropic, humanistic and socialist discourses have been replaced by neo-conservative ones saying much the same about the importance of family life and natural parenthood (1989: 204). In the 1940s and 1950s, 'experts' such as Winnicott and Bowlby advocated encouraging and rationalizing the natural expertise of mothers, to ensure the welfare of the child.

> They established a perceptual system and a vocabulary by means of which mothers (and others) could speak about and evaluate their selves and their emotions and relations, and the self of the child as well. Infant feeding, for example, becomes not a task to be learned but a 'putting into practice of a love relation between two human beings'. The life of the baby, and the life of the mother, become 'inherently difficult' (Rose 1989: 203).

Such a vocabulary also provided a forum for the law, for social sciences and for welfare agencies to intervene discursively within families. More recently, such outside interference has been challenged by conservative and radical voices. Rose (1989: 207) suggests that these challenges represent a new, individualizing discourse which recognizes the *rights* of parents and children:

> from this time forth, the ideal relation of psychological expertise to its subjects will be outside the legal domain, in the private contractual relations between individuals concerned about their families and experts seeking only to assist them in their search for adjusted selves, relationships and children.

A discourse on family privacy coincided with moves within social welfare agencies to maintain and support families, substituting long-term care with notions of 'shared care', 'inclusive fostering' and the rapid return of children to their family after being taken into care, to promote the integrity, identity and autonomy of the family (Rose 1989: 208). This new discourse on child welfare, Rose (1989: 208) concludes, has led to a governmentality of the modern family, achieved not through coercion or social control, but through

> the promotion of subjectivities, the construction of pleasures and ambitions, and the activation of guilt, anxiety, envy and disappointment. The new relational technologies of the family are installed within us, establishing a particular psychological way of viewing our family lives and speaking about them, urging a constant scrutiny of our inherently difficult interactions with our children and each other, a constant judgement of their consequences for health, adjustment, development and the intellect. The tension generated by the gap between normality and actuality bonds our personal projects inseperately to expertise.

In Rose's account, welfare is problematized. It is no longer a value which – however relative – is to be fine-tuned or radically revised for the greater good. Welfare impinges on the government of the soul, subjecting it, creating subjectivities, inscribing bodies. It is a consequence of expertise, not vice versa. Where there is expertise, there will be welfare (or health or whatever). From this perspective we may understand the organization of care as the organization of technologies of expertise, the (attempted) organization of subjectivity itself.

In this section of the book, I have tried to demonstrate the ways in which truth-claims about health, illness and healing are constituted, and how the rationalist project of organizing care has contributed to a discourse through which the figure of the patient or client emerges, inscribed and made a subject of power/knowledge. In Part 2, I focus not upon the 'how' of this discourse of care, but upon the detailed micro-politics of the caring relationship. More specifically, I turn to the possibility of resisting this subjection, and how a postmodern theory of health might contribute to retheorizing the contact between carer and cared-for. I shall return to a commentary upon modernist organization in Chapter 6, when I address issues of ethics and politics in care and in social theory.

PART 2

REPETITIONS AND RESISTANCE

In the next two chapters, I want to explore the ways in which a postmodern social theory conceptualizes the possibilities of resistance to the discourses of the body outlined in the last section. In doing so, I shall focus upon the element of the caring relationship which postmodernism identifies through its critiques: the repetitions by which caring comes to resemble other relations, and principally the oedipalized familial relationship between parent and child. Deconstructing these repetitions opens up the potential for new 'readings' of care which are based not upon dependency but upon generosity.

The principal ideas which will be introduced in this section are described in the following.

Desire

In questioning rationalist 'explanations' in social theory, postmodern writing has addressed the unconscious and, in particular, the desire which motivates agency. Psychoanalysis has – particularly under the influence of Jacques Lacan – understood desire as the effort by which a subject tries to achieve or regain that which has been lost: the object of desire. Lacan's (1977: 203) 'unconscious which is structured like a language' seeks this object, yet, in the same way as in language meaning is always deferred, always finds that this object of desire recedes, is unattainable.

A quite different conception of desire emanates from the writing of the philosopher Deleuze and the psychoanalyst Guattari. In their conception, desire is not a lack at all, but a positive force, which enables and which 'de-territorializes' the body inscribed in discourse, allowing it to become other than it is, and to thereby resist.

In Chapter 4, these two versions of desire inform a rereading of Parsonian sick-role theory, supplying a framework for exploring the processes within the contact between carer and cared-for which contribute to discourses of control, and which – if reconstituted – might enable resistance to such control.

Repetition

Counterposing the form of desiring which seeks something which fills a lack, with the desire which is a real presence, focuses attention on the strategies by which the former kind of desire is mediated in various discourses of care. Crucial to these strategies is the *repetition* of earlier themes in interaction. An interaction in the here and now is to be seen (in the first kind of desire) as a recapitulation of an earlier interaction. Perhaps it has been distorted, and no doubt the actors are unconscious of part or all of their repetition, which has been repressed and is now played out symbolically.

Caring relationships, it will be suggested, have co-opted a structure of repetition to mediate the power relations of dependency and control.

Challenging these repetitions, or refusing to model care relationships as repetitions of parent–child or master–slave discourses, opens the possibility for a positive desire of carer towards cared-for. In the latter part of Chapter 4, examples from the literature of some of the repetitions in caring are deconstructed, opening the way for discussions of how resistance can become possible.

The Gift

Relationships based upon control and dependency may be seen as a form of property relation, by which the empowered party possesses the dependent. The poststructuralist feminist Cixous opposes such 'Proper' relationships with what she calls Gift relationships. The latter are open-ended, trusting, relations of *generosity*, in which a person invests another with the gift of her/his desire – the kind of positive desire described earlier.

It is suggested in Chapter 5 that the Gift relationship provides the basis for contact between carer and cared-for which enables, which offers the possibility for the cared-for to resist the discourses of health care, and perhaps to become other, to move towards the *arche-health* mentioned in Chapter 2, in which the body of the cared-for is invested not with discourses on 'health' but with its own power to become.

Intertextuality

Developing the perspectives offered by these three ideas, I return to the practicalities of resistance. For feminist post-structuralism, writing has been important in enabling, in creating space for a subjectivity which is not the outcome of the discourse of the (male) other. I take up this argument, and relate it to the postmodern interest in intertextuality – the play of one text (book, film, body) upon, within or beside other texts. The inscribed body described in Chapter 2 collides with other textualities, which have the effect of 'de-territorializing' it momentarily, enabling transformation and 'becoming' other.

In the caring relationship, intertextuality is the means by which the cared-for may attain the space to resist the discourses of health and care. The latter part of Chapter 5 is concerned with ways in which intertextuality may be used positively, including a focus upon writing as a creative, resisting force.

These four ideas constitute the theme of resistance which in Part 3 of this book will open up the more general positions on ethics and politics which the PSTH entails.

4

REPETITION, DESIRE AND PROFESSIONAL CARE

The sociology of health and illness has defined itself, at least in part, through its illustrations of the darker side to caring relationships. The healers are exposed as manipulative and/or oppressive characters, quick to make judgemental and moral evaluations of their patients, or as agents of a deterministic social or political system. Admittedly, Talcott Parsons was an admirer of the medical profession (and I shall turn to a reading of Parsons later in this chapter), but from Eliot Freidson onwards there can have been few passages emanating from the pens of medical sociologists which have dwelt on the positive aspects of medical practice. I have myself contributed to this theme of what might be termed 'doctor-bashing' in the first part of this book: the PSTH has its own critique of medical power/ knowledge, the gaze and governmentality, as has been seen.

It is hardly surprising that sociology should have taken this negative approach. Firstly, it was legitimate and well overdue to appraise critically the positions emanating for medical discourse, which for at least two hundred years had been promulgating its own claims to authority and prestige. The analyses of Dubos and McKeown pricked the bubble of medical assertions that the profession could take the credit for bringing health and happiness to the modern world, while the quip that the surgeon's motto was that 'the operation was a success, but the patient died', struck a chord which has resonance in an era of the hi-tech. Medical sociological critiques of medicine articulated with a general disillusion with establishment values and centralized systems: to knock the powerful was trendy and progressive.

Secondly, as I have suggested in Chapter 1, modernist sociology had constituted its position in opposition to the natural, and has generated models of nature which have enabled it to sustain its unique perspective. The romantic subject, in particular, supplied a sociologized version of the biological individual to be exhibited as the downtrodden victim of oppressive forces, be they the forces of capitalism, patriarchy or medical dominance. The validity of medical sociology was, in part, to be measured through its capacity to generate critiques of these societal forces.

These sound *disciplinary* reasons for a focus upon the negative in appraisals of medical practice have led to an opposition between medicine and health care as the negative, controlling discipline, while the SHH has been defined (and privileged) as the positive, empowering discipline – on the side of the oppressed and vulnerable. I have already deconstructed this opposition in Chapter 1, and do not need to repeat the postmodern position which demonstrates the disciplinary character of sociological 'knowledge' itself. Suffice it to say that from the standpoint of the PSTH, it is a false opposition, which has variously constructed a human subject which is essentialist and/or over-socialized or determined.

While the preceding chapters have identified, from postmodernist perspectives, the ways in which patients and others are inscribed by power/knowledge, and by organizational strategies, in them I sought to demonstrate how the social, while constitutive of human subjectivity, was also open to challenge and to resistance. In them I did not spell out the character of this resistance, and it is to this which I wish now to turn.

In particular, I want to open the way towards an understanding of how relationships between carers and the cared-for might potentially be empowering for the latter, based not in discourses on the role of 'the medical', but in relations of trust, generosity and confidence. Whereas structuralist and modernist analyses found the negativity of caring in the dominance arising from closure, patriarchy, capitalism or bureaucracy, postmodernism emphasizes a much more intimate effect of power and control – constituted in knowledgeability: I have already addressed this position at some length.

I now wish to push this intimacy one step further, to suggest that we understand this power/knowledge and control as *inextricably associated with the body of the carer*. The consequence of this is that power and control in the interaction between carer and cared-for are not an epiphenomenon of the positive 'care' which is being administered, but *are part of that care*. Care is power, and the possibility of resisting that power entails a refusal of care *qua* care, and of the very meanings which are associated with professional carers – which, if you like, are inscribed upon the bodies of carers.

In the pages which follow I intend to go some way beyond the analyses of power in caring interactions which have recently been ably set out by Hugman. Hugman (1991: 113–34) suggests that caring professions dominate their clients through labelling them 'clients', 'patients', by controlling them through such institutions as the sick role, or more coercively, in total institutions, by control of access to precious resources of care services, and by sustaining an ideological split between carer and cared-for. He suggests that resistance to this professional power is to be achieved through collective action by clients/patients, by the use of advocacy, and through a move to a consumerist ideology of care services (1991: 135–44). None of these seem to Hugman satisfactory, and he suggests:

> An alternative approach to the empowerment of service users must be one which recognises mutual collective interests between service users and members of caring professions ... as a 'power *sharing*', going beyond the relationships between individual professionals and service users, necessary as that is in everyday practice (1991: 144–5, emphasis in original).

Hugman's (1991: 145) focus upon 'a reframing of professional and organisational structures' displaces the focus of what such power-sharing means away from 'everyday practices'. What I will try to show is that, unless it is at this intimate, individual, everyday level of interaction that the sharing of power occurs, resistance will not replace dependency on the part of the client, and (*pace* Hugman) professional power/knowledge will remain intact.

So in this chapter and the next, I am going to focus not upon structure, but upon the micro-politics of what happens between carer and cared-for. The impact of the exploration of the possibilities of resistance to the power/knowledge of the medical (that portion of the discourses of the social concerning themselves with health and healing) is far-reaching, entailing so radical a re-evaluation of the carer role that the role will be fragmented irrevocably, to be replaced by a relationship with the cared-for (a role whose own dissolution is the objective of the resistance), based not in dependency but in generosity and a positive *desire* invested by each upon the other.

It is this notion of desire and the related theme of the unconscious which supply the starting point for this element of the PSTH.

Desire and the unconscious

If, as Turner (1992) has suggested, 'the body' has been absent in medical sociological discourse, then 'desire' and 'the unconscious' are terms which are as absent, if not more so.

What does it mean for social theory to study desire and the unconscious? To put it otherwise, if we wish to study desire, how is this possible within discourses constituted in reason? The difficulties of such a manoeuvre were discussed by Derrida (1978) in his critique of Foucault's *Madness and Civilisation* (1967). Foucault's attempt to provide a history of irrationality from within reason led him (in Derrida's view) to recapitulate the logocentrism which originally created madness as its opposite (Derrida 1978: 37). Just as Foucault saw madness as that which *cannot be said* (Derrida 1978: 43), so it is with desire. That, one might conclude, is sufficient to explain the silencing of the unconscious in modernist social theory.

It is possible to read the progression of Foucault's thought as a response to Derrida's critique. Despite his concern with resistance, he found himself writing always the genealogy of power and repression. I discussed in Chapter 2 how, in his later work on sexuality and the care of the self, there no longer seemed room for resistance at all, with the consequence that liberation became merely a further discourse of subjectivity. The result was a delibidinized actor, in which desire played no part at all (Lash 1991: 260).

The problems of such an account can be seen in a recent discussion of medical power (Maseide 1991). This author describes a 'control model', which, in Maseide's view, draws on Foucauldian positions to describe how an 'adequate' clinical practice is achieved:

> power is thought of as always necessary to the clinical encounter, and in that respect *often benign*. It enables the doctor to act as situationally and institutionally competent. Such competence is often demanded by patients and it is legally and professionally prescribed ... Power is made effective through forms of control and methods of domination ... As such, they are essential resources for the doctor's ability to do his or her clinical work adequately ... The impact of power is effective to the extent that doctor and patient share a system of knowledge and assumptions that facilitates relatively conflict-free interaction and effective patient compliance. In this sense, medical power is largely a cognitive phenomenon (Maseide 1991: 552–3, emphasis added).

The version of Foucauldian post-structuralism used here constitutes a kind of linguistic-based functionalism, emphasizing rationality and the conscious. Clinical competence, Maseide (1991: 558) concludes, is developed within hegemonic rationalities and moralities, and it by recourse to such cultural and cognitive sets that what is necessary, rational and moral in clinical practice is established. Presumably, it is from within such a rationalist standpoint that the author is able to define medical power as benign.

The recruitment of this sociologized Foucault to support such rationalist explanations of medical power suggests the need for a counter-move, questioning this hegemony of reason (see the critique of the 'strong programme' in Chapter 1 of this book). By excluding a serious investigation of desire, as a force of unreason, modernist sociology is condemned to recapitulate this reasonable activity, in which one always finds that rationality is constituted in an essential actor, a determining structure, or some Giddensian structuration which mediates the two poles through a 'bounded knowledgeability' (Giddens 1984).

In the discussion of desire which follows, I am going to depart in one dramatic way from the 'standard' readings of desire which have been generated in post-structuralism. The *rapprochement* which has been evidenced in some writings between feminism, post-structuralism and psychoanalysis (see Gallop 1982; Sayers 1986; Grosz 1990; Hekman 1990; Game 1991) has drawn for its inspiration the perspective on desire and the unconscious deriving from Jacques Lacan's writing. Despite the 'turn to language' in Lacan, I do not find his readings of desire persuasive, indeed I view them as problematic, and follow those writers who have seen Lacan's work as illustrative of aspects of logocentrism which postmodernism has sought to challenge (Rosenau 1992: 45; Butler 1990; Fraser 1992).

In place of a Lacanian position, I shall explore the radically different reading of desire deriving from Deleuze and Guattari, whose *Anti-Oedipus* (as the name suggests) rejects this psychoanalytic model of desire, as did Foucault (Sawicki 1991: 38). The work of Deleuze and Guattari has yet to receive the critical attention in the English-speaking world which it deserves. As will be seen, its challenge to the 'repetitions' of psychoanalysis, and its wider model of the territorialization of the body (the Body-without-Organs) by discourse and its de-territorialization by desire makes their contribution to postmodern theory particularly important.

It is from this reading of desire that I shall build in Chapter 5 a practical politics of resistance, using the work of the feminist post-structuralists, and in particular Hélène Cixous' (1986) notions of 'the Gift' and 'the Proper', and the perspectives on intertextuality which return the discussions to Derridean notions of *différance*. To begin this enterprise, I shall briefly set out the differing positions on desire in Lacan and in Deleuze and Guattari.

Desire and the symbolic in Jacques Lacan

I cannot hope, in the space available, to present anything approaching an adequate assessment of the impact of Lacan upon psychoanalytic theory. In the sketch which follows I have been most dependent on Forrester's (1990) appraisal of Lacan, which, while generally favourable towards psychoanalysis, deconstructs – in my view brilliantly – some aspects of Freudian theory, and explores the intertextuality in Lacan's readings of Freud and Derrida's readings of Freud and Lacan (see also Moi 1985; Grosz 1990). My own reading is less concerned with the minutiae of Lacan's reading of Freud than with its intertextuality *vis-à-vis* the anti-oedipal, anti-psychoanalytic desire of Deleuze and Guattari.

One might begin an exegesis of Lacan with his famous dictum that 'the unconscious is structured like a language' (Lacan 1977). The attractions of his dictum are twofold. Firstly, given that speech is the medium of psychoanalysis (Forrester 1990: 108), it means that the psychoanalytic process is capable of identifying unconscious processes at work: psychoanalysis is acting in the same register as the unconscious it would explain. Secondly, we can understand the attractiveness of a linguistic model for a post-structuralism which similarly sees language as the medium of power. Lacan privileges the signifier over the signified in the same way as the decon-structionist. To use Forrester's example, when Freud's patient, 'the Ratman', compulsively seeks to lose weight, this is a symptom acting at the level of the symbolic, and mediated by the equation of *dick* the German for 'fat', with *Dick*, the name of an American hated by the Ratman. In this kind of analysis, meaning is deferred, as one signifier takes the place of another. Condensation and displacement, Freudian processes by which the un-conscious creates realms of symbolism in dreams or slips of the tongue, in Lacan's writing are equated with metaphoric and metonymic tropes of language. The analogy with Derrida's *différance*, difference and deferral, is clear.

It is in this chaining of signifiers that desire, for Lacan, is constituted. Lacan distinguished three realms of relations between the Ego and the Other: the Real, the Imaginary and the Symbolic (Grosz 1990: 59ff.). The first of these is the realm of human 'need', the basic instincts of survival: food, warmth, shelter, freedom of movement. Need is satisfied by real objects (milk, the mother's body). The second – the Imaginary – is the arena of 'demand', which replaces need as the dominant relation of the organism with its entry into language, and is always formulated in lan-guage, tying need to concrete and specific items, and linking the Ego to the Other (initially the mother-figure) through the demand 'Give me . . . '. While demand is conscious, Lacan's third element, 'desire', which inhabits the Symbolic realm, is unconscious.

The entry into the Symbolic realm is initiated through the triadic rela-tionship Mother–Father–Ego. While demand and its satisfaction meet the needs of the organism, demand goes beyond need, for it is also the demand for the Other (the giver). The original lack, in Lacan's view, is the differ-ence between the child's general demand for satisfaction and love from the parent, and the particularity of what is supplied to satisfy it (Dews 1987: 81–2). Desire recapitulates the loss which the child experiences in the bosom of its family. It is hence intricately associated with the psychoana-lytic conception of oedipality.

With the oedipal separation of child from mother, desire takes the form of a *wish*: it is constituted in relation to an absence or lack of its object, it is the *excess of demand after basic need has been met*. It is the yearning for something which is absent, and which – when the absent is made present – slips off onto another object of desire. In a world of commod-ities, it is the acquisition, the wish to possess. The second element of the Oedipus process, the identification with the father, is not with a Real or idealized father, but with the *Name of the Father*, the symbolic, always already absent signifier.

In opposition to demand (and in accordance with need) desire is beyond conscious articulation, for it is barred or repressed from articulation. It is structured like a language, but it is never spoken as such by a subject. Its production through repression is one of the constitutive marks of the unconscious, upon which it bestows its signifying effects. Desire undermines conscious activity; it speaks through demand, operating as its underside or margin ... desire requires mediation. It is intrinsically inter-subjective ... Desire desires the desire of an other. Desire is thus a movement, an energy which is always transpersonal, directed to others (Grosz 1990: 64–5).

Desire therefore acts in the symbolic, in the language-based unconscious, in which signifiers relate to other signifiers, where the object of desire is continually deferred, continually unachievable. It is a desire for an Other which exists not in the Real but in discourse. The lack which characterizes desire is the same lack which is the consequence of the chaining of signification in language.

At this point we may introduce the second dictum, Lacan's claim that *the unconscious is the discourse of the Other*. From the preceding discussion it is now clear that this discourse arises in the entry of the child into the Symbolic, and this, in Lacan's schema, is a function of the process of Oedipus, the separation from the mother and identification with the father. It is not a discourse of an abstract Other, but of the father, whose sins and mistakes are recapitulated in the child and acted out in his desire, attitudes to authority, values and beliefs (Forrester 1990: 256). This oedipalization of desire turns all desire, and relations with others into recapitulations of Mother–Father–Ego. And it is this recapitulation, this *repetition*, which in the psychoanalytic session is repeated back to the analyst (although the client does not realize that it is a repetition), which enables psychoanalysis to work.

Desire and anti-Oedipus in Gilles Deleuze and Félix Guattari

The critique of this model of desire deriving from the writing of the philosopher Deleuze and the psychoanalyst Guattari may be summed up as follows.

Firstly, they are critical of the positioning of desire as constituted in the Symbolic. They see desire not as a lack, an absence, but as a presence, and furthermore, a Real, material presence (Lash 1991: 267–8), a *productive* force:

> the traditional logic of desire is all wrong from the very outset: from the very first step that the Platonic logic of desire forces us to take, making us choose between *production* and *acquisition*. From the moment we place desire on the side of acquisition, we make desire an idealistic (dialectical, nihilistic) conception, which causes us to look upon it primarily as a lack: a lack of an object, a lack of the real object ... If desire produces, its product is real. If desire is productive, it can be productive only in the real world ... Desire

does not lack anything: it does not lack its object. It is, rather, the *subject* that is missing in desire, or desire that lacks a fixed subject ... Desire is not bolstered by needs, but rather the contrary; needs are derived from desire: they are counterproducts within the Real that desire produces (Deleuze and Guattari 1984: 25–7).

As Butler (1990: 57) comments, in Nietzschean terms, Lacan's symbolic desire – which is bound to fail – is a slave mentality, of which one must ask: what is the power which sustains such a fiction? To that question, Deleuze and Guattari would respond that it is sustained by the social relations of capitalism, and the family form. Lacan's version of desire is disempowering, while desire as real presence is equivalent to Nietzsche's will-to-power, affirmative, creative and giving (Bogue 1989: 23–4), a channel for resistance to discourse.

Secondly, and following this resituating in the domain of the Real, they challenge the dictum that the Other of desire is always a repetition of the oedipal Mother–Father–Ego triad. It is upon this basis that they refute psychoanalytic theory, and what is more, go so far as to attack it for making a virtue of a process which they see as a pathological symptom of commodification under capitalism (Butler 1990).

To these we might add a third criticism, which derives from the centrality of the phallus in Lacan's model, as the 'transcendental signifier' to which the signifiers of desire relate, and which generates the Symbolic in the moment of Oedipus (Butler 1990: 44; Forrester 1990: 110). This phallogocentrism is inimical to post-structuralism (Massumi 1992: 5).

Desire then, in Deleuze and Guattari's scheme, is quite unlike Lacanian desire. By setting its own version of 'desire', it does not deny the existence of the kind of 'desire' described by Lacan, but wishes to say that this desire is restricted and 're-territorialized'. In Chapter 2, I touched upon the elements of the Deleuze and Guattari scheme, but I will recapitulate these briefly. As readers will recall, Deleuze and Guattari's theory of desire entails an understanding of the play of the social and of desire upon a political body – a body quite unlike the medical body – the *Body-without-Organs* (BwO). It is upon the surface of the BwO that discourse is inscribed (Deleuze and Guattari 1984: 9ff.), alongside one's own desire, and that of others.

Desire is the product of 'desiring machines' (1984: 26). This idea of a machine suggests the active process involved in desire: desire is not something produced by the action of another upon the body, it is the active flow which is the *power of becoming* of the body. Desire is polyvocal, offering a multiplicity of possibilities (1984: 112). Desiring-machines attach themselves to the BwO to form a grid, inscribing the possibilities of action of the BwO.

But the BwO is a locus of contestation, between desire and the social – 'there is only desire and the social, and nothing else' (1984: 29). The discursive productions of the social inscribe upon the body 'figures' of the discourses of power and knowledge, the expertise and the politics of 'the social'. These figures are the product of the collision between the social and the body: surveillance, discipline, the technologies of the self, all constitute figures on the surface of this Body-without-Organs. They govern our thoughts and our practices (Lash 1991: 265), they constitute our subjectivity, by channelling desire into prescribed pathways (Bogue 1989: 94–5). The social relations of production *re-territorialize* the desiring-machines of the BwO, determining how that BwO will behave. This process can be seen as analogous to the Foucauldian description of the effects of technologies of discipline (such as the panopticist gaze of the hospital or the self-care of the 'healthy lifestyle') in producing a docile body. Desire can be seen as the body's will-to-power, opposing the discourse and subjection of the phantasms of the social world (Bogue 1989: 20–4).

The Other's desire, for Deleuze and Guattari, is a positive material investment, which may sometimes be co-opted in the struggle for the Body-without-Organs, alongside one's own desire, against the social. The outcome may be a *de-territorialization* of the BwO, out of which is produced a *nomadic subject*, a point of intensity which enables becoming, or to put it otherwise, enables resistance, enables the realization that things could be different.

On the other hand (and it is at this point that Deleuze and Guattari articulate with Lacan's notion of desire), in the era of modernity – under the social relations of capitalism – the Other's desire may, *through investment in the realm of the Symbolic* contribute to the re-territorialization of the BwO. The doctor is invested as a figure of authority, a father-figure, recapitulating an earlier territorialization of the BwO. This 'oedipalization' or constitution of a familial model of authority turns the Other's desire into phantasy. In the hands of psychoanalysis, this process becomes a virtue:

> psychoanalysts invent nothing ... All that psychoanalysts do is to reinforce the movement; they add a last burst of energy to the displacement of the entire unconscious ... a transference Oedipus, a consulting-room Oedipus of Oedipus, especially noxious and virulent, but where the subject finally has what he wants, and sucks away at his Oedipus on the full body of the analyst. But Oedipus takes shape in the family [even if] Oedipus is not made in the family [but by] all the forces of social production, reproduction and repression ... very powerful forces are required to defeat the forces of desire (Deleuze and Guattari 1984: 121–2).

Lacan's desire, it turns out, is a restricted and restricting desire, a discourse of the social which attaches to people or things a *repetition* of familial rivalry in Mother–Father–Ego. Deleuze and Guattari do not deny Lacan's 'desire', but they see it is as discursive: emanating from power and control.

As Foucault's analysis of the history of sexuality showed, desire (and subjectivity) is constituted in discourse, it is not immanent within a subject. The object of sexual longing is created discursively – in the social. It is the opposite of the will-to-power and to resistance.

Imagine these rival versions of desire as people in one's life. On one hand, there is 'Desire that is a lack'. S/he is saying ' . . . be this . . . do this for me . . . I want you to be like this . . . '. On the other, 'Desire which is a real positive force' is saying ' . . . here's some space for you . . . go for it . . . get on with it . . . I trust and have confidence in you'.

It is this duality in the character of desire – invested either in the realm of the Real, or in the Symbolic – which I wish to focus upon in this chapter. For Deleuze and Guattari, desiring is the process by which de-territorialization of the BwO comes about. The discourses of the social which were examined in detail in Chapter 2 in relation to health and healing, are contested in their re-territorializations by desire acting in the Real world. This desire derives both from the subject and from possible investments of desire by an Other. But the Other's desire, if transformed in the symbolism of the Oedipus complex into a *lack*, a desire for what has been lost, a *repetition*, a sign of a sign – in short, a Lacanian kind of desire – contributes to the inscription of the social upon the BwO. In Lacan's scheme, there is no possibility of resistance or emancipation (Fraser 1992: 59).

Desire and the unconscious in the sick role

While on the topic of the unconscious, one might wish to ask what is the continuing force of Talcott Parsons's theory of the sick role and doctor role, that it still seems to haunt the modernist SHH (Turner 1992: 161). On the other hand, we might also wish to enquire why, as Gerhardt (1987) has pointed out, the elements of his theory which derive from psychoanalysis have been generally ignored in the medical sociology literature. In the light of the previous discussion, I shall now suggest that we can see these phenomena as related: that, with his description of the strategies by which Western societies try to cope with illness, which he idealized in the sick role and doctor role, Parsons hit upon the *repetition* which the doctor–patient contact recapitulates: the repetition of Oedipus.

This discovery, which deserves to be reconstituted at the centre of any theorizing of the doctor–patient contact (although not in the way that Parsons might have wished it), implicitly determines that this contact will be one of imbalance, between authority and dependency, master and slave. But it is this discovery, that the relation is a repetition, that SHH theorists have been unable to address. Instead they have sought to displace the source of the power relation on to the State, professional closure, patriarchy, and so on. With their love–hate relationship with medicine, SHH theorists have been able to refocus attention away from the body of the doctor, on to these other agencies.

In the discussion which follows I would acknowledge Gerhardt's (1979; 1987) exegesis of the psychoanalytic element in Parsonian theory. However, I shall try to move the analysis on by reading Parsons first through Lacan, and then through Deleuze and Guattari. The intention of this exercise is to explore how the oedipal repetition of desire may constitute discourse within the doctor–patient contact, and then to examine the proposition that it is this oedipalization – *contra* Parsons's own view – which is the limit to the patient's desire, which must be the focus of her/ his resistance, and which the health professional can collaborate against in the 'becoming' of desire.

Identifying the psychoanalytic paradigm in Parsons's work is straightforward. At the beginning of his article 'Illness, therapy and the modern American family' (Parsons and Fox 1952: 31–2), it is stated that

> there are intimate psychodynamic relationships between the processes which occur in the normal system of family interactions, and those which obtain in the doctor–patient relationship . . . The elements of correspondence are perhaps best approached in terms of two analogies: on the one hand, the similarity between illness and the status of the child in the family; on the other hand, the overlap between the physician's role and that of the parent . . . Both child and sick person differ [from the non-sick adult] in two primary respects. The first is the capacity to perform the usual functions of an adult in everyday life . . . The second . . . is that they are both dependent: needing and expecting to be taken care of by stronger, more 'adequate' persons. Thus, in these two senses, illness is not unlike more or less complete reversion to childhood.

Health professionals are analogous to parents, they go on.

In the following discussion, Parsons and Fox outline the roles of the modern American family and the strains upon these roles under capitalism and patriarchy, and generate the proposition that illness is an attractive means of escape from these duties. It must be said that the discussion is remarkably non-psychoanalytic in tone, and indeed the Oedipus complex is mentioned almost in passing, in a footnote (1952: 37n). Despite the claims of gender equality within the family (1952: 36), the wife-mother is described as prone to 'seize upon illness as a compulsively feministic way of reacting to her exclusion from the life open to a man' (1952: 35), while it turns out that adult responsibilities are 'adult masculine' ones (1952: 36). Recourse to the sick role is described as a rational response to the pressures of family roles, or, in the case of the child, of socialization into adulthood.

An episode of illness in this perspective is motivated by a desire to recapitulate the needs-dependency of the pre-oedipal stage, in psychoanalytic terms, a repetition. From the previous discussion of Lacan's reading of Freud, one can understand this repetition as motivated by the desire for that which was lost in the entry into the Symbolic, the realm of language. It is the lack which is a consequence of the creation of the unconscious structured like a language, in which what one desires is always already absent; the surfeit of desire over need.

The part which the doctor plays in sickness, as described by Parsons and Fox, is to mediate this desire. The therapeutic relationship they describe emphasizes the psychoanalytic transference (see also Parsons 1951: 453), and in considering each of the four phases they describe, it is worth dwelling on the transference – as it is described in Lacan's position.

The first phase is a *permissiveness*, 'encouraging the patient to express deviant ideas, wishes and fantasies' (Parsons and Fox 1952: 40). Here, then, is the recognition that the content of the analysis is the material by which the cure will be achieved: the rule is to keep talking. With this material, the patient will repeat the primary repression; from this will come the recognition which will lead to recovery.

The second phase is one of *support*, 'valuing the sick actor as a person in his role: accepting him as a bona fide member of the therapeutic system because he is deemed worth helping' (1952: 40). The therapist in this phase permits the development of the transference, a powerful attachment of dependency, recapitulating the needs-dependency of the patient which has been repressed and which is now repeated in the therapy. The desire of the patient now comes to have the doctor as its object. In Lacan's phrase, the unconscious is the discourse of the Other – the symbol of the Father (the Name of the Father). In therapy, the Name of the Father is transferred on to the therapist.

The third phase is the withdrawal of the therapist into *professionalism*, refusing to respond to the tranference with a counter-transference of her/his own upon the patient (1952: 41). In psychoanalytic theory, the transference (desire) must be declined, but it must not be rejected (Forrester 1990: 83), a difficult balancing act which must be achieved to enable the therapy to succeed. I will return to this point in a moment.

The final phase is a *disciplining* of the patient's desires, by which s/he 'gradually gives up his [*sic*] deviant orientation and comes to embrace maturity in its stead' (Parsons and Fox 1952: 41). The therapist reaffirms the Oedipal crisis, by which the child gives up the Mother and orientates her/his desire upon the Name of the Father, and in doing so, enters into the realm of the Symbolic in which for the first time the child orientates not towards the Self in the narcissism of the Mirror stage, but outwards, towards the Other.

In their article, Parsons and Fox emphasized that the doctor's role in reorientating the patient away from the child-world into adult life was necessary, due to the danger that if left to the family, the reintegration might be inhibited by forces within the family which would allow needs-dependency to be sustained. In another significant footnote, they identify the Oedipal context of the doctor role as associated with the Name of the Father:

> The role of the physician however is more closely analogous to the father role than to that of the mother ... mother, father, therapist may be said to vary over a continuous range; with the mother giving the highest level of permissiveness and support; the physician, the greatest incentive to acceptance of discipline (1952: 42n).

I think, from this reading, that the Oedipal aspect of the doctor–patient contact, as outlined in Parsonian theory, is clear. Further, the emphasis on the contact as a *repetition*, mediated through the transference, has been brought out. But most significantly, in my view, is the identification of the doctor with the symbolic Name of the Father. The professionalism of the relationship is the means by which the association is made not with the Mother, satisfier of need, but with the Father, symbol of lack, which desire will seek to fill, but which is destined for ever to be unrequited. The *attributes of the doctor role are the attributes of this professionalism*, by which the transference is sustained. Without these attributes, the doctor would be at the mercy of the seduction of the patient, whose transference on to the person of the doctor threatens to turn 'therapy' into some other relationship. (For a discussion of the development of a psychoanalytic professionalism to cope with the transference, see Forrester 1990.)

In this reading, the authority of the professional is not a consequence of knowledge (Parsons and Fox 1952: 31), but an essential attribute of the role which s/he plays out in repressing the conflict of Oedipus, which the regression to a childlike dependency during illness brings with it. Without that authority, the professional would not be a suitable object for transference.

Of course, we cannot leave this analysis to stand, with its deterministic explanation of medical dominance, particularly as I began this chapter with the intention to explore the possibility of a positive relation between carer and cared-for. Turning to the very different rereading deriving from Deleuze and Guattari, this Lacanian analysis is turned on its head.

First, the repetition which Parsons and Fox describe in the doctor–patient or therapist–client contact is rejected as the basis for cure. Deleuze and Guattari deny the similarity between the child–parent dyad and that of client–therapist. They see no value in recapitulating this Oedipal drama; on the contrary, it is simply the inscription of the Body-without-Organs by the social, a further imprinting of discourse. The transference is a relation of domination, imbuing the client or patient further with a slave mentality of dependency.

Second, and consequently, the engine of medical dominance is precisely the power of this repetition. Deleuze and Guattari do not reject the existence of the Oedipal crisis, in which the child enters into the Symbolic, but they do reject it as the source of desire. Desire for them is a productive rather than acquisitive force, enabling the BwO, not inscribing it in discourses of lack. But, because oedipalization of the child occurs in capitalism, with the consequent inscription of the BwO in the discourses of a desire created as possession, there will be a tendency to repeat the Oedipal crisis, playing out the parts of Mother–Father–Ego. In situations where there is a dependency, such as in illness, the relations will be attracted towards such a repetition. (I have gone along with this notion of oedipalization, following Deleuze and Guattari. In Chapter 5, I introduce Cixous' notion of the realm of the Proper, meaning the masculine, possessive, commodifying force. Either this notion, or simply the notion of logocentrism, might be substituted, in my view, for the more specific Oedipus.)

And what of the desire of the doctor? Similarly a product of Oedipus – one might speculate, constituted in a professional subjectivity which exudes the repetitions of Oedipus – s/he will be faced with the demands to sustain her/his dominance as the Name of the Father. Constantly challenged by the resistance of others, it will be as second nature to play out the Oedipus in the relationships, using the dependency of the patient or other staff to assure authority. The desire of the doctor is directed away from the positive desire of becoming, towards repetition, the wish to possess that which is lacking, or that which at any moment may be lost.

Thirdly, the force of a positive desire allows that things can be different. Once the professional is seen not as the essential requirement for a successful transference, but a fabrication of the discourse of the social, repeating a message first enunciated in the Oedipal crisis, then the possibility emerges of a relationship between carer and cared-for based not in dominance–dependency, but in the force of becoming, of resistance.

The force of this reading of Parsons is that, stripped of its functionalism, this model of the oedipalized contact between doctor and patient suggests not the way things *ought* to be, or how they *need* to be for the successful functioning of society or capitalism, but a description of how things often *are*. What Parsons mistook for a valuable attribute of a professional service is in fact an epiphenomenon of the oedipalization of capitalist relations in general, and indeed a negative one at that. From this perspective, the Parsonian sick role is best seen as the desire (by the professional) for an oedipalizing relationship enabling the repetition of her/his authority.

Yet the force of positive desire still enables resistance. It is hardly surprising, consequently, that the sick-role model often does not describe empirical situations (Twaddle 1969; Arluke et al. 1979). It is a normative desire for control and dominance, as is illustrated well in Jeffrey's (1979) discovery that the four attributes of the sick role are also the attributes by which a group of medical personnel defined legitimate patienthood.

I spoke at the end of Chapter 2 of the idea of 'arche-health', which could best be thought of as a becoming, a liberation from the discursive inscriptions of the social, of what Deleuze and Guattari call 'nomadic subjectivity'. What I hope these readings of Parsons suggest is that arche-health is not to be found in a professional discourse on health and healing based in a repetition of authority and logocentrism. The rest of this chapter is devoted to the possibilities for resisting such repetitions in medical care, and making possible the becoming of arche-health.

The caring relationship: resistance versus control

The impact of Deleuze and Guattari's model of desire upon the PSTH is important for the reading of the caring relationship (or, as I would prefer, contact). To recapitulate very briefly: this position denies the passiveness of the human body 'totally inscribed by discourse'. The inscription is active, the outcome of desire and its territorialization by the social (discourses on power/knowledge).

Secondly, it asserts that desire acts in the Real, not in the Symbolic. The force of desire is material, it is not transcendental, nor an idealist representation of reality, whether mediated in an individual or collective consciousness, but productive, the capacity of the organism to act on its environment. Nor is it the creation of the unconscious structured like a language.

Thirdly, because it is real, its consequences are real, and the strategy for its exploration cannot be psychoanalysis. Psychoanalysis colludes to re-territorialize the Body-without-Organs. If desire is a real productive force, then while it is itself in the realm of the unconscious (Bogue 1989: 89), as something real, it must mediate in the material world, indeed in the world of social production. Deleuze and Guattari's project is political: concerned with empowerment and disempowerment. Under capitalism, desiring/production can have three outcomes: the production of nomad thought (enabling, becoming something other); through the fragmenting effect of commodification, a de-territorialization of desire, subject to the economic rules of rationalized capitalist production; and through oedipalizing repetition, a re-territorialization of desire within restricted, familial, models.

This emphasis upon desire as the primary force opens up a *politics of resistance*. Whereas Foucault took power as his focus, for Deleuze and Guattari the restricted re-territorialized form of desire in capitalism is the regime of power, with its disciplines of school, clinic, workplace, family. Unlike Foucault, they are thus able to recommend a de-territorialization which would create the nomad thought of becoming (Bogue 1989: 105–6).

This rather abstracted discussion now needs to be explored through examples of the doctor–patient caring contact. These examples are intended to identify the re-territorialization of desire in these contacts, and identify the possibilities of de-territorialization and resistance.

Towards the end of the case study of surgical ward-round interaction in Chapter 3, I reported a contact between the surgeon Mr D and a patient during a post-operative ward round. In this extract, each of Mr D's statements reflect his desire.

Mr D: (to patient, looking at chart) 'Hallo Mr Y. Well we want to send
    you home, but I don't like that raised temperature.'
Patient Y: 'No.'
Mr D: 'I don't know what can be causing it. We've cultured the wound
    and there's no infection there. I just don't know what's causing it . . .
    Are things ready for you to go home?'
Patient Y: 'Yes, my wife can come and collect me today.'
Mr D: 'Can you go to bed, and she can look after you?'
Patient Y: 'Yes.'
Mr D: 'I don't like that raised temperature. Phone your wife and you can
    go home now.'
Patient Y: 'Thank you very much.'

As I commented previously, what struck me about this interaction was the interesting repetition by Mr D of the phrase 'I don't like that raised temperature'. While in its first context the phrase might be interpreted as meaning that the raised temperature was a possible complication to be resolved before discharge, the second time the phrase is used differently, to signify an annoying datum, which Mr D 'does not like', because it does not fit in with his desire to discharge the patient.

This desire is enunciated in Mr D's very first comment when he begins this interaction, and is repeated in every subsequent comment he makes. The desire which Mr D is investing in his patient is productive, having the effect of recategorizing the latter, following a major piece of surgery, as 'healed', a success of his surgical prowess, a marker that he has done his job. But the raised temperature is getting in the way of this desire. In his second utterance, Mr D clarifies the irrationality of the temperature, it is incomprehensible. He admits (and this could be seen as a failing in another context) that 'I just don't know what is causing it'. Perhaps from experience, Mr D knows that raised temperatures do occur (PUO – pyrexia of unknown origin – is a legitimate medical diagnosis!), and so he is able to rationalize it (the irrational) out of consideration in terms of managing the case. In other words, he uses a technical discourse (of experience, of acceptance of a degree of uncertainty in medicine) to justify his claim to expertise over the discharge of his patient.

His third comment is seeking information about the patient's home situation: if there is care and a psuedo-hospital setting available, then Mr D can further calm his anxiety over discharge. With the confirmation that the patient will be cared for at home, Mr D allows his desire to be fulfilled. He defines the raised temperature as the enemy of his expertise, discounts it as unworthy of attention, and tells the patient he may go home.

This deconstruction of the non-rational, unconscious element in Mr D's commentary may be seen as contributing to the organizing force of the discourse. But, from Deleuze and Guattari's position, this interaction should be read not as an investment of positive desire, but as a desire which inscribes – re-territorializes – the patient in Mr D's expertise. The patient's discharge – while in some senses a liberation – is circumscribed in terms of how the patient and his wife must behave once he is discharged. Responsibility for the raised temperature is firmly placed upon the patient: it is nothing to do with the surgery, there is no infection, it is irrational. The patient must accept the verdict of the expert: he is expected to be grateful for his release, and for the evidence that this supplies that he is a success of surgery, and he owes this all to Mr D.

The patient here is inscribed as part of the surgeon's desire: precisely the process described in Chapter 2. Mr D's desire (wish) is to mark his success as a surgeon, and along the way this means that the patient's BwO is inscribed within this realm of surgical expertise. The patient thus becomes a *repetition*, another in a long line of success stories. His subjectivity is territorialized within a framework which is discursively constituted in Mr D's desire to be surgeon. For Deleuze and Guattari, it is an oedipalization of the relationship between surgeon and patient, a relation of dependency, of dominance and of control – in short, it is the activity of the social, not of desire. It has nothing to do with a positive desire, which, when invested in the Other, de-territorializes, allows the creation of the *nomadic subject*, able to become, to resist, to see that things can be otherwise.

Substituting a non-oedipalizing, positive desire, the interaction documented here would be very different. Needless to say, it probably would not happen in such a situation at all, nor would 'surgeon' and 'patient' mean the same. If this positive desire were more to the fore in caring relationships, perhaps it would not be necessary to write this book. Later in this chapter I will explore the possibilities of a non-oedipalizing positive desire.

Oedipus and the co-opting of family values

As a second exploration of the re-territorialization of desire in caring contacts, I want to look at Strong's (1978) ethnography of paediatric clinics. This study identified what Strong called a predominantly bureaucratic mode of relation on the part of doctors. Doctors related to parents in a manner which Strong perceived as 'medical gentility', offering courtesy and politeness in their contacts (1978: 41). Parents were generally constituted as responsible and competent adults, to be consulted, if not entirely agreed with, during consultations concerning their children.

Strong's (1978: 212ff.) own explanation of this bureaucratic model of medical gentility is a fairly unconvincing history of medical practice, seeing it in part as a throw-back to the different relationship between doctor and patient in private practice in an earlier era, and in part to do with the perception of the patient as a consumer of health care.

A reading which draws upon the perspectives developed in this chapter is rather different. In the paediatric clinic, the doctor–parent–child relationship alters the usual doctor–patient dyadic contact in significant ways, and one must challenge Strong's (1978: 194) assertion that the model can be generalized to doctor–patient contacts. The doctor–patient contact itself is strangely absent in Strong's work: was it recalcitrant to sociological rewriting, one might wonder? The contact is mediated (at a discursive level) via the parent, and hence implicates the parent–child relationship. This latter, in general, is one invested both by a positive desire, of love, delight, encouragement, and so on, and by a relation of property: the child is under the auspices of the parent, and this familial relation of possession and control is legitimated in law. So the clinical authority of the doctor must take into account the authority vested in the parent with regard to the child. Potentially this rival authority is a threat.

In such a situation the doctor is faced with a number of possibilities. Firstly, s/he may challenge the authority of the parent. Strong documents a number of occasions (he calls them the 'charity' model of interaction) where there is a direct challenge, but more often the strategy entails some organizational work which serves to set an agenda which articulates with medical as opposed to parental authority. These constitute the bulk of Strong's extracts, and are equivalent to the organization described in Chapter 3 of this book.

Secondly, the doctor may go along entirely with the wishes of the parent concerning the child, as grounded in the property relationship between parent and child. Given that these authority relations may counter medical wisdom, this is a problematic situation, threatening to undermine the doctor's medical expertise. But given the analysis of Parsonian theory earlier, it is possible to recognize a congruence in the authorities, both oedipalizing: the parental, in some weird reversal, becoming a repetition of the medical.

These interactions may be organised within a discourse acknowledging natural or competent parenthood:

Social Worker: How will she [the mother] know if he [the child] has attacks? She may miss them.
Doctor: (to mother) I don't think you miss them very easily, do you? Because you can tell by the way he breathes.
Mother: Yes, he has funny breathing, yes.
Doctor: And you sleep fairly close to him, don't you?
Mother: Yes (Strong 1978: 50).

---

or the rights of parents to control the care of their children:

Dr I: Make an appointment for me then, and I'll just check her over again.
Mother: Well: if you don't mind me asking, will this take a long time?

Dr I: Oh well, we might have to do it until we are absolutely sure.
Mother: Well, I know I shouldn't have asked this question.
Dr I: Well, it's a fair enough question. It's just that we are unable to answer it (1978: 96).

---

or their skills and abilities as measured against a medical standard:

Dr H: So we're well on he way to winning but we've not found the right adjustment yet.
Mother: As I say, I've been giving him 20 ml a day but that turned out to be too much.
Dr H: Too much?
Mother: Yes, it was like dirty water. We gave it a try but it wasn't any good.
Doctor: Well, I feel we've reached the stage where you're almost the doctor and I'm just watching what you're doing (1978: 176).

In all these examples, the parent is invested with the doctor's desire. But it is an oedipalizing desire, establishing a metaphor of the doctor's role in relation to the parent role. This repetition allows the doctor to assert her/his power via a discourse on responsible parenthood. This 'chaining' of signification is of course an instance of Derridean *différance*. Perhaps it also helps to understand the 'charity' model instances recounted by Strong, in which a doctor chastised a parent for irresponsibility: for example, when a mother nervously laughed while reporting that her child chewed cigarette ends (1978: 44). In such cases, the doctor is unable to assert authority via a co-option of parental responsibility, and indeed is placed in direct opposition to behaviour which cannot be countenanced by medical discourse.

A third strategy for these contacts – unrepresented in Strong's study – would entail an avoidance of these oedipalizing forces in the parent–child relation, instead investing parents with trust and confidence, not as parents with rights over their children but as people of goodwill. In place of a relationship which is expected to be a repetition of the doctor's caring, they might be enhanced in their possibilities, enabling them to 'become', to de-territorialize their subjectivity. In a study that reports similar strategies in the child–parent–professional triad, Silverman (1983) concludes that empowerment of the child would inhere in an emphasis on choice and possibility.

The desire for (of) repetition

So far in this chapter, I have sought to explore the processes by which professional–patient contacts always seem to end up in a situation of imbalance. That such contacts do not readily lead to a positive investment of desire suggests that the caring relationship between professional and patient (and the very differentiation between these terms supports this) is constituted in ways which deny such investments. I have used Deleuze and Guattari's analysis to focus upon the *repetitive* characteristics of the doctor role. This role both repeats others, principally the Oedipal role of the Name of the Father, and seeks in others a repetition. Those who have contact with the doctor (and perhaps all professionals) are encouraged to repeat the parts played out by those who have come before, as well as the complementary child role. *The sick role is simply the deal which is struck between professional and the person who undertakes this repetition.*

From a functionalist perspective, this is a desirable arrangement for social continuity. In criticizing it, I am recapitulating ground which has been covered many times before in the SHH. What derives from the focus on desiring, however, is the *absolute necessity of this repetition for expertise.* As has been seen, it is not essential for the professional or the expert to control and dominate, indeed it is much easier for her/him to collaborate with a discourse which already constructs a subjectivity, so long as this is one which can be redefined as a repetition of the professional expertise. In the examples from Strong above, the oedipal relation of parenthood is used to create a quasi-clinical discourse: the mother's care becomes a repetition of professional welfare and healing expertise. In the next chapter I will report on efforts to help doctors take patients' lay understandings of illness into account (Tuckett *et al.* 1985). Such motivation, while in itself laudable, and potentially opening up the possibility of the kind of positive investment that I have been discussing, may also allow a co-option, a repetition, in which patients' beliefs are channelled into medical discourses: encouraged so long as they do not run counter to received clinical wisdom.

Such a repetition may be seen in relation to recent emphasis on living within a healthy lifestyle, and upon 'health promotion' in primary care services. Health and illness are to be experienced in a family context. One might conjecture that the rise of 'family medicine' during the present century can be seen not only as extending a clinical gaze into the community (Armstrong 1983), but also as returning medicine to an arena in which it can directly articulate with the oedipal desire which models medical expertise, and which, more and more, is modelled upon it.

As a final example – of the potency of such an alliance of discourse – I will look at Waitzkin's (1989) study of medical encounters. Waitzkin emphasizes the extent to which such encounters bolster traditional domestic roles and role contradictions, drawing upon ideological constructions of class, race, age and gender to achieve these repetitions.

One of the examples Waitzkin cites concerns a woman who visits her doctor complaining of palpitations and shortness of breath, which are preventing her from doing housework. Because of her role obligations, this has led to anxiety and distress. However, in the consultation, the doctor asks the woman to exercise, takes an electrocardiogram, and ignores the psychological processes by which she has become anxious. The doctor prescribes a drug for the heart condition and encourages the woman in trying to keep a tidy household (1989: 234). Waitzkin's interpretation emphasizes the ideological character of medical discourse, while from the perspective developed here the emphasis would be upon the oedipalized desire to reproduce familial roles. But Waitzkin's interpretation of the outcome of such encounters is important. He suggests (Waitzkin 1989: 236) that in such situations doctors

• offer technical solutions to ideological problems
• fail to criticize ideological relations
• exclude collective action challenging ideology
• encourage consent to status quo.

I am not primarily concerned here with arguing the case of the postmodern reading over the structuralist account offered by Waitzkin, although I hope it will be clear to the reader that the work of theory in this chapter does offer an alternative reading of control and resistance to that offered by the Marxist analysis. In place of a medical profession ideologically committed to capitalism, patriarchy, and so on, the postmodern reading seeks the repetitions which expertise generates, and in this case, the articulation with a familial model of responsibility and dependency.

This last study brings out the wider implications of an oedipalizing expertise. It suggests that professional care is – by its need for repetition – implicitly conservative in character. Perhaps it is no more than common sense to suggest that therapy is about return, about bringing about the situation which existed before the episode of illness, to try as best it can to normalize the anomaly. I said in the introduction to this book that the concern was to be with the politics of health-talk. This chapter has shown how professional care is implicated in a politics of repetition, identity and sameness: that is the reality of the micro-politics of care. In the search for a politics of difference, of becoming, professional expertise on caring offers no possibility (within its own discourse) for resistance. And, as the SHH has frequently demonstrated, when it comes to a struggle for dominance, the vulnerability of the cared-for makes it a very unequal encounter.

But that is still not to say that within contact between carer and cared-for there is no possibility of the positive desire which can enable resistance. It is the practical politics of this possibility with which the next chapter is concerned.

5

RESISTANCE AND
THE GIFT

Resistance to power/knowledge is a becoming other, a rejection or fragmentation of identity, a movement of difference. That is the sense in which
to understand Deleuze and Guattari's conception of *desire* – as production
and performance. Desire is not a lack which the object-of-desire aspires to
fill. Desire is not the wish to *possess* the Other, to 'eat it up', to ingest
rather than invest.

In thinking about Deleuze and Guattari's conception of positive, productive desire, one cannot but notice how many words which describe the
possibilities of relations between people have these possessive qualities,
and how few suggest what one might mean by a positive investment of
desire.

This distinction is reflected in the feminist post-structuralist Hélène Cixous'
(1986) opposition of what she has called the realms of the *Proper*, and of
the *Gift*. Feminism's dissolution of the personal/political opposition of
modernist social theory supplies important lessons for postmodern readings
of health. The fruitful associations between feminism and post-structuralism
supply much of the theoretical underpinning of this chapter, although towards the end, the discussion returns to Derrida's concept of *différance*, and
the related notion of *intertextuality*. In keeping with this latter emphasis,
the structure of the chapter will entail reading a series of texts alongside
and through postmodern positions.

The opposition between the Proper and the Gift, Cixous suggests, is
between a negative male, *possessive* desire, and a feminine desire which is
based in *generosity*.

> Proper – property – appropriate: signalling an emphasis on self-identity,
> self-aggrandizement and arrogative dominance, these words charac-
> terize the logic of the proper according to Cixous (Moi 1985: 110).

Cixous' reading of desire derives from her Lacanian psychoanalytic background: her critique of Lacan is feminist – seeing his concept of desire as masculine, with the Otherness of the feminine as something to be negated so that the masculine subject may achieve presence. An alternative feminine desire accepts rather than negates Otherness: it goes out to otherness, and continues without end (Game 1991: 80). Despite the similarities with the positive desire of Deleuze and Guattari, I am unaware of any acknowledgement by Cixous of such similarity; and whereas the former authors conceive their desire as a real force, for Cixous desire acts in the realm of the Imaginary (in psychoanalytic terms the pre-oedipal, pre-symbolic phase of representation).

For this reason it is not possible simply to equate these different theories of desire. Yet for both, desire is a political process. For Cixous, the desire manifested in the realm of the Gift acts upon the body (the BwO?), disrupting the patterning of inscription generated by masculine, symbolic, discursive desire, enabling new possibilities for action and resistance, precisely the becoming of Deleuze and Guattari's de-territorialized, nomadic subject.

Despite the paucity of words to describe what is entailed in a gift relationship, one might suggest:

generosity
trust
confidence
love
benevolence
commitment
involvement
delight
allegiance
esteem
accord
admiration
curiosity

How easily many of these words elide into other (possessive) relations: trust becomes dependency, esteem becomes reverence, generosity becomes patronage, curiosity becomes the gaze. But perhaps of more immediate interest is the remarkable extent to which these words fail to conjure the way in which the professional, the healer or the expert is usually described as relating to the subject of her/his activities. While these words may suggest the investment of a client or patient, many of them, if applied to the professional, would not only be seen as unusual, but possibly even inappropriate or 'unprofessional'.

Professional care as 'the Proper'

Chapter 4 concentrated upon the repetitions involved in professional care. With this notion of a Gift relationship, I wish to continue the explorations of the character of care but now focusing upon possession. Dependency provides de Swaan (1990) with the starting point for his analysis of how caring becomes a relation of dominance and disempowerment for those who are cared for. When people fall ill, they are often unable to work, and because of sickness's conditional legitimacy, they are allowed this dispensation.

> As the disease progresses, sick people can do less and less for others and less and less for themselves. When it is said of people that they can take care of themselves, what is usually meant is that such persons can make sure that others will take care of them, that they can return every favour with a counter-favour which is considered its equivalent. Such people buy what they need ... and if they do not pay for services of others, then they will make sure to return the favour soon (1990: 27).

Care is provided by professionals, but also by family, who receive no pay, and expect no immediate favours in return: the sick soon become heavily indebted to those around them. Eventually any expectation of repayment of favours disappears.

> Increasing dependency goes with status anxiety and loss of status: sick people become the lesser, the asking party, who need more from others while having less to offer them (1990: 27–8).

In societies which operate on the basis of exchange (the realm of the Proper), where goods and services possess value and can be used as a resource to be possessed or dispensed, one might – perhaps only for heuristic purposes – distinguish between formal and informal caring relations in terms of the Proper–Gift opposition.

The professional or formal relation between carer and cared-for would be sustained within the realm of the Proper. The carer, paid by the individual, by the State or by insurance schemes, expects a reward for their effort in care. In addition to a financial remuneration, this might entail some commitments on the part of the cared-for. As de Swaan suggests, the sick become incorporated within a set of values emanating from the professional: constraints on lifestyle and expectation are to be accepted. Increasing dependency continually forces the cared-for further into this value system, until s/he is part of the carer's possessions. The medicalization of life could be understood as the appropriation of the body of the patient – in my terms, an inscription of the political BwO.

Informal carers do not usually calculate their care on the basis of exchange in the same way (Graham 1991: 65). Of course, they may inscribe the cared-for in other ways, and it would be foolish to romanticize the relations between cared-for and informal carers. Carers may extract non-financial rewards from their charges, and these may be demeaning or emotionally painful for the cared-for. Derrida's recent reflections upon gifts have identified the subtle calculations which are obscured in many donor–recipient relationships (if I give this, then I will be seen in this way, and she will be grateful . . .). The true gift is the one that someone does not realize s/he is giving (Derrida 1992).

Yet, despite these more realistic reflections on obligations and secondary gains, it is possible to see in informal care – in opposition to professional care, at least – elements of the Gift. Despite the inability to repay the favours, and the increasing indebtedness, the care is offered as a Gift. Whether the cared-for is an infant, a child or spouse with functionally impaired abilities, a sick relative or friend or an ageing parent, the generosity of the carer and her/his investment of love, trust or delight means that the favours are not calculated, for repayment at some future time.

The Gift as source of resistance

The force and value of this distinction between the Gift and the Proper in the discussion of caring rests in its suggestion that, when it comes to professional–patient relationships, *things could be different.* It offers the potential for a politics of care. While Cixous, sustaining the Lacanian position, maintains that the Gift works in the psychic realm of the Imaginary, I would suggest that it is in fact possible to see it – in the situation of care – as a real gift: it has real consequences, and is part of a material, practical politics. The Gift is thus equivalent to the positive productive desire of Deleuze and Guattari. The Proper, possessive relationship may also have real consequences, but it works in the Symbolic: constantly requiring of its object that it behaves in certain ways, is defined (as 'patient', 'client'), and repeats the patterns of those who have been the objects of 'care' before. Jolley and Brykczynska (1992) have argued that the constitution of an impersonal HCS in the West provided the opportunity for a discourse on 'care' to supply the distinctive 'profession' of nursing. One might conclude that expertise and 'professionalism' are particular forms of power/knowledge, which *transform the object of their holders' desire from the Real into the Symbolic realm.* In place of a relationship of generosity, there is imposed a relationship of possession.

Caring services, under the regime of liberal governance, may obscure the exchange relationship by insurance or taxation schemes, but the relationship between carer and cared-for remains underpinned by expectations of reciprocity. This expectation is often managed through compliance and docility on the parts of patients, or by a 'gratefulness' for the expertise of the doctor. But if patients come to see that the reciprocity is fake, they are humiliated, degraded or stigmatized. They may try to offset their dependency with demands, complaints and accusations (de Swaan 1990: 36).

In the realm of the Proper, a gift is threatening, because it establishes an inequality, a difference, an imbalance in power. The act of giving becomes an act of aggression, an exposure of the Other (Moi 1985: 112). (This is the earlier sense of a gift relationship as developed by Mauss.) But a Gift is not given with any expectation of reciprocity; in the realm of the Gift, those who care do not expect gratefulness or even an acknowledgement of their effort.

The ethics and politics of care might thus derive upon a replacement of the Proper by the Gift in caring relationships. If this is easy to say, then it seems that it is far harder in practice. A review of the literature suggests that we have been writing the history of a care grounded in the Proper (Graham 1991). Much of the rest of the chapter will thus have a rather negative feel to it, as I document studies which demonstrate the difficulties facing this fundamental shift in perspective on caring.

However, the ease with which a Gift relationship can become one of possession and repetition can be clarified by recourse to an example. Bond (1991) examined some of the consequences of rationalization and formalizing of informal caring – for family or friends – as a result of recent UK legislation encouraging moves away from institution care, towards 'care in the community'. This legislation provides the possibility, among other policies, of financially rewarding informal carers, and providing training to ensure standards of care are achieved. Paradoxically, Bond argued, this professionalization of informal care leads to a loss of the 'caring' element of the relationship.

Within the framework developed above, this process could be interpreted as the loss of the positive investments which carers supply in caring – of love, admiration, commitment, accord, involvement, generosity – substituting these with a relation of possession, in which the cared-for is the property of the carer, upon whom the carer 'does' care. In place of the trust, confidence, esteem on the part of the cared-for towards the carer – investments which make care synonymous with the relationship – the cared-for enters into a relation of negative dependency. Instead of a positive desire invested in the subject of care, there is a political inscription of the 'body of care', mediated through the discourse of 'professional care' which smothers and envelops (White 1991: 92).

At the end of this chapter I will reflect further upon 'community care'. But it is perhaps worth commenting at this point that there is an idealism of familial care in Bond's commentary. Following Deleuze and Guattari, I would question whether the family can sustain these positive elements of desire towards a cared-for member without oedipalization – transforming them into repetitions of the power struggle of Mother–Father–Ego. Graham's (1979) illustration of how mothering has been exploitation, supplying care on the cheap, suggests the complexity of the processes of desire within the family. One might conjecture that part of the attraction of 'community care' is that it draws on these restrictive, repetitive, familial models of dependency.

Expertise takes control, possesses, the object of its desire. Healing requires of its subject that it takes on the character of the healer's wish: namely, to be 'healed'. Recalling the discussion in Chapter 4 of the encounter between surgeon and patient, expertise may thus be seen as motivated by an investment of desire for the Other, but a desire constituted in the symbolic realm, oedipal or otherwise. As such, it cannot but re-territorialize its object according to its particular discursive technique of metaphoric representation. Only if this symbolic investment is reconstituted in the Real, in the realm of the Gift, can the interaction substitute control with 'becoming', a territorialized subject with a nomadic subject.

Educating for the Gift: meetings between experts?

It is possible to see this possessive character of professional expertise in many studies in the SHH. To read the literature is to identify the unwillingness of professionals to invest the kind of positive desire which I have been describing in these pages. To take an example, *Meetings between Experts* is a study which documented an effort to introduce British doctors to the possibility that patients' own beliefs and values could contribute to their care (Tuckett *et al.* 1985). Despite efforts by the study team to intervene to persuade doctors to this view, they found that doctors saw lay beliefs as a useful way of 'getting the whole picture', so as to discover the real problem; to avoid appearing superior and as an aid to communication; to provide clues so that doctors could give appropriate reassurance; or as a waste of time, and only worth listening to on grounds of courtesy (1985: 198–9). Nor did the doctors see how they could incorporate these beliefs into the 'explanations' they gave to patients concerning the management of their treatment. The possibility that such a belief might form the basis of care was not even on the agenda.

This study concluded that the medico-centrism of their behaviour was a consequence of the urge to make a diagnosis and the urge to stay in charge (1985: 201). These desires are those which were identified in Chapter 4 as associated with the transference within the doctor–patient contact. I am reminded of the classic ethnographic extract in which a mother's claims to have a son and a daughter are challenged by a doctor who cannot bear to accept the mother's version over the version (two daughters) in his notes (Graham and Oakley 1986: 111).

Is it feasible to seek to short-circuit this desire? From the interpretations in this chapter, some suggestions for such a project would involve:

- a recognition of the desire for repetition in the doctor's contact with her/his patient;
- a recognition of the possessive character of that contact, and the possibility of a relation of generosity in its place;

- an emphasis always upon contacts which will foster de-territorialization, opening-up of possibilities;
- a willingness to respond to investments of trust and confidence, by inscribing not dependency, but a reciprocal goodwill.

In Lynam's interviews with young people with cancer, she found that they identified particular characteristics of supportive relationships which seem to bear upon some of these elements of the Gift. The kinds of positive relationship they desired were *reciprocal*, in which both they and the other party took an active part in constituting the support.

> In order to participate effectively, the families and friends, potential supporters, needed to be educated. Many of the [young people in the study] took responsibility for educating the people around them about their illness. They chose to share aspects of their illness experience with others either because the others were seen as able to understand or they were seen as caring about them and needing to understand (Lynam 1990: 184).

In addition to this reciprocity, Lynam found that *evenness* was a characteristic identified as necessary in a supportive relationship (1990: 187). This was important because the fear and uncertainty created situations in which the patients felt very vulnerable. In such circumstances, evenness ensured this vulnerability was not compounded. Evenness in relationships helped the young people to take more control over the impact of the disease on their lives – to de-territorialize some of its associations, making it less central to their lives (1990: 189). (For further discussion of this in relation to pain, see Chapter 7.)

In Lynam's study, the professionals were often criticized for failing in these attributes of reciprocity and evenness: it was family and friends who provided the supportive Gift. The literature appears to be very short on examples of such professional–patient contacts, but Danziger (1986: 315) documents one among many interactions between a female patient and a doctor.

Patient: Oh I have something else. I'm planning to breastfeed the thing and ... when do they have you start, right away or after a day or so?

Doctor: Whenever you want to.

Patient: Well, which is best?

Doctor: Oh, it depends. It's better for the milk coming in to start as soon as possible. But if you're not up to it, you don't have to ...

Patient: But then they give it formula?

Doctor: No not necessarily. Listen, the whole thing about breastfeeding is *not* to worry about it and to really want to do it. If you have *any* doubts about it, chances are you'll have trouble ...

In this instance, the health professional, for whatever reason, is keen to enhance the patient's personal choice. Perhaps, as Danziger suggests, this willingness is also part of the doctor's construction of the patient as a competent decision-maker, but it is still the case that the consequence of this is to open up the woman's possibilities, and to act generously towards her desire to choose how to feed her baby.

In general, it seems less certain that this kind of rationalist approach could be relied upon to foster relationships of generosity between health professionals and those for whom they care, for the very reason that expertise and professionalism invest so heavily in the repetitions of the Symbolic. One text which has sought to address the symbolic desire of the doctor is Glin Bennet's interesting book *The Wound and the Doctor* (1987).

Vulnerability and the Gift: the wounded healer

The psychiatrist Glin Bennet explored the problems within the professional–patient relationship by reflecting upon the dual attribute attached to many healers throughout history, of being both wounded and capable of healing. The healer may have recovered from a wound or have learned to live with it: but in either case s/he has related to the would creatively, so that through it others can be healed (Bennet 1987: 212). The healer is both a weak figure, and on imbued with a strength of power. It is this duality – present in *everyone* – which is often ignored in modern Western medical care, Bennet (1987: 214) argues. In place of what Bennet calls the 'doctor-patient' – a constellation of attributes which recognizes both the knowledgeable, competent 'doctor' and the frightened, dependent 'patient' in *everybody* – the Western carer suppresses the patient pole of the duality altogether, resulting in the 'familiar, brash all-knowing doctor, who dispenses treatments, advises and carries out surgical operations' (1987: 215). What is suppressed is the fear, helplessness and desire for care of the 'patient' part of the healer. Alternatively, these attributes are projected on to the patient: the healer's weakness is shifted on to the patient, who must now bear her/his own weakness and that of the doctor:

> This kind of doctor is dominating and all-powerful, and he [*sic*] pushes his patients into the utterly supine and helpless position familiar to so many sick people today. The doctor has all the information and the patient knows nothing. Such a doctor requires helpless and un-informed patients to carry his unacknowledged weakness for him ... (1987: 216).

Just as there is a 'patient' pole within every healer, within all sick people there is a healer pole. The potential for self-healing, says Bennet (1987: 216) rests with this healer pole, if only it can be activated. This cannot happen when the healer is suppressing or projecting her/his own dependency on to the patient.

While this focus upon the human vulnerability of the professional is of interest – for instance, suggesting the urge to deny death among the medical profession – Bennet's arguments do not articulate straightforwardly with the positions developed here. Deriving from a psychoanalytic model, Bennet's 'patient' pole is the repetition of the dependency of the Oedipal relationship, while his 'healer' or 'doctor' pole is the adult controlling element, repeating the Name of the Father. This repetition leads Bennet (1987: 216) to perceive the onus as continuing to remain with the healer, as the key facilitator of the patient's capacity to self-heal (ibid). Perhaps Bennet's own suppressed desire requires him to try to retain control in the hands of the healer.

However, stripped of this psychoanalytic gloss, Bennet's argument is subtly transformed. What Bennet calls the 'patient' pole is not concerned with dependency, fear and helplessness, but with openness, trust and sharing: the Gift. What Bennet calls 'weakness' is weak only if transformed in Oedipal repetition into dependency. What Bennet demonstrates is how professional carers either suppress this generosity, or transform it (project its negative oedipal form) into a demand for dependency. What Bennet calls 'self-healing', which in his writing apears almost as a mystical or supernatural process, is the de-territorialization of the body, so that – no longer constrained by dependency and helplessness – the sick person may resist the discourses on the Body-without-Organs constituted by professional care.

Bennet (1987: 219) suggests that, in practice, this means carers recognizing their own vulnerability, their potential to be wounded, to be human, frail and weak, by acknowledging their own blemishes. Some of the circumstances suggested by Bennet (1987: 219–20) to enable carers to achieve this perspective seem rather unattractive: illness, a bereavement, divorce or other personal tragedy, a medical error leading to a patient's death, while his vision of a reshaped medical perspective is liberal and individualistic, and does not in itself challenge medical power (1987: 245); nor does it suggest ways patients might become active in resisting it. But the emphasis upon reflexivity on the part of carers is important, and, for this reason, Bennet's work may have suggested to the medical profession that it needs to take account of its desire. (For another study of 'wounded healers', see French 1988.)

Bennet's study sometimes sounds as if 'mind over matter' will resolve our ills and pain. I have been concerned throughout this book to challenge rerepresentations which transform pain and suffering into social epiphenomena. Any project to develop caring relations built on generosity rather than the realm of the Proper must address the reality of suffering of the subjects of care. Within the contact between carer and cared-for, there is a two-way flow of desire. Many of the attributes of the positive desire, the generosity of the Gift which I have been speaking about, may characterize the response of patients towards health professionals. There is a vast amount

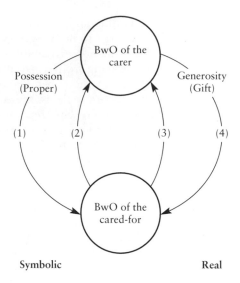

1 Oedipalizing desire for repetition of authority and control.
2 Oedipalizing desire for repetition of dependency or anger.
3 Positive desire in trust, confidence, commitment, etc.,
  enabling 'becoming' in the carer.
4 Positive desire of generosity, trust, delight, etc.,
  enabling 'becoming' (creation of arche-health) in the cared for.

Figure 1 Positive and negative flows of desire in the caring relationship

of goodwill and trust, confidence and involvement invested by patients in their carers, and if the sociological literature has focused on the negative responses of patients, some studies have identified this positive aspect (for example, Calnan 1987: 170ff.; Tuckett *et al.* 1985: 162).

So while health professionals may be investing their patients with the oedipalizing desire described above, and patients may in turn be responding by repeating their oedipal dependency, the latter may also be investing their carers with a Gift at the same time. Consequently there are many possible variations within this dyad, contingent upon the extent of these relations of the Proper and the Gift. These are summed up in Figure 1.

We might expect that an investment in one direction in one realm might facilitate a similar investment in the other direction, but this is conjectural. Indeed, it is quite possible to imagine how the BwO of a doctor, enabled by the trust and confidence of her/his patients, is re-territorialized so as to be even more oedipalizing, even more in the realm of the Proper! There is no guarantee that resistance means a more democratic or more emancipatory subjectivity. The complexity of the contact between carer and cared-for requires that we explore the positive investments made by patients in their carers, enabling *them* to 'become', to resist; and whether such investments are negated by the oedipalization which professionalism seeks.

The Gift subverted by suffering

The body of the patient is inscribed by the desire of the carer, but this is secondary to, or at least concomitant upon, its inscription by its pain, and by the anxiety and fear which this pain provokes. This history of their illness is continually rewritten through pain and by fear (Kleinman 1988: 48). In such situations, the potential for Gift relationships in caring may be swamped by the repetitions which the sick are forced to live out from day to day.

De Swaan's study of a cancer ward suggests the difficulties of contemplating a caring relationship based on generosity. Here, as de Swaan describes it, is a libidinal economy in which positive desire is hard to achieve. The anxieties of staff caring for people who are dying are displaced – translated into medical terms. Patients' bodies are cared for, while their emotions go untended. Staff do not discuss their upset with colleagues. Doctors and nurses learn not to become attached to seriously ill and dying people: the investment of care, affection and generosity by a member of staff in a patient goes 'unrewarded' when one day the person is dead (de Swaan 1990: 42–7).

In this economy, the patients' desire is overwhelmed by their fear and their anger. The healthy become the targets of jokes in which they are degraded, tortured or described as animals:

Healthy visitors must be thrown in the canal, floored with a boxing punch, their necks twisted, put on the table and made to sing (1990: 52).

Patients negate the good intentions of the staff. A patient wrote

a children's joke: 'A man comes to the drugstore for a bag of Reckitt's blue balls. The druggist kicks him in the groin: "that will give you blue balls"'. [This] may well be read as 'That's what you get, when you ask a healer for help' (1990: 54).

They displace their unease and fear, somatizing their discontent, translating it into physical symptoms to which they demand attention and treatment (1990: 42). Yet, as de Swaan documents, there are examples of generosity, enabling patients to 'become'.

To patients it means much when doctors and nurses know how to handle their wounds competently and without fear ... The nurse patiently [!!!] washing a dilapidated patient, changing his clothes, is also the only one who dares touch him without disgust or fear, who quietly and competently handles the body which so torments and frightens the patient . . . [who] knows how to deal skilfully with the wounds and lumps, in doing so liberating the patients for the moment from their isolation (1990: 48).

Perhaps this last extract suggests how one is to understand the force of the Gift, and Deleuze and Guattari's 'investment of positive desire'. The Gift is constituted in an open-endedness. It stands in place of discourse, even a discourse on liberation or emancipation, which tells the Other *how* to be freer or more sexy or more something else, and of course in doing so, closes down the possibilities, making the Other an appendage of the discourse, inscribed with the power of the Word. It does not say what something is, or is not: it allows, for a moment at least, a thing to become multiple, to be both something and another thing and another.

Generosity, trust, love, affirmation, confidence blast the Body-without-Organs out of the subjectivity which has been inscribed by the social upon its surface. For a moment, the subjectivity is free to wander over this surface – the nomad subject becomes. Then it settles back, but in a different configuration, as the process of signification seizes upon the new patterning of intensities. Both for Cixous and for Deleuze and Guattari, such a moment can be achieved through disruption of the mentality which imbues a subjectivity. Both see their own writing as channels for such positive desire: for Cixous *écriture feminine*, for Deleuze and Guattari their schizoanalysis. The latter was conceptualized as involving transformation, from one level or plateau to another:

a plateau is reached when circumstances combine to bring an activity to a pitch of intensity that is not automatically dissipated in a climax leading to a state of rest. The heightening of energies is sustained long enough to leave a kind of afterimage of its dynamism that can be reactivated or injected into other activities, creating a fabric of intensive states between which any number of connecting routes could exist . . . That never lasts more than a flash, because the world rarely leaves room for uncommon intensity, being in large measure an entropic trashbin of outworn modes that refuse to die (Massumi 1992: 7–8).

That is how it is possible to resist. And that is the part which desire plays, not the negative desire created in a Lacanian lack, in Oedipus, in the desire to repeat, but in a positive desire which is a gift, which does not say 'be this', 'be like me', 'desire me too'.

De Swaan's description of the cancer ward shows how far the realm of the Proper, of Oedipus, has extended into the clinic. In this situation, the Gift is overwhelmed, extinguished even when someone fleetingly invests her/his generosity. To change this set-up is not simply a matter of brightening up the ward, or training the staff to be nice, because what is going on does so in the unconscious. In such a situation as de Swaan described, the sick hate the healthy, in whose health their own disease is defined. They hate their disease and their pain and their suffering which mark their difference. They hate the expertise which forces them to be repetitions of all those who went before, and repetitions of the enslaved, whose master finds a subjectivity in this relation of dominance and dependency. They hate the institutions which create them as subjects of the clinical gaze, they hate their bodies which are inscribed in that gaze. And they hate their hate, for using them up and leaving nothing behind.

There is nothing rational here, nothing which can be sorted out with a new more rational, more socially aware, more democratic medicine. That is to sustain the realm of the Proper, of property and propriety – in Cixous' terms, in a masculine desire which possesses and controls, in Foucauldian terms, to contribute further to the total inscription of the body.

If for no other reason than this, the rationalist project of modernist medical sociology is doomed to repeat the territorializations of the Proper.

Difference and intertextuality

Having said which, it must be clear to the reader that I cannot set out some kind of detailed programme to ensure the overthrow of professional discourse and the substitution of relationships which de-territorialize and enable. But with the perspectives on desire and upon the Gift developed here, what is quite feasible is the elaboration of some of the strategies of a practical politics of resistance.

In the final part of this chapter, I will look at some specific issues in this politics of care. These I shall explore, with the help of the theoretical perspectives developed here, through the themes of *difference*, *différance* and *undecidability* as they impinge on the practice or philosophy of *intertextuality*, the play of texts upon and within each other.

Earlier in this book, I considered Derrida's theorizing of *différance*, the simultaneous referral and deferral of meaning which signifiers carry with them. These traces of that which a signifier is *not* result in the radical undecidability of language, and in turn to the possibility of textual deconstruction: the process of opening up the traces, allowing texts to conspire with other texts to reveal new possibilities.

Consider this text: I have played off Deleuze and Guattari's perspective on desire and territorialization with Cixous' notions of Gift relationships, and the various example from the SHH literature, to open up new readings on issues of caring and health, allowing the undecidability to provide us not only with what these authors intended (how can we know this anyway – it is always already deferred), but with all sorts of new textualities.

And you, the reader, rewrite my words as you read them, as the play of the text which is your Body-without-Organs inscribes the BwO of this book. You in turn are inscribed, rewritten. That is intertextuality.

The commentary by Massumi (1992) quoted on page 102 concerning the de-territorialization of the Body-without-Organs, suggests what – in Deleuze and Guattari's model – can be achieved when the established frameworks of meaning are broken. De-territorialization allows the patterns to be dissolved: for a moment there is a nomadic subject wandering upon the political surface of the Body-without-Organs, before it falls back, re-territorialized elsewhere as the discourses of the social establish their new pattern of intensities, some weaker than before, others stronger, others not previously present newly established. *What Deleuze and Guattari speak of here is also intertextuality.*

They make this quite clear in the pages of *A Thousand Plateaux*, a book which is designed as a plant-like 'rhizome', ceaselessly achieving multiplicity, refusing to follow a single chain of signification (1988: 7–9). Reading their book is intended to de-territorialize, allowing becoming, like a rhizome connecting any point to any other point (1988: 21).

> We call a plateau any multiplicity connected to any other multiplici-
> ties by superficial underground stems in such a way to form or
> extend a rhizome. We are writing this book as a rhizome. It is
> composed of plateaus . . . Each plateau can be read starting anywhere
> and can be related to any other plateau (1988: 22).

The objective – maybe – is to orchestrate enough intensities upon the reader's Body-without-Organs that new connections become possible, a new plateau is achieved, so the reader can say 'So that's what it's about'. Their book is also an incitement to write:

> Conjugate deterritorialized flows. Follow the plants: you start by
> delimiting a first line consisting of circles of convergence around
> successive singularities; then you see whether inside that line new
> circles of convergence establish themselves, with new points located
> outside the limits and in other directions. Write, form a rhizome,
> increase your territory by deterritorialization, extend the line of flight
> to the point where it becomes an abstract machine covering the entire
> plane of consistency (1988: 11).

If it has been suggested that Deleuze and Guattari's notion of positive desire is too closely associated with a foundationalist (maybe even biological) will-to-power, standing somehow beyond discourse, these passages offer a much closer affinity to the Derridean conception of intertextuality, and indeed to Derrida's proposition that there is nothing (knowable) beyond the text – be that text a book, a set of practices or a body. If Deleuze and Guattari have invested their positive desire in their writing, then it acts in the material relationship which a reader has with the body of the book.

What is also clearer is that Deleuze and Guattari here owe more to Derridean positions than to those of Foucault. But it also makes a connec-tion with a concern with *writing* which feminist post-structuralists have developed as a strategy of resistance. I shall briefly review these positions, as part of this reflection on intertextuality as de-territorialization.

Feminism, post-structuralism and writing

The impact of post-structuralism upon feminism has been to challenge the essentialism which elevates women's experience as authentic or even natural, and to question whether there is a single category of 'women' which can define a collective response towards oppression (Butler 1990: 4; Fraser 1992: 65). Coupled with an insistence which has distinguished feminist theory that the political cannot be separated from the personal, the readings which have emanated from feminist post-structuralism (FPS) supply a perspective on resistance generated within a politics of difference and of lived experience.

The part which writing as a political practice plays in FPS needs some exploration. An eloquent description of the empowering character of a writing project was outlined by the Boston Women's Health Book Collective in the introduction ('A Good Story') to *Our Bodies, Our Selves* (1978). This book came about after a conference.

> As we talked we began to realize how little we knew about our own bodies, so we decided to do further research ... The results of our findings were used to present courses to other women. We would meet in any available free space ... as we taught we learned from other women, and as they learned, they went on to give courses to others. We saw it as a never-ending process always involving more and more women ... We formed our group as individual women because we wanted to. Since most of us had patterned our lives around men, working together was a liberating experience ... Probably the most valuable thing we learned was to speak for ourselves and be ourselves. Many of us feared discussing personal details of our lives and relationships ... By facing up to our ambivalent feelings and being honest and open, we were able to build up more trusting relationships ... We no longer feel the need for constant support from our families, particularly our men. We can choose to be alone and to seek support when we need it: we realize we are no longer powerless, helpless children (1978: 11–16).

Of course, what is being spoken about here is as much to do with collaboration and closure as with writing *per se*, and one can deconstruct within this text political agendas and an essentialism which characterize modernist feminism. But, in the context of the book which follows, it also suggests a political re-territorialization which perhaps for the authors was as much part of the 'health' they write about as the biomedical detail.

This fairly unreflexive writing about the process of writing contrasts with FPS discussions which have theorized writing variously. Julia Kristeva's poetics and Cixous' *écriture feminine* both oppose the kinds of writing which they advocate with the phallogocentric realm of masculine discourse.

The poetic is not governed by the rules of syntax, which are constituted in the masculine symbolic realm of Oedipus, but in what Kristeva (1986) calls the 'semiotic'. While the semiotic, feminine principle inhabits all texts, it is marginal, playing guerrilla tactics with a text's meaning, but always doomed to fall back into the register of the symbolic. I find echoes of Deleuze and Guattari in this description: the nomad thought which is re-territorialized, although for Fraser (1992: 64) at least, this submission of the feminine is inexcusable. So, too, is there an echo of undecidability: for Kristeva it is the semiotic or the poetics in a text which contributes its undecidability, against the hegemonic meaning which the masculine dis-course of the Symbolic has constituted.

However, it is in Cixous' position on writing that there is perhaps most to offer in this discussion. *Écriture feminine* is a writing practice which is concerned with the openness of texts and multiplicity in place of closure and univocality (Game 1991: 80), and as such is closely related to the Derridean concept of *différance*: 'feminine texts' strive to undermine oppo-sitions, to deconstruct textuality itself. Feminine texts are not necessarily the product of women (Moi 1985: 108), although Cixous (1990: 318–20) writes:

> I write woman: woman must write woman. And man, man . . . it's up to him to say where his masculinity and femininity are at: this will concern us when men have opened their eyes and seen them-selves clearly . . . I mean it when I speak of male writing . . . writing has been run by a libidinal and cultural – hence political, typically masculine – economy . . . where woman has never had her turn to speak – this being all the more serious and unpardonable in that writing is precisely the *very possibility of change*, the space that can serve as a springboard for subversive thought, the precursory movement of a transformation of social and cultural structures (emphasis in original).

Écriture feminine needs to be understood, says Cixous (1990: 320–1), as writing the body:

> By writing her self, woman will return to the body which has been more than confiscated from her, which has been turned into the uncanny stranger on display . . . Censor the body and you censor breath and speech at the same time . . . To write. An act which will not only 'realize' the decensored relation of woman to her sexuality, to her womanly being, giving her access to her native strength: it will give her back her goods, her pleasures, her organs, her immense bodily territories which have been kept under seal – tear her away by means of this research, this job of analysis and illumination, this

emancipation of this marvellous text of her self that she must urgently learn to speak.

This is about as far as I shall develop Cixous' position on writing. Toril Moi's powerful critique of Cixous, which addresses the aforementioned Lacanian influence in her work, questions whether there is an elision here between writing as the vehicle of resistance and as the enactment, the end-point itself (Moi 1985: 125). Cixous swings between the deconstructive version of writing as a system which displays its own inauthenticity (Warning: this writing will auto-deconstruct in five minutes ...), and thus opens up possibilities for new interpretations, for multivocality and de-territorialization, and an essentializing of feminine writing as the product of the pre-oedipal realm of the Imaginary, of the female line by which daughters are in contact with mothers: 'a woman is never far from "mother" ... There is always within her at least a little of that good mother's milk. She writes in white ink' (Cixous 1990: 322) – a writing denied to men by their enforced entry into the realm of oedipal lack.

Writing as the practice of difference

Throughout this book – with its subject-matter of the reality of suffering – I have been concerned with the material and the real: hence the interest in Deleuze and Guattari's conception of real positive desire. Both for Cixous and for Kristeva, it would seem that their efforts to resist phallogocentrism are compromised by their adherence to the psychoanalytic opposition of Symbolic and Imaginary (see p. 75), and an unwillingness to recognize desire as a real force (Moi 1985; Butler 1990; Fraser 1992). These writers seem ultimately to recapitulate the essentialism of Lacan's phallic logo-centrism, but in reverse.

However, while this Lacanian influence is marked throughout claims to a feminine writing, there is a second relation discernible in Cixous' writing – to the Derridean critique of logocentrism (discussed in Chapter 1). It will be recalled that part of the logocentric claim to authenticity and authority was the phonocentric emphasis upon the privileging of the spoken: the voice of the authority, over the dead manifestations of the *logos* in the written word. The presence of the speaking subject is demonstration enough of the facticity of what is being claimed, while writing always carries with it the seeds of its own overthrow, in the shape of *différance*. Writing, or textuality, acknowledges the free play of the signifier and opens up what Cixous sees as the prison-house of patriarchal language (Moi 1985: 107). The relationship between the Gift and this attribute of feminine writing can be seen here, whereas masculine writing inheres in the realm of the Proper:

A feminine text cannot fail to be more than subversive. It is volcanic: as it is written it brings about an upheaval of the old property crust, carrier of masculine investments; there's no other way ... it's in order to smash everything to shatter the framework of institutions, to blow up the law, to break up the 'truth' with laughter (Cixous 1990: 326).

A 'feminine text' – whatever its modality – might thus be defined as one which encourages (unlike speech) the play of textuality which will deconstruct its claims to authority and presence.

And, we might ask, if speech possesses this illusion of self-presence, how much more so does the body itself, totally imprinted by history as it is? The sheer *facticity* of the human body written into discourse on gender, race, age, health, beauty: all the desire that can be produced. The human body is so *convincing*. That is why it is the focus of discourse. It is so tempting to inscribe a body, which will thereafter so authentically bear witness to the power which inscribed it. It is so *habit-forming*, the more we do it, the more we need that pleasure. In this sense, inscription and the power which comes from inscribing can be understood as a fundamentally masculine – or Proper – principle. (For a reading which emphasises this linkage, see Nead's (1992) book on the genealogy of the female nude.)

The importance of the FPS critique, and in particular, the focus which Cixous and Kristeva place upon writing, is within the context of *inter-textuality*: the play of one text as deconstructive of another, itself in turn dissolved or reread. In such a context it is also possible to discern the significance of *difference* in this politics of resistance. Many philosophies of resistance, including Marxism and modernist feminism, have grounded their logic of resistance in *identity*. Readers will recall that, in the introduction to this book, I documented the construction of a sociological self, victim of power and control, waiting to be freed (by sociological insight) into some essentialist state of grace.

The reading of the 'sick role' in Chapter 4 – as repetition – suggested the processes by which the identity of the sick are inscribed upon their Bodies-without-Organs, constantly recapitulating old relations, denying difference. What the FPS critique denies is any claim that this is somehow a 'false' identity, masking some other interior or transcendental identity, essence or soul:

> The figure of the interior soul understood as 'within' the body is signified through its inscriptions *on* the body, even though its primary mode of signification is through its very absence, its potent invisibility. The effect of a structuring inner space is produced through the signification of a body as a vital and sacred enclosure. The soul is precisely what the body lacks (Butler 1990: 135).

For the FPS, patriarchal (Proper) politics – reactionary or radical – is equated with a search for identity, for closure: around nationality, race, class, gender or interest. In contrast, FPS seek difference, engage with it,

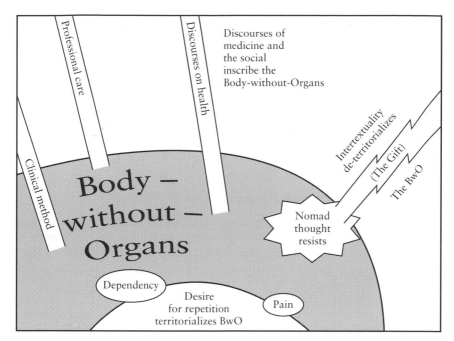

Figure 2 Territorializing and de-territorializing the Body-without-Organs

revel in it, fail to find a common denominator (Butler 1990: 15; Westwood 1990). There is no essential subject to be released from the prison of discourse. All there is, is the play of inscription upon the political surface of the Body-without-Organs. Resistance is the *becoming* of the BwO, not something which can be done for it, although something which perhaps may be facilitated by relationships in the realm of the Gift. *Power, discourse and resistance are all functions of the patterning of the BwO.* Which is another way of saying that all three are mediated by the play of the text on text – of intertextuality.

In Figure 2, I have attempted diagrammatically to summarize the dynamics of power and resistance which has been developed in this section of the book.

My strategy in this chapter has been to read various texts alongside each other, using the very intertextuality I am describing. In the play of text upon text, new possibilities are opened up, perhaps a new 'plateau' can be glimpsed. As an intertextual practice, writing has particular attractions. Writing provides a forum for positive agency: space to act in a world where is it more usual to be the subject of writing. Writing's relative permanence paradoxically makes its less permanent – able to be changed, rubbed out, refined or trashed. Writing enables reflection: it can be returned to, contextualised, reread (Bolton 1994). In addition, writing can be deconstructed: it cannot make such strong claims to authenticity as speech or the lived body. The undecidability of the text is much clearer in writing: there is always a further reading of any writing.

Intertextual practice (in this chapter, for instance) may thus enable de-territorialization: the momentary liberation of the nomadic subject upon the surface of the BwO. In a moment I will look at two examples where writing plays an explicit part in this de-territorialization. But to make the point that it is one technique, I want to refer briefly to two studies in the social theory of health, both of which, in different ways, also address gender.

Intertextual practice in health settings

I want to look at an extract of interaction from a study by Maura Hunt (1991), which looked at the care provided by nurses in the homes of people with terminal illnesses. The main drift of Hunt's argument is that professional carers tend to marginalize family carers, in a discourse which has as its objective ensuring patients died at home, not in hospital or hospice, sometimes against the wishes of relatives. However, in two extracts, this territorialization of the patient seems to be replaced by something else. At the end of one visit, the following occurred (1991: 386):

Nurse: I've got to get on . . . it's been a busy day today . . . actually I've got to do my shopping as well sometime and I've got quite a few more patients to see yet . . . and then go and get some food.
Patient: I haven't got that worry today.
Nurse: The men don't have that worry do they . . . ?
Patient: No, I give them a list . . . what to get.
Nurse: Yes, you see but I bet you've got to think what to put on the list, haven't you?

In another instance, when a patient is frustrated because she cannot do housework:

Nurse: So frustrating yes, when you want to do things.
Patient: My husband says 'Oh leave it'.
Nurse: Yes, but women can't, can they, you know women can't (1991: 386).

My interpretation of these extracts is in terms of the play of two texts: one on relations between carer and cared-for, the other on 'women's lives'. The latter has the effect of – momentarily – changing the former. Perhaps the nurse enters into a more Gift-like relationship in these shared experiences.

The second study explores the possibilities for a medicalization of menstruation. Els Bransen (1992) challenges the proposition that this aspect of women's experiences of their bodies will eventually become part of a medical discourse. She found that women construct their own stories to make sense of menstruation. Firstly, they may generate an 'emancipation' story, in which they are in control of their menstrual symptoms, coping 'well'. In the second genre, the body is something bothersome, to be ignored most of the time until medical advice has to be sought. In the third, the menstruating body is natural, and the functions of the menstrual cycle are seen as beneficial and necessary (1992: 101–5). In all three genres, there is an articulation with the medical profession, but only in the second is the doctor more expert than the woman herself, says Bransen (1992: 106).

These stories provide women with a strategy to play with the texts on menstruation with which medicine might territorialize their bodies. No doubt, in a society where there is a clinical discourse on menstruation, there is a possibility of this kind of discourse to inscribe a woman's BwO. But through intertextual play such as this, medicalization may be resisted.

These examples illustrate some of the arguments I have been developing concerning the politics of resistance in relation to settings of care. What has become clearer is that resisting is fraught with difficulties – many of which derive from the ideology of professional expertise which has invested the field of care. But it has also – I hope – become clear that the over-determined subject which has emerged from the Foucauldian strand of post-modern discussion needs to be revised in relation to some of the discussions emanating from Derrida, the feminist post-structuralists and from Deleuze and Guattari.

In the final pages of this chapter I want to discuss some further prac-ticalities of resistance. The first two readings take up the general perspective on intertextuality in relation to writing, which may indeed suggest strat-egies for creating 'space' in caring relationships. The third reading tries to integrate some of the perspectives which I have introduced in an exploration of moves towards a system of 'community care'.

Narrative and resistance

In *The Illness Narratives* (1988), the anthropologist and psychiatrist Arthur Kleinman uses his concept of the explanatory model in the exploration of the experience of chronic illness, but now taking the sense of 'illness as text' as his starting point. This is a book which works at several levels. It has narrative as its subject-matter, it has many sections which are narrative in structure, and, furthermore, one has the feeling that it is Professor Kleinman's own narrative which we are reading here. In almost every sense, the conceptual framework of the book goes against the perspectives developed in postmodernism. Kleinman's actor is a modern one, of the romantic sort – suffering the existential angst of suffering and mortality. And his health professional is similarly disembodied: engaging at the level of mind with the patient. But Kleinman's discussion of the textual character of illness is helpful, motivated by a perspective which recognizes the possibility that health care may contribute to the inscription of the patient:

> The role of the health professional is not so much to ferret out the innermost secrets (which can easily lend itself to a dangerous form of voyeurism) as it is to assist the chronically ill and those around them to come to terms with – that is, accept, master and *change* – those personal significances that can be shown to be operating in their lives and in their care (1988: 43).

Episodes of chronic illness have their signifiers (symptoms), and those involved (patient, family, professional) use these to provide explanatory accounts of the disease. Kleinman sees these accounts as fundamentally narrative in character.

> the chronically ill are somewhat like revisionist historians, refiguring past events in light of recent changes ... interpreting what has happened and why and prognosticating what might happen, make of the present a constant, self-reflective grappling with illness meanings (1988: 48).

In the language of the PSTH, they inscribe a subjectivity – based in the discourses available. Kleinman (1988: 48) goes on:

> The chronically ill become interpreters of good and bad omens. They are archivists researching a disorganized file of past experiences. They are diarists recording the minute ingredients of current difficulties and triumphs. They are cartographers mapping old and new territories.

Kleinman sees this process as myth-making: a way of making the experience existentially tolerable. And he suggests that 'a core clinical task is the empathetic interpretation of a life story that makes over the illness into the subject-matter of a biography'. The health professional uses the patient's myth (explanatory model) to understand what the experience of the illness may be like (1988: 49). Yet a paragraph later, Kleinman (1988: 49) comes very close to the postmodern position.

> The illness narrative is a story the patient tells ... to give coherence to the distinctive events and long term course of suffering ... Over the long course of chronic disorder, these model texts shape and *even create experience*. The personal narrative does not merely reflect illness experience, but rather it contributes to the experience of symptoms and suffering (emphasis added).

Story and pathology combine, collaborate, refine each other to generate subjective experience, Kleinman (1988: 55) argues. This position allows Kleinman (1988: 53) to consider the potential for 'narrativization' of illness to be part of the therapy, and also demand of clinicians that they unpack their own narratives in the care relationship.

But Kleinman's book, like that of Bennet (1987) – see pp. 98–9 – is aimed at the physician, not the chronically ill person, and his imperatives are aimed at the professional. For instance, in relation to pain, professionals often

> come to question the authenticity of the patient's experience of pain. This response contributes powerfully to patients' dissatisfaction with the professional treatment systems . . . the training and methods of health professionals appear to prevent them from effectively caring for the chronically ill (Kleinman 1988: 57).

To compensate for these shortcomings, and building on the narrative theme, Kleinman (1988: 230–40) recommends that physicians become skilled in the art of the anthropologist – taking a 'mini-ethnography' of the patient, a life history in the style of a biographer, and an elicitation of the explanatory models a patient has generated. The responsibility continues to rest with the professional: one feels at the end of all this that it is just another exercise in achieving compliance. From the postmodern position, the gaze is being extended, the sick person is more firmly inscribed within systems of power/knowledge – Kleinman (1988: 242) is convinced that 'laymen possess alternative forms of knowledge, not merely insufficient scientific knowledge'.

It is only a small step to change the agency for these 'therapies', so now it is the sick person who writes her/his autobiography, is trained in the skill of ethnography as applied to her/his own life situation, who writes, rewrites, transforms her/his explanatory models.

The notion that sick people 'write themselves' is discussed briefly in Howard Brody's book *Stories of Sickness* (1987), which in many ways takes an equivalent position to Kleinman's concerning the role of meaning and explanation in being ill and being healthy.

> suffering is produced, and alleviated, primarily by the meaning that one attaches to one's experience. The primary human mechanism for attaching meaning to particular experiences is to tell stories about them (1987: 5).

Although doctors have the privileged stories in Western culture, they are by no means the only people who produce such narratives (1987: 7), and the possibility of rewriting illness endlessly is a theme in Brody's book. Brody explores fictional accounts of illness to elucidate his position, and in the final chapter of this book I shall similarly look to see what fiction might bring to the exploration of 'health' and 'illness'.

Kleinman's writing demonstrates his belief in the importance of textuality in inscribing and resisting inscriptions of health and illness. Negative examples of intertextual practice among professionals are well documented. Anspach (1988) suggests that doctors rarely communicate their assumptions to the people most needing to know how they are being territorialized: the patients themselves. Perhaps in their dealings with those for whom they care, it is the doctors who need to write their autobiographies and explore their explanatory models. This is the use to which textuality has been put in the 'Stories at Work' programme.

Stories at Work: intertextuality as 'professional therapy'

The postgraduate programme in primary and community care at the University of Sheffield caters primarily for caring professionals from a range of disciplines, using student-centred approaches to learning (see Fox: forthcoming). An optional part of the master's programme is a series of workshops entitled 'Stories at Work', developed and facilitated by writer and educator Gillie Bolton (1993; 1994).

Stories at Work may be described as fictional-critical writing or narrative-making. Although there are educational goals associated with the programme, the underlying objective is to enable participants to reflect on their work and lives through exploratory fictional writing. Needless to say, for many, the workshops provide the first opportunity to write in a fictional mode since English lessons at school.

The course runs as a closed group, enabling supportive, critical discussion of participants' own and other members' writing. The workshops help the professionals to begin writing, to discover their stories, and, to an extent, take ownership of them. They write fictional accounts based on issues in their present or past lives, often minutely embedded within practice. The writing takes a variety of forms: straight accounts, descriptions, poems, ramblings and fragments (Bolton 1994). They read these, and discuss them at each meeting. Bolton (1994) argues that

> our lives are a mesh of our own and others' stories. In the telling and retelling, they flex and develop as we create and recreate ourselves. The impulse to tell is strong in us all, but . . . valued stories are all too often told by the powerful . . .

Writing as a member of a group provides support and a framework for the necessary discipline. This can, of course, have a down side. Writers are occasionally reluctant to read aloud passages which expose difficult or painful issues, they may reject some topics as too painful to share – although they may write these as well, as unsharable, personal pieces. Bolton encourages the emphasis upon the *fictional* character of the writing, both in writing and discussion. This, she suggests, creates a necessary confidentiality, and the possibility to write safely and without inhibition – about a character, rather than about oneself.

The content of the workshops usually involves participants reading part of their writing which they produce in their own time between meetings, often on a topic agreed by the group the previous week, such as 'In control', 'Change', 'In between' or 'Home'. Trust and confidence tend to grow as the course progresses, with participants becoming more willing to share their writing, and also more willing and able to express and expose themselves. The course notes suggest a range of techniques for facilitating writing:

- Intuitive writing – write non-stop for six minutes. Allow no time for thinking or constructing a finished piece.
- Journal writing – all kinds of material, drafts of poems or stories, intuitive writing, recalled dreams, lists, descriptions etc. This provides raw material for re-drafting and editing.
- Unsendable letters – letters which will never be read by the addressee, living or dead.
- Writing games – writing under headings: a misunderstanding, a conflict of loyalties, a matter of integrity, a frustrating episode; lists; sentences beginning 'I know that . . .', 'If only . . .'; finishing part-overheard conversations; invent lives or rewrite characters from fiction etc.

I have devoted some space to this programme because of its articulation with the post-structuralist approach to subjectivity. The programme rejects psychoanalytic models of therapy: what is created here is not repetition but resistance, difference not identity. I feel that it illustrates some of the possibilities of writing – particularly where the emphasis is upon fictional or creative production.

I have tried in this chapter to mingle the three ideas of *de-territorialization* of the BwO, the positive desire and generosity of *the Gift*, and of *intertextuality*. Stories at Work reflects, in my view, one way in which explicitly intertextual activities provide the possibility, particularly in a shared and supportive environment, in which relations are of trust and generosity, not of control or possession, for a de-territorialization. The potential, using this fictional writing as a medium, to become other, also bears upon the kinds of writing practice advocated by feminist post-structuralists such as Cixous and Kristeva, which I reviewed earlier. It is an example of a practical way of using intertextuality in professional situations to reflect upon the work of care in which participants are involved in their work.

Commentary: community care and resistance

In the final section of this book, I shall investigate some of the practical implications of the postmodern approach to health and healing which has been developed in the last five chapters, in relation to particular topics. However, at the end of a dense and theoretically complex discussion of resistance to discourse, I want to explore one issue in some detail now. The purpose is to illustrate the extent to which the perspective raises questions concerning the constitution of care within a politics and a knowledgeability, and the strategies by which these may be contested.

In the UK, community care (CC) became part of the rhetoric of welfare discourses in the 1980s, and in the 1990s can be expected to be a practical issue of great complexity – partly for the reason that, as with health and welfare in general, it has been politicized. Escalating health costs and a demographic shift towards an ageing population throughout the developed world have also brought discussion of 'community care' on to the agendas of European and North American governments (Brownlea 1987).

From the positions developed in this book, the following are some of the issues which I see postmodernist theory (specifically) generating in relation to community care.

The first issue is the creation – in the term 'community care' – of a 'floating signifier', the meaning of which is continually redefined and rewritten to serve particular factional interests. As a concept it appears to be defined in terms of its opposition. The privileging of CC may be deconstructed as dependent, definitionally, upon institutional care, or care which is 'uncaring' and depersonalized, or care which detaches the client from her/his 'community', whatever that might mean, or care provided less economically in hospitals. Which of these definitions obtains depends upon the interests of those using the term.

The worrying thing about this, is that potentially CC may be redefined in ways which are quite detrimental to those who are cared for under its auspices. On the other hand, it suggests that it may be developed in ways which may indeed benefit its consumers. The undecidability permits the intertextual play which opens up all kinds of new readings (including this one).

The second issue is the fabrication of a metanarrative of a heritage in which the aged, handicapped and sick were cared for in family groupings or in 'communities'. With the previous point in mind, it is possible to discern in CC an ideology which draws some of its potency from an imagined past where things were done differently, more wholesomely, more in tune with the way things were supposed to be. Capitalism has been criticized (often by those who are its staunchest supporters) for destroying the family. As I write, the ultimate family, the British Royal Family, seems to be on the point of disintegration as a model. Social theorists have pointed to the inexorable move away from familial relationships grounded in rights, towards commodified relations, as a consequence of the rise of the capitalist mode of production (Sennett 1980). This theme has been taken up in postmodernism (see, for example, Rose 1989: 226–8). Deleuze and Guattari (1984: 34) suggest that the family is the final territorializing force in a market of free exchange.

The significance of our history, or rather 'our heritage' as we must learn to call it, has been reviewed by Game (1991: 153–66). Because this supposedly shared heritage is in common, difference is denied, and identity is constituted. CC is thus ideologically constructed as above petty differences, a universality to society in which we all – regardless of income or social status – will receive the care we need. At the same time, the discourse obscures the difficulties of introducing family- or community-based care at a time when these social forms are fragmenting (Laslett 1992). It may also hark back to a former time when 'families cared', despite the questionable historical authenticity of this claim (Anderson 1980).

The third issue is the oedipalization of care through its location in familial or quasi-familial settings. I have already discussed his, in relation to the article by Bond (1991) on the professionalization of informal care (see pp. 95). The oedipalization theme in the writing of Deleuze and Guattari emphasizes the re-territorialization of relationships into repetitive relations of possession. The cared-for, although no longer under the auspices of the institutionalized caring system, become part of a system of relationships ideologically constituted in the dependency relations of child–parent. Even where family members are not involved in care, the quasi-familial model might be expected to generate the obligations of dependency of Oedipus. It is possible, though improbable, that this location of care may strengthen the familial model in Western societies (Ungerson 1983; see the previous point).

The fourth issue is the extension of a gaze into the community, and the location of health and illness within the family. Organizing care 'in the community' entails systems of control and surveillance to monitor the care which is provided away from the centralized institutions. Under current legislation in the UK, family practitioners and social service departments have been designated for these tasks. Those involved in caring – be they family members or commercial contractors – will be subjected to monitoring. In conjunction with the previous point, this may lead to a new emphasis on the management of family life within normative frameworks.

Armstrong (1983) has documented the extension of a medical gaze into the community during the twentieth century. The introduction of community care may mark the fabrication of a new medical sub-discipline, and is certainly a potential means for family medicine to enhance its status. We might expect an increased 'visibility' of the subjects of CC: the old, handicapped people, those with learning difficulties and the chronically ill. While – in Foucauldian terms – this will constitute more rigorous subjectivities in these people, it may also be argued that politically, enhanced visibility may have some political benefits.

Lastly, there is the possibility of de-territorializing dependency relations between carer and cared-for, and the potential of a new conception of care as facilitation and empowerment. As has been suggested throughout this part of the book, professional caring is imbued by discourses on expertise which make it hard to relinquish a desire based in repetition and control.

The opportunity for a decentralized system of CC does not necessarily end this relationship, nor – as has been suggested above – does the informal familial relationship lead to a de-territorialized BwO (May 1992).

However, legislation in the UK has been constituted so as to generate a consumer-like relationship between cared-for and carers. The formulation of care plans on the basis of economics, with those needing care receiving – in effect – a sum of money which they can spend on care as they wish, or at least with a degree of flexibility, places those needing care in a more powerful position than when dependent either on central services or upon goodwill in informal care relationships. The creation of a 'market in care' may, in this sense, enable people who need care to make choices, to de-territorialize, to choose to have the 'health' they wish inscribed upon them (Clode 1991; Wiles 1993; Hoyes and Means n.d.).

Further, it is possible that in such a situation, professionals will reorientate their roles away from expertise towards facilitation. Within the UK community-care legislation, the model of 'care management' may lead to professionals, and in particular social workers, working very closely with those in need of care to develop individual and personalized care packages across a wide range of provider agencies (Department of Health 1991: 31).

PART 3

DIFFERENCE AND ENGAGEMENT

Postmodernism generates not only distinct positions concerning some of the contested questions of social theory – subjectivity, knowledge, power and the social itself – but also a requirement for a different attitude towards politics and ethics – that is, in terms of how one uses these positions to *engage practically* with the world. In the final part of this book, having set out the theoretical positions which have informed a postmodern social theory of health in earlier chapters, I wish to consider the political and ethical impact of the postmodern, and some strategies for practical engagement. In Chapter 7, these politics and ethics will be applied – from my particular perspective – to a range of topics in health and health care. The title of that chapter: 'De-territorializing health and illness', is intended to signify the intrinsic link between political engagement and the micropolitics of inscription and resistance.

The tension which develops in postmodern ethics and politics is between a responsibility to act in the world and a responsibility to difference or otherness (White 1991). The dialogue between these two political imperatives informs a number of different readings in Chapter 6. I shall suggest, following Stephen White, that the ethics and politics of postmodern social theory are mediated through a mood of 'grieving delight', grounded in a response to difference and to finitude. One further concept will also be introduced here: that of the 'eternal return'. This Nietzschean notion has influenced post-structuralist and postmodern writing, and perhaps it is helpful to understand this idea in relation to the repetitions which were discussed in Chapter 4. Whereas repetition looks to the past, the eternal return is the desire that renews itself into the future: a becoming which never ends in fixity or identity.

As an ethical doctrine, the eternal return is the rule 'whatever you will, will it in such a way that you also will its eternal return' (Bogue 1989: 31).

With such an orientation, supposedly, it becomes possible to live a commitment to the Other, to difference. The eternal return and the mood of grieving delight are more fully explored in relation to a study of health promotion interventions.

Arche-health

Readers who puzzled over the reference to 'arche-health' in Chapter 2 – an idea which at that point it was inappropriate to theorize except at a fairly basic level – will be reassured that at the end of Chapter 6 it is discussed in greater detail, in the context of the ethics and politics of the PSTH. Arche-health is the 'becoming' of the Body-without-Organs, a resistance to discourse and mastery. It is not a prior or privileged kind of health, but a state of becoming which resists definition, which inheres not in an identity, but in difference. Arche-health is perhaps no more than a rhetorical flourish, making the point that a PSTH questions any 'health' or 'illness' created discursively by medicine – or by sociology.

Taking up this last point, the final section of this book is thus also implicitly, and sometimes explicitly, a critique of the modernist sociology of health and healing. I return to the argument introduced in the introduction: that this modern discipline is implicated in the control and construction of health and of those in need of care, alongside medicine and welfare disciplines. One objective in these pages is to juxtapose the ethics and politics of modernism and postmodernism. In Chapter 7, setting out my 'manifesto' by means of some specific discussions, this juxtaposition will – I hope – clarify the extent to which the postmodern social theory of health diverges from its modernist counterpart.

6

THE POLITICS OF
ARCHE-HEALTH

Postmodernism has been challenged as to its politics, usually from the Left. In the era of post-Marxism, these attacks have become less frequent, but postmodern positions have been associated with reaction, with complicity, with capitalism and consumerism, and culturally with the pop, the low-brow and with mediocrity (White 1991: 28). Other critics have leapt upon the unashamed abandonment of the metanarratives of truth and progress to accuse it of courting the 'black hole of relativism' (Rosenau 1992: 189).

The difficulty with these criticisms is not so much that they are incorrect, but that they miss their target. What postmodernism and post-structuralism have disclosed is not their own lack of political and ethical allegiances, but the failure of modernism to generate a morality which does not reflect partial, political interests. Derrida's critique of logocentrism may be seen as a critique of the textual practices within which humans have been created as ethical beings – whether the philosophy is humanist, liberal, paternalist, Marxist or fascist. These discourses have in common their efforts to construct their ethical human in terms of an identity or as in some way essential. Once thus constituted, one may derive an ethics *de facto*. Deconstruction shows this human up as merely an effect of discourse.

This difference between a postmodern and a modern ethics has been described by Stephen White as the difference between a *responsibility to otherness* and the modern *responsibility to act*. The latter is

a moral-prudential obligation to acquire reliable knowledge and act to achieve practical ends in some defensible manner. This responsibility derives from the character of being in the world both physically and politically ... What the postmodern thinker want to assert here is that meeting this responsibility always requires one, at some point,

to fix or close down parameters of thought and to ignore or homo-
genize at least some dimensions of specificity or difference among
actors (White 1991: 20–1).

What is at work in modernism is an unacknowledged will to mastery.
It is upon this critique that I have based my challenge to the modernist
sociology of health and illness to be other than a further discourse on the
human body. Post-structuralist theory discloses that *everything* is political.
Texts are written for reasons of power, and every reading of a text is an
act of power, maybe empowering the reader, maybe causing disempowerment. It has been argued that there is an implicit politics entailed in such
deconstruction, which 'always takes what is claimed to be authoritative,
logical and universal and breaks those claims down, exposing arbitrariness,
ambiguity and conventionality' (White 1991: 16).

In the writing of Derrida and Foucault we are led to recognize that
discourse is driven less by reason than by power. Traditional political
choices, between Left and Right, individualism and totalitarianism, are
deconstructed to expose the discursive strategies which constrain us within
such oppositions. The reaction of those 'radical' groupings which, when
deconstructed in these ways, respond by labelling postmodernism as reactionary is understandable.

Postmodernism in this view is subversive of what Massumi calls 'State
philosophy', the discourses on sameness and constancy which create identity and deny difference and otherness. Deleuze and Guattari's 'nomad
thought' and the feminist poststructuralist 'phallogocentrism' – both of
which have been discussed in this book – are aspects of State philosophy
(Massumi 1992: 4–5).

It is this 'responsibility to otherness' which I shall explore more fully in
the coming pages. As will be seen, this simple term does not supply an
immediate over-arching framework for an ethics and politics: it is the kind
of non-concept that dissolves as soon as one tries to pin it down (like
différance – it is processual rather than conceptual). For these reasons, I
shall approach it in a series of tangential moves. Before doing so, I wish
to make one other comment.

If post-structuralism reveals the politics of textual practices (in the sense
of claims as to responsibility to act), then post-structuralist texts are themselves similarly political: they cannot somehow be free of the force which
invests all other texts. Post-structuralist texts sometimes go to great lengths
to try to shake off any vestige of responsibility to act: for example, by
appropriating the metaphor of the poetic to replace representationalism,
or by using stylistic devices to challenge authorial voice. In my own view,
what makes post-structuralism postmodern is not only the recognition of
the responsibility to otherness, but also a continuing responsibility to act
as an explicit politics (and a concomitant ethics). But it is a politics which
must be worn on the sleeve, in full view, available for deconstruction,

willing to say 'OK, I admit it, I have written this or done this for political reasons. No, I don't presume to make you share my politics, that's for you to choose.'

For these reasons, the PSTH which has been developed so far in this book possesses a politics and an ethics which is available for deconstruction. Indeed, were it to deny this, it would not be postmodern. Modernism pretended that it could go beyond politics. If only it could be rational, objective, scientific enough, it could be value-neutral, could tell us who we were and what we were really like. Oh, those books on methodology: sociology's answer to religion. How to maximize validity, exclude bias, and so on. Postmodernism *must* be open about its own politics, that is what makes it postmodern.

The arguments raised by White and Massumi concerning the denials and negations which inhere in modern thought suggest the exclusionary and hierarchical character of modernist discourse. It may be argued, however, that in and of themselves, these objections are not sufficient to consign modernism to the dustbin of history. In terms of ethics, modernists – from liberal humanists to Marxists – have made certain claims concerning the impact of rationality and the search for knowledge: namely, that – in comparison with non-rationalist perspectives and the kind of post-rationalism which postmodernism advocates, rationality and science have provided humanity with a system which incorporates humanist values of 'reason' and the search for truth, and as such amounts to a 'civilizing' ethics and politics (for a thoughtful review of this position in relation to science, see Grim 1982).

If that is so, then postmodernism would indeed have to justify its ethics of otherness. Specifically in relation to health care, modern disciplines have regarded rationality and rationalization as the best chance to maximize the civilized treatment of those unfortunate enough to need care. If a PSTH questions modernist SHH's epistemology, does it also throw out the benefits of rationality in care?

Earlier in this book I explored postmodern positions on organization, but at that point did not directly address the morality of modern organization. It is clear from what has just been written that it is important that this issue is addressed. The morality of modernism has been taken up and subjected to rigorous critique recently in Zygmunt Bauman's brilliant reading of the part which modern organization played in the Jewish Holocaust. It is through his reading that I will look at the claims of modernism to supply an ethics and politics based in reason, and address the distinction between 'formal' and 'substantive' rationalities.

The dark side of modern 'rationalization'

Bauman argues in *Modernity and the Holocaust* (1989), that the Nazi extermination of 6 million Jews was not an *aberration* within a fundamentally progressive and humanizing project of rationalist modernity, but the contrary. Firstly, the extermination programme was a *logical rational activity* intended to achieve a particular end as a consequence of a calculated set of means. Secondly, it was an enterprise *achievable only under modern forms of bureaucratic organization*, which could marshal resources to undertake the project, and by dividing the task into a series of operations (guarding prisoners, driving transport trains, delivering poison gas, operating the gas chambers, and so on), in a strict hierarchical line of command, desensitize the actors from the morality of the task – turning it into just another organizational problem to be solved.

This analysis, in addition to its horrifying implications for a world which organized according to modern principles, arsenals of megadeath weaponry, brings together elements of the critique of modernity deriving from Weber's (1930) writings on the 'iron cage of bureaucracy' in an entirely novel reading. Weber's analyses of rationality and of bureaucracy become, in Bauman's hands, a negative image of modernity which far surpasses Weber's own rather gloomy view. Because Bauman is arguing from a Weberian perspective, it will be useful to identify briefly the fundamentals of this position on the relationships between organization, bureaucracy and rationalization.

Weber saw the iron cage of bureaucracy as an inevitable consequence of the division of labour within modern societies. An administrative system became necessary to regulate the economic and political system of capitalism, with its 'formal rationality' based upon accounting techniques which enabled the rational calculation of profits and losses in terms of money. A labour force which was 'free' to sell its labour power as it wished, and an open market for the exchange of goods were further requirements for the development of capitalism in Weberian analysis. These were achieved as part of a philosophical rationalism, as opposed to some 'natural' law of social and economic organization (Weber 1930: 60ff.), and this leads him to make the distinction between *formal* and *substantive* rationalities. Formal rationality refers primarily to the *calculability of means and procedures*, while substantive rationality refers to the *value* – from some explicitly defined standpoint – of *ends or results* (Brubaker 1984: 36).

Formal rationality, however, is in perpetual tension with substantive rationality, meaning rationality from the point of view of some particular substantive end, belief or value commitment. Claims to rationality entail judgements of human activities.

> From the point of view of a given *end*, an action or pattern of action is rational if it is an efficacious means to an end, and irrational if it is not. A judgement of rationality or irrationality is in this case a judgement about a causal relation – or lack thereof – between an action considered as a means and a given end-in-view ... from the

point of view of a given *belief*, an action is rational if it is consistent
with that belief, and irrational if it is not (Brubaker 1984: 35).

For Weber, modern capitalism embodies the principles of a formal
rationality of action. The problem of irrationality, of why actions which
would most effectively maximize the attainment of a particular goal, such
as the effective treatment of a particular group of patients, or the arrangements for conducting surgery, are not universally chosen, was answered
for Weber by the growth of bureaucracy. Because capitalism requires a
rational legal State to administer the processes of exchange and legal procedures to ensure equality between participants in the market (formal
rationality), this has led to the growth of a bureaucratic State. But the
abstract rationalizations which seek to eliminate entrenched privilege, to
ensure the 'rationality' of the market, constitute a monopoly in themselves
(a substantive rationality), in which privileged strata of bureaucrats
develop (Giddens 1971: 180–2). This, for Weber (1930: 181), was the
'iron cage' of bureaucracy.

A slightly different formulation asserts that formal rationality favours
economically powerful groups (Brubaker 1984). While freedom of con-
tract in the capitalist market is a condition of formal rationality, in practice it is not neutral, for it guarantees the economically advantaged the
opportunity to use their resources without legal restraint to achieve power
over others. While this may lead to an 'iron cage' which ironically aims to
sustain the interests of the powerful in maximizing formal rationality,
economically threatened groups have an equally strong interest in subjecting the market to substantive regulation, and thus reducing formal rationality. But in both perspectives, formal rationality is compromised by
substantive rationalities reflecting value or belief commitments of groups
within the market. Indeed, taking a Weberian perspective, the application
of rational calculation does not lead to the furtherance of definite moral
or political goals, for example the meeting of particular needs. The morality invested through a *substantive* rationality may be the morality of a
powerful minority, be it a bureaucracy or a dominant grouping.

In *Modernity and the Holocaust*, Bauman (1989) outlines the nightmare
scenario of a group coming to power which held a substantive rationality
in which European Jewry was seen as a pollutant to be eliminated. The
German National Socialist Party's anti-Semitism was not distinctive, Bauman
argues, it merely replicated 1000 years of prejudice. What was distinctive
was that it was translated into the Final Solution of mass extermination
and genocide. And this, Bauman concludes, was achieved through two attributes of modern organization not available to other anti-Semitic regimes.

Firstly, the world-view of the modern era enabled the Final Solution to
be recognized as similar in character to the solution to any other problem.
Despite its repulsiveness for anti-Nazis, it is a *rational* solution to a

problem of organization. How to murder a race? Organize the trains, the extermination units, the labour camps, a system of incentives, all of which promote a docile population walking to its own death (1989: 106).

Secondly, modernism organized itself via a bureaucratic, hierarchical chain of command of people each doing a small task as part of a larger task they may not have understood or even known of, and implicitly following orders. In modernist organizations, as Bauman (1989: 101) has it, the morality of the task inheres not in what *end* it serves, but in its *efficient* achievement.

Together, these elements meant that Hitler could have told his subordinates to find a solution to the Jewish problem, and with a substantive rationality which was anti-Semitic, a formal rationality which enabled the rational use of resources efficiently, effectively, and calculably to match a procedure to an objective, and finally an administrative system which utilized the machine metaphor of organization to divide a task 'scientifically' and achieve it to a schedule, could have overseen the extermination of 6 million people within a space of years. The extraordinary absence of knowledge about what was happening at the time may also be explained by this combination of elements of modern organization. Like the factory or the school, organization in the modern world often takes place in relative private, with few in a position to see the overall picture (1989: 97).

Bauman finds in his analysis nothing to suggest a morality which grows from the principles upon which modernity is founded. Indeed, there is an absence of morality which may be sequestrated equally by evil or by good. We have been persuaded that the latter is more common: Bauman's thesis challenges that belief, and sees lesser versions of the Holocaust in the techniques of modern warfare such as the napalming of Vietnam (1989: 98), or, we might add, the bombing of Iraq during the 1992 Gulf War.

Returning to the context of health and welfare, despite the wish to impute good intentions to those who care, Bauman's reading removes any grounds for expecting that good intentions will be bolstered by an inherently progressive modern project of rationality. Substantive rationalities of a quite local and unattractive mien may supply a morality, bolstered by a formal rationality which efficiently match means to end, and scientifically achieve the goal of the moral order. Interests are dressed up (or obscured) with scientific pretensions, or often, in the case of clinical enterprise, by technological pragmatism: 'such and such procedure works, so we will do it despite not knowing quite why it works'. It is, of course, the deconstructive concern of the PSTH to expose the politics of those interests.

An interesting example from health care is supplied in a recent study of health economics discourse (Ashmore *et al.* 1989). Health economists base their input to debates on clinical management upon a claim that, unlike other interest groups such as clinicians or managers, they possess an Archimedean spot from which to analyse health care. In Weberian terms, their model of 'economic man', who acts so as to maximize the attainment of given ends through the efficient application of means, possesses not substantive, but *formal* rationality. This is *rational* action, *ergo* economic analysis is rational! Economic analysis cuts across interests held by clinicians to provide a 'true' picture of how means can be tailored to meet particular ends. Ashmore *et al.*'s intent is to challenge this argument, suggesting that economists' contribution is partial and socially located, deriving from the limited model of social action in academic economics (1989: 204). While their position is perhaps paradoxical, as they would criticize this model from a similarly partial and socially located model deriving from sociology, it is possible to follow a slightly different tack from Ashmore *et al.* which does not privilege a new *logos*.

The economistic model assumes a rational economic actor who always selects the most efficient means (through the acquisition of commodities or services) to ensure the attainment of her objectives. Consequently, if values can be ascribed to these commodities (both means and ends), then a formally rational strategy to match means to end efficiently and effectively can be derived, free from substantive rationalization. So, for example, the health economists' Quality Adjusted Life Year (QALY) is regarded as a tool to assess the relative cost-effectiveness of differing medical technologies upon patients' extent and quality of survival.

Within the interpretation developed from Bauman's analysis we may see here a formal rationality (the estimation of a QALY score); a bureaucratic mode of action in implementing a QALY-based regime of implementation of scarce medical technology; and a substantive rationality – which might be that of a managerial policy, a clinical perspective, or of course the methodology by which the QALY scores were originally constructed. These elements together fail to offer any guarantee of the morality of the care deriving from this effort at rationalization. Indeed, it is all too easy to see how a substantive rationality which has a very doubtful morality (from another interest perspective) might be adopted. Even if economists themselves administered the organization of resource allocation, this could not insulate the procedures from the vested interests of economic discourses, or of those in a position to influence the economists' judgements. In their book, Ashmore *et al.* (1989: 60–81) reproduce some of the sceptical media responses to Maynard's development of the QALY and the claims of health economists to possess formal rationality.

This example suggests that, from Bauman's rereading of the rationalizations of modernity, the argument that modernism supplies – through rationality – a strategy for achieving truth and progress, founders on the distinction between formal and substantive rationality. (This distinction, made by Weber, is deserving of far greater attention. For a fuller discussion, see Fox 1991a.) However formalized the method of calculating ends, the underlying values by which these calculations come to have political significance determine the ethical engagement. When coupled with the other element of rationalization – bureaucratic organization – the potential for an ethical-political engagement which is far from liberal, humanistic or 'rational' is created. If there were no other argument for questioning modernism, this one seems persuasive to me.

Affirmation and scepticism in the postmodern

It has been suggested by Pauline Rosenau (1992) that the diverse movement of postmodernism can be understood in terms of those who are *affirmative*, as opposed to those whose postmodern perspective makes them *sceptical*. Sceptics offer a negative gloomy assessment, seeing postmodernism as bringing

> fragmentation, disintegration, malaise, meaninglessness, a vagueness or even absence of moral parameters and societal chaos . . . No social or political 'project' is worthy of commitment . . . there is no truth, then all that is left is play, the play of words and meaning.

Affirmative postmodernists are 'open to positive political action (struggle and resistance) or content with the recognition of visionary, celebratory personal nondogmatic projects' (1992: 15–16).

Both these aspects of the postmodern disjuncture may be seen as deriving from the writing of Nietzsche, whose influence has been acknowledged by many postmodern writers, including Derrida, Foucault and Deleuze. The significance of Nietzschean thought will be addressed more fully in the next part of this chapter. The scepticism reflects Nietzsche's desire to free Western culture from the straitjacket of scientific thought, whose misguided optimism has denied the possibility for humanity to achieve its potential. Truth – for Nietzsche – was a conventional fiction, created through a language which had lost its power to affect us emotionally. Only by cutting free from this rationalism might a new vibrancy be introduced into human relations (Asher 1984: 170–1). The affirmation derives from the joyous playfulness and innocence of becoming, without truth, origin or centre (Derrida 1978: 292), the creativity of the will-to-power which is exercised with no fixed or preconceived notions of where this will may lead us (Asher 1984: 173).

These two positions suggest somewhat different political stances in relation to policy. Rosenau makes some interesting comments on the impact that postmodernism – in its two forms – might have on social science (her term). Affirmative postmodernism would construct a 'broad-gauged and descriptive rather than predictive and policy-oriented' corpus, which would 'underscore novelty and reflexivity as it looks to the richness of difference and concentrates on the unusual, the singular and the original' (1992: 169). In contrast, sceptics 'view the universe as impossible to understand, and this discourages them from efforts at building a post-modern social science' (1992: 170).

Rosenau utilizes her sceptic–affirmative opposition to address the consequences of the dissolution of the essential human subject in postmodern perspectives. For the sceptic, advocacy is prohibited, and

> only a few sceptics dare to contemplate institutional and societal reconstruction along lines compatible with the views of their post-modern individual. Those who do, for example, call for a community that does not impose collective choices or democratic decisions on its members . . . (1992: 171).

Non-participation in politics is a rejection of the corruption of represen-tation and a modern politics which is remote and irrelevant. Only political acts which violate modern conceptions of the normal or are contemptuous of the political are of interest to the sceptics (1992: 140–1). Affirmatives, on the other hand, revise rather than reject the modern subject out of hand. Affirmative postmodernism leaves room for a socially sensitive, active human being, groping for a new politics (1992: 171), and focuses upon people

> on the margins, the excluded, those who have no control over their lives, and those who have never known what it is to be an author . . . or a post-modernist reader (active, creative and inventive). Their goal is to speak for those who have never been the subject (active, human), but who are rather so often assumed to be objects (observed, studied). They would include new voices and new forms of local narrative but not in an attempt to impose discipline or responsibility (1992: 173).

They would be critical of representative democracy as a sham, and may reject emancipatory politics in favour of an ill-defined 'life politics' which abandons efforts at general prescriptions or coherent programmes, explor-ing the politics of intimacy, self-actualization and identity, the interpretive and intertextual. Social science [sic] must go beyond rules and methodol-ogy to be interventionist, spontaneous and unpredictable (pp. 146–8).

There is virtually no mention of ethical considerations in Rosenau's text, and her strategy throughout is curiously unengaged, and by no means exemplary of the kind of perspectives which she reports. While an inter-esting textual ploy, her opposition of affirmation and scepticism is remi-niscent of Weberian 'ideal types'. Her approach might also be criticized for erring on the side of inclusiveness, with every theorist who has engaged with discussions of modernity, from Baudrillard to Giddens, from nihilist to New Age philosopher, incorporated under the heading 'postmodern'.

It is helpful to read Rosenau alongside the discussion by White cited at the beginning of this chapter. White, it will be recalled, considered the politics of a responsibility for otherness which – in post-structuralism – substitutes for a politics of the responsibility to act. The dimension of affirmation–scepticism may perhaps be deconstructed as the undecidability inherent in postmodern texts concerning the engagement – as an ethical subject – with the world, of how far one extends one's 'radical suspicion'.

Reading Rosenau suggests that the responsibility to otherness is necessary but not sufficient for the construction of a postmodern politics and ethics. It establishes what could be called the 'concerns' of post-structuralism – the deconstructed and reprivileged interests in difference and diversity, finitude and chance – but leaves open the question of how to act in the world. The justification for political action will be under-determined by the responsibility to otherness, and will – as such – be subject to deconstruction. This suggests that in terms of the practical politics which derives from a postmodern social theory of health, these will be contested and pragmatic, eliding of the realms of the 'political' and the 'personal', and entirely divorced from rationality.

What, then, are the 'necessary' elements of the responsibility to otherness? It is upon these which I now wish to focus, exploring the 'postmodern mood' and the ethics of the 'eternal return'.

Finitude and the eternal return

The attractions of a politics based in a responsibility to otherness, Stephen White argues, is its relevance to the need to respond to suffering. Postmodern writers, he says, have generated 'imaginative, unorthodox ways to remember the unofficial, unprivileged concrete other' (White 1991: 113). In his efforts to develop a postmodern politics of care, White suggests that we can understand the imperatives of the responsibility to otherness in terms of a mood of *grieving delight*. Quietly allowing the recognition of mortality and limitations in human affairs into everyday life, this sense of finitude

> would come alive in the spacing between the self and otherness. The delight with the appearance of the other brings with it the urge to draw it closer. But that urge must realize its limits, beyond which the drawing nearer becomes a gesture of grasping. And that realization will be palpable only when we are sensitive to the appearance of the particular other as testimony of finitude. Then delight will be paired with a sense of grief or mourning at the fragility and momentary quality of the appearance of the other (1991: 90).

Grief sensitizes us to *injustice* – to the added burden of needless suffering, while the element of delight deepens the concern with *fostering difference*. Difference is no longer something to be normalized or tolerated, but to be celebrated. In turn, a caring for difference affirms our humanity, our finitude (1991: 129). Grieving delight, while a consequence of the postmodern responsibility to otherness, White suggests, constitutes the conditions for an ethical-political engagement with modernity, and an attitude towards the responsibility to act.

> Large complex societies will always be heavily constructed around organizational routines and institutional projects, from the perspective

of which the appearance of difference will often elicit more irritation than delight. The more the sway of the responsibility to act dominates a situation, the more this will be the case. The real issue is how to relax the pull of this responsibility before, within and after such routines and projects; how to create slack and space within which the mood of delight can flourish (1991: 129).

In this sense, the responsibility to otherness creates a critical distancing from any ethical and political engagement in the world – a moment for reflection before acting. The skein of postmodernisms discerned by Rosenau, from extreme sceptic to extreme affirmative, reflects the different evaluations of the appropriate balance to be achieved.

I see characteristics of the realm of the Gift discussed in Chapter 5 in this 'mood of grieving delight'. Both act in a generosity towards the Other, and a sense of the fragility of human experience. But it is possible, also, to see parallels here with the Nietzschean idea of the *eternal return*, in particular, as elaborated and clarified by Deleuze.

The conception of the eternal return was introduced by Nietzsche as a question: whether, if told that your life would be repeated over and over as it has been lived and you are living now, in every detail, you would throw myself down and gnash your teeth in despair, or you would exhilarate in that knowledge. The thought of eternal return may be the heaviest burden upon all your actions – it may crush you, it will certainly transform you, in the question 'Do you want this, again and again, without end?' The burdensomeness of the eternal return will depend how you are disposed towards yourself – on how you view your life (White 1990: 67).

This proposition is not one of ontology or cosmology, but is intended as a way of asking of oneself whether there is a way of being disposed towards ourselves and others which would allow an affirmative response to the question of eternal return (1990: 68). It is not a desire for repetition, or for a cyclical return of the same, but the opposite: an affirmation of becoming and difference (Bogue 1989: 28–9). The eternal return needs to be read within Nietzsche's philosophy of a will-to-power, an active principle of becoming other, as opposed to reactivity and passivity. Deleuze's reading of Nietzsche makes the connections between the will-to-power and the positive desire which was discussed at length in Chapter 4 of this book.

Becoming entails flux and multiplicity, chance and chaos: the nomad thought of Deleuze and Guattari. Nomads impose no fixed boundaries, they occupy a space according to their capabilities, and then move on (Bogue 1989: 11). The affirmation of the eternal return is the affirmation – as in a game of dice – not only of the range of possibilities of a throw, but also of the specific outcome of a throw. Accepting the eternal return entails accepting the outcome, whatever it may bring, as the desired outcome

(1989: 29). The eternal return is the *affirmation of difference*, one might also say, a *delight* in difference.

What is suggested through the notion of the eternal return is not just a strategy for self-reflection, but an ethical principle. Quoting Deleuze's book *Nietzsche and Philosophy* (1983), Bogue summarizes this as follows:

> As ethical doctrine, the eternal return functions as a selective princi-ple that issues in a practical rule: '*whatever you will, will it in such a way that you also will its eternal return*' ... This, the *thought* of the eternal return, makes possible the elimination of all the half-desires and hesitant yearnings, the qualified excesses and provisional indulgences, of a cautious and calculating will (Bogue 1989: 31).

A person who advocates the eternal return, as it is becoming, recognizes that life is the will-to-power, that we constantly overcome ourselves, even if we do so by reaffirming ourselves as we have been. The advocate of the eternal return lives dangerously, continuing to toss the dice, accepting the pain or the pleasure, to see what one may become. This is the Nietzschean model of how humans should live.

> living, for human beings, is soul-making, but after recognizing that I am the creator of my soul, I must still decide what soul I will struggle to create, given the material and talent available to me, and how that soul will relate to other souls also in the making (White 1991: 104).

This new, active way of life is 'the affirmation of the being of becoming, the unity of multiplicity, and the necessity of chance' (Bogue 1989: 32).

The relationship between the eternal return and the de-territorialization of the Body-without-Organs described by Deleuze and Guattari is recog-nizable here. The 'plateaux' are strategies for becoming, for affirming the eternal return. But I am more interested here in the ethical aspect of the eternal return. Trying to read the eternal return alongside White's 'grieving delight' suggests that – in relation to suffering and to care – fostering of difference and a sensitivity to injustice supply an ethical-political position not only in terms of one's own actions, but also in relation to others.

The adoption of the mood of grieving delight comes through a recog-nition of finitude – one's own limited span of experience, of perspective, of life. Willing the eternal return in what one does in the world similarly entails a recognition of finitude. Bauman makes the point about the will to action through Jorge Luís Borges's parable *The Immortals*. Once mortal, the immortals have lost the desire to act, they do nothing, they do not write or even speak. Having once striven to achieve, now they are contemptuous of all actions or thoughts – which now cannot be unique as they were when mortal.

> The understanding that circumstances and changes are infinite and therefore *worthless* could appear only in so far as one remembered

that the circumstances and changes were once finite and thereby *precious*; if one knew the value that was once born of finitude (Bauman 1992: 9–10).

The eternal return is not immortality, which is the continuation of unchanging being. How can there be an eternal return when there can be no becoming?

A mood affirmative of the eternal return might thus possess a congruence or convergence with the 'grieving delight' of the responsibility to Otherness. Or put another way, the principle of affirming the eternal return supplies an ethics which orientates towards (I will resist saying equates) a responsibility to Otherness, and in particular a sensitivity to injustice and a fostering of difference. It provides some kind of touchstone to address the responsibility to act, as weighed against the responsibility to Otherness. This proposition also allows a rereading of Nietzsche's misused version of the outcome of affirming the eternal return and 'becoming': the *Übermensch* ('overman').

I have tried once again in this section to read some philosophical propositions alongside each other, in the hope that this might illuminate and offer new potentials for analysis. For example, while I see the eternal return as interesting and important to the ethics of postmodernism, it may be hard – concretely – to affirm one's particular actions in this way. What does it mean, when confronted by a situation of care, to say that one wills one choice through an affirmation of its eternal return? For those of us starting out on the effort at 'becoming', contemplation of the mood of 'grieving delight' may be more instrumental!

I am conscious of the 'sheer weight' of theory involved in these complex notions. To explore these readings less abstractedly, I will now address the ethics and politics of a particular topic through these positions: how the PSTH might inform involvements in interventions around 'lifestyle' in health promotion.

A question for the PSTH: the politics of 'lifestyle'

How should the postmodern social theorist of health articulate with the social epidemiology of diseases, and the so-called 'lifestyle'-orientated responses which have been generated by medicine and by 'health promoters'? For example, in Sheffield, a project entitled 'Heart of Our City' has been concerned with addressing issues around coronary heart disease (CHD) in some inner-city areas. While identifying some of the 'material' causes of CHD to do with poverty and other social conditions, the emphasis in terms of its interventions is aimed at changing individual behaviour: reducing levels of smoking, of intake of cholesterol and saturated fats, encouraging exercise, reducing stress and also promoting medical check-ups to identify early signs of CHD (Heart of Our City n.d.). This programme is in many ways typical of a large number of interventions in health promotion which target at the level of individual prevention, and in particular focus on changing behaviour away from higher-risk towards lower-risk behaviour.

Such programmes have attracted much attention in modernist sociology of health, and sociologists have often become key members of programme teams, using their knowledge of the sociology of illness behaviour and their methodological expertise in researching social processes to develop and implement health promotions. The theoretical writings on 'lifestyle' interventions are varied, ranging from critiques of the ideological implications of such programmes (Townsend and Davidson 1982; Davey-Smith *et al.* 1991), through assessments of the 'medicalization of life' which they entail (Zola 1972; Crawford 1986; Miles 1991) and methodological discussions (Calnan 1987) to accounts which begin to merge with epidemiology (Hart 1985; Fitzpatrick 1991). I shall not even attempt to document the many discussions which have been raised in this literature.

I take as a fundamental (and I will return to this in the next chapter), that as social theorist I am not in a position to make informed clinical judgements as to the efficacy or problems with any particular intervention. I must perforce leave these to clinicians and medical scientists. Despite my suspicion of the truths which these disciplines have derived, I will confine myself to the arena of social theory as informed by postmodernism: principally the effects of discourse in constituting subjectivity and the possibilities of resistance.

I will address these issues in the context of 'care' and the constitution of 'health', to identify some of the positions which the PSTH generates concerning such interventions, and to try to move towards an ethical-political engagement. To avoid an entirely abstracted discussion, I will take as an example (for no particular reason) the Sheffield Heart of Our City initiative to encourage knowledge and awareness of CHD, and a range of self-initiated changes related to heart health, including diet, smoking, exercise and stress in the population of their target area through community initiatives and health education (Heart of Our City n.d.: 28).

Initial questions are those which are to be asked of any topic in the PSTH. Whose voice is being heard in the discourse on lifestyle? What authority is being spoken here, what body of expertise is being cited, what are the conditions of promulgation of these messages through and by which we are asked to accept the authenticity of the discourse? Answering these questions can begin to identify the form of territorialization which is being attempted. (In this particular case, both medical and community development discourses seem important in defining the objectives and the criteria for outcomes.)

More specifically, concerning the proposed interventions, what benefits are being suggested from the behaviour change? The concern here is not with some kind of cost–benefit evaluation: what are the benefits in health or the cost of health care, as weighed against costs in choice, enjoyment, and so on? I am more interested in identifying hidden benefits: for example, will intervention lead to additional primary care clinics which will generate income for family practitioners under the National Health Service incentives for prevention? Will there be spin-offs for community development in other health and non-health arenas? What will be the longer-term effect for funding such initiatives? This will give me a wider picture of the local alliances and conflictual positions which the intervention will engender. (For a detailed example of analysis of such alliances in the control of surgical services, see Fox 1991.)

I will now begin to deconstruct some of the arguments which are involved in the intervention. For example, and fundamentally: 'health promotion'. This term glosses the individual person in an interesting way. What is being promoted? The answer might be: a healthy person. But it is not promoting personhood, or people in general, but the 'healthiness' that the person carries with her/him. Health promotion is forced to delimit some attributes as to do with 'health'. The delimitation may be very wide – to incorporate mood, sexuality, security, and so on, or it may be much narrower. Feasibly the delimiting will involve attribution of 'those behaviours (the lifestyle) which are involved in health'.

However, such a behaviourist interpretation may be problematic if the intervention seeks to influence lifestyle. Glassner (1989) has argued that discourses on health and fitness require a thinking subject, capable of agency. So there is a double movement here. Firstly, a notion of some things as delimitable as 'health' is constituted. Second, a subjectivity is situated in relation to this health. There is a dissociation between the person and her/his health: they are constructed in a dialectic. In this perspective, the subject has the potential to act rationally to influence her/his health. On the other hand, 'health' has the potential radically to affect the subject – who, though separate, depends upon it for survival. This dissociation provides the potential for victim-blaming: the person is the victim of her/his health turned nasty, but also the agency responsible for this state of affairs. It is a dissociation, incidentally, with which modernist sociology has colluded, in its continued mind–body separation.

In a recent article, Bauman (1992) has begun a deconstruction of death and the efforts which people make to avoid it. Health promotion and illness prevention discourses contribute to a rationalizing away of our finitude.

> The truth that death cannot be escaped is not denied – it cannot be denied; but it could be held out of the agenda, elbowed out by another truth: that each *particular* cause of death (most importantly, death which threatens the particular person, me at the particular moment, now) can be resisted, postponed or avoided altogether. Death as such is inevitable, but each concrete instance of death is contingent

... All deaths have causes ... We do not hear of people dying of mortality. They die only of individual causes ... I can do nothing to defy mortality. But I can do quite a lot to avoid a blood clot or a lung cancer. I can stop eating eggs, refrain from smoking, do physical exercise, keep my weight down ... And while doing all these right things and forcing myself to abstain from the wrong ones, I have no time left to ruminate that the effectiveness of each thing I am doing, however foolproof it could be made, does not in the least detract from the uselessness of them all taken together (1992: 5–6).

This is another element of the mind–body differentiation, another element of subjectivity to be inscribed on the Body-without-Organs of the person living a 'healthy lifestyle'.

It would be possible to continue the deconstructions which are involved in an intervention, and no doubt collecting commentaries from people involved might provide further material in the play of intertextuality. For example, we could examine the issues raised by this comment from a GP surveyed by the project: 'I'm sure it's very useful but the problem that I see is that it's getting the wrong people, the ones not at risk. The people at risk don't seem interested' (Heart of Our City 1992: 26).

I shall look briefly at one further element, the characterization of the contact between health promoter and 'promotee'. I wrote at some length about the oedipalization (repetition) of such contacts in Chapter 4. Preventive contacts do not necessarily have the same discourse as curative or caring contacts. Szasz and Hollender (1956) would probably put it within the realm of 'mutual participation', where a professional helps a client to help her/himself. This is supposedly an adult-to-adult relationship. The extent to which a non-oedipal, non-repetitive contact can be sustained may depend upon a number of factors:

1 the context and personnel involved (non-clinical personnel can take on many aspects of promotion, avoiding moves towards the dependency of the clinician–client contact);
2 an emphasis on choice, responsibility and calculability of costs and benefits will tend to de-territorialize the interaction, while inputs which introduce fear, or dwell on the technicalities of the disease and/or the intervention, will re-territorialize within a repetition of dependency;
3 whether the intervention draws upon familial health-promotion roles as part of its programme (for example, targeting mothers as the people responsible for providing a healthy diet – see Graham's (1979) critique of health promotion).

These elements also suggest the conditions of resistance to the inscriptions which a health promotion of lifestyle might entail. The opportunities for relationships of generosity, and the challenge of professionalizing discourses of care would need to be assessed in making judgements on the ethical-political involvement.

On the basis of these deconstructions, the question becomes how to act within the responsibility to Otherness, or, to put it otherwise, with an appropriate lightness of care deriving from the mood of 'grieving delight'. Such a response would entail at least: an emphasis which would act very locally, as opposed to more indiscriminate or totalizing interventions; programmes which enable people to make active decisions about the lives they lead; a celebration of diversity in the target population, rather than a perspective which sees individuals as deviates from some norm of behaviour; involvements which take advantage of spaces in routines and lives to explore new possibilities for activities and identity; and programmes which do not detract from the finitude of those who are clients, for example, by an overblown emphasis on 'being healthy' as opposed to 'becoming this or that'.

Taking the position of affirming the eternal return of one's own choices, a personal involvement would entail making such contributions to a programme which would facilitate the just-mentioned elements. As with all other involvements, the personal and the ethical-political are dissolved as separate realms.

I have tried to show in this section the kinds of ethical-political analysis which are entailed in choosing a responsibility to act. As I mentioned earlier in this chapter, in the postmodern there is no excuse for action. Unlike the modernist, who makes claims to rationality or to organizational imperatives, that (mythical) latitude is denied. Regardless of how much an action seems to flow from a responsibility to Otherness, one will still be held to account. There is no longer any *logos* which can legitimate action. The deconstructive activities of the PSTH do not possess the authority of science: they celebrate undecidability. That is why I have been at some pains in this chapter to develop a fairly sophisticated analysis of the conditions for ethical-political action.

If it is possible to act within the PSTH, then there are no unquestionable imperatives for activity, and within the example readers may discern a 'radical suspicion' concerning health. The unitary notion of health or illness dissolves in the postmodern mood, to be replaced by something which is very fragmentary and indeterminate. The discussion in this chapter demonstrates the decentring which a politics of responsibility to Otherness entails. In place of health or its absence, one is left only with *difference*. I have called this indeterminacy *arche-health*. Arche-health was mentioned in Chapter 2, when I first addressed the possibilities for resisting the inscription of the Body-without-Organs. To round off this chapter, I return to this topic.

Arche-health

I have made the comment at various points that the subject-matter of my text is the 'politics of health-talk'. This suggests that what it is *not* about is trying to define 'health' or 'illness', but rather to look at the ways in which these terms are used discursively. As I have suggested, the inscription of the Body-without-Organs by health and illness is affected by the organizational processes of health care (Chapter 3), the repetition of dependency in the contact between carer and cared-for (Chapter 4) and the failures of trust and generosity in the caring setting (Chapter 5). In each of these domains, these inscriptions are contested and may be resisted as the play of indeterminacy and intertextuality opens up new possibilities for the BwO.

It is in the contestation of the BwO that the PSTH becomes political, and it is a 'political anatomy' that must therefore be of interest. Some people who work in the modernist SHH have seen a contribution to be made, through their sociological skills and knowledge, to the enhancement of health or to limiting illness. But if these terms are no more and no less than discourses, elements of power/knowledge inscribed on the BwO, is there any way in which a postmodern social theory can engage with these practical concerns? For example – as in the case of health promotion above – what is the significance of this scepticism about 'health' and 'illness' for an ethical-political commitment to action?

This scepticism provides the ground for the radically different conception of human potential which I have christened 'arche-health', and which derives from the postmodern positions which have been examined throughout this book. The perspectives on engagement which were investigated in the case study of health promotion need to be read through this notion of arche-health, rather than through any other definition of health or illness.

It is hardly breaking new theoretical ground to identify the cultural meanings which are attributed to health and illness: to demonstrate that – despite supposedly signifying some biological state, maybe reflecting pain and suffering – they serve moral purposes (Grim 1982; New 1991). The SHH has pointed out many of these contextualizing definitions, and from a post-structuralist analysis it would be straightforward to begin to deconstruct these meanings and the ways in which they are used discursively.

In the medical model, health has typically been defined through its opposite, and then in terms of a series of operationalizing definitions: days in hospital, days off sick, and so on (Doyal 1981: 241). Outside medical discourses, health is rarely now defined simply as an absence of illness. 'Complete physical, mental and social well-being' is the slogan of the World Health Organization (WHO 1985), while New (1991) documents Oliver Sacks's view of total health (in Parkinson's disease patients when first administered L-DOPA) as an 'awakening'. In this book we have heard of de Swaan's (1990: 22) version of ill health as a 'notion of increasing dependency'. Canguilhem (1989) sees illness and health as negative and positive biological values, while Sedgewick (1982: 30) identified illnesses as socially constructed definitions of natural circumstances which precipitate death or a failure to function according to certain values. Other definitions cite an anthropological phenomenology of 'what it is to function as a human', with illness defined (somewhat tautologically) as circumstances of a failure to function which continue to be seen as human (Wright 1982). New (1991: 11) defines health functionally: a healthy person is 'someone who is not prevented by any internal state from functioning normally, and who can be expected to continue that way'. The recognition of this normative element underpinned the Parsonian conception of the sick role, and has been a topic for analysis in much medical sociology literature. Ethnomethodology took as its subject how people 'do' health and illness convincingly, while structuralists saw the categories as opportunities for exploitation of people by the medical profession, industry or the State.

All these definitions have a politics associated with them, all try to persuade us to a particular perspective on the person who is healthy or ill. I described, in the introduction, some of the 'grotesques' by which sociology has defined the 'natural': these discursive strategies are applied in the SHH discourses on health and illness. All definitions of health and illness are thus implicated in the inscription of the BwO. The politics of health-talk is about these inscriptions and resistances, which include the inscriptions of modernist social sciences alongside medicine and health disciplines.

This is the reason for the suspicion concerning political engagement with health-care interventions. I have shown in this chapter how rationality and organizational arguments substitute an unacknowledged *will-to-mastery* for any justice of action. This can be seen in the emphasis in modern medicine upon the heroic, where the attempt to succeed is held in greater esteem than any possible benefits of action. At the root of any such claim to justify intervention (a responsibility to act, in White's terminology) there will lie a *logos* – sometimes acknowledged, other times not – by which the authenticity of the discourse is articulated. The postmodern substitution of this responsibility to act with a responsibility to Otherness is the rejection of a will-to-mastery, and the replacement of this Proper, identity-seeking discourse with a Gift relationship to difference.

The discussions of the mood of grieving delight and the ethics of the eternal return in this chapter generate the very different conception of human potential or its failing, in place of the notions of 'health' and 'illness' with their discursively constructed efforts at inscription. Arche-health is about a will-to-power, a becoming, a de-territorializing of the BwO, a resistance to discourse, a generosity towards otherness, intertextuality: all the things which I have outlined throughout this text.

Arche-health is not intended to suggest a natural, essential or in any way prior kind of health, upon which the other healths are superimposed. The reason for the term is its homage to Derrida's (1976: 56) notion of '*arche-writing*', which he developed in his discussion of *différance*. Arche-health is that which refuses to be discursive: it is intertextual, *différance* – that which differs and is deferred. Arche-writing, argues Derrida, is that which supplies the possibility of writing – based on a system of difference.

> This arche-writing, although its concept is invoked by the themes of 'the arbitrariness of the sign' and of difference, cannot and can never be recognized as the *object of a science*. It is that very thing which cannot let itself be reduced to the form of *presence*. The latter orders all objectivity of the object and all relations of knowledge (Derrida 1976: 57).

So it is with my concept of arche-health. Arche-health is the *becoming* of the organism which made it possible for the first time to speak of health or illness. It is present, in the sense that a trace of it is carried, in every discourse on health, however and with whatever *logos* that discourse has constituted itself. It can never become the object of scientific investigation, without falling back into discourse on health/illness. It is not the outcome of deconstruction of these discourses, it *is* deconstruction or intertextuality, difference and becoming. It is real in a way that health and illness can never be real. It is the nomad thought on the surface of the BwO, momentarily de-territorialized, blasting the BwO out of fixity, into multiplicity and the possible. In this sense, it is synonymous with the will-to-power of the BwO. It is the principle of action, the apotheosis of reactivity. It is multiple in its effects, and, as a form of *difference*, cannot be spoken of in terms of unity or of its division. Every BwO has an arche-health, which is its becoming. Whereas health and illness territorialize the BwO with their discourses (see the beginning of Chapter 2), arche-health is the force of desire, of resistance.

An ethics of becoming

I hope that the discussions in this chapter of the eternal return and the postmodern mood of grieving delight – as strategies for ethical-political involvement – become clearer as a consequence of this comparison of 'health' and 'arche-health'. What I have argued is that one's responsibility to act be guided by the responsibility to otherness which has as its objective the facilitation of becoming, of arche-health. It should also be clearer why the postmodern involvement with such things as health promotion is not straightforward. 'Health' promotion for one person may facilitate arche-health, while for another the same intervention territorializes within a discourse. Arche-health is possible only by the de-territorialization of the BwO. The inscriptions on that BwO – by organization, by repetition, by expertise, by pain or fear – territorialize it, against arche-health.

There is no guarantee that acting in the world will lead to this facilitation of becoming. Sometimes one's own becoming may territorialize another: hence the ethics of the eternal return. The positions in this book have suggested what is entailed in the territorializations of the BwO, and

the possibilities of resistance in caring settings offered by intertextual practice. The ethics and politics of arche-health concern engagement with BwOs:
always on the side of the nomad thought, of responsibility to difference
and Otherness, against identity, and in support of generosity against mastery.
Unsurprisingly, this is not simple.

DE-TERRITORIALIZING
HEALTH AND ILLNESS

This text has created the Body-without-Organs (BwO) as the locus for a postmodern social theory of health. This political surface is distinct from the anatomical body, and from the sociological reconstructions of the body to which I alluded in the discussion of 'the natural' in the introductory chapter. In comparison, there has been a failure in modernist medical sociology to engage critically with the construction of the body in medicine and health-care discourses. This failure threatens, as Nettleton (1992: 147) suggests, to submerge the SHH into these disciplines, as an adjunct utilized to theorize medicine's newly fabricated 'biopsychosocial' model (see also Perakyla 1989: 131). This tendency – to accept the anatomical body as the site of discourse – also seriously impoverishes the so-called 'sociology of the body', which – largely through a sociological reading of Michel Foucault – appears to have rediscovered flesh and blood.

The BwO is – as its name suggests – unlike an anatomical body-with-organs. But, as Deleuze and Guattari (1988: 149–50) say, we all have one (or several).

> At any rate, you make one, you can't desire without making one. And it awaits you: it is an inevitable exercise or experimentation, already accomplished the moment you undertake it, unaccomplished as long as you don't. This is not reassuring, because you can botch it.
>
> The BwO is real, it is not an idealist conception. Of course, it is fabricated, it is human-made, through material practices, just as one would make a hatchet or a piece of music.
>
> You never reach the Body-without-Organs, you can't reach it, you are forever attaining it, it is a limit ... But you're already on it,

scurrying like a vermin, groping like a blind person, or running like a lunatic: desert travels and nomad of the steppes. On it we sleep, live our waking lives, fight – fight and are fought – seek our place, experience untold happiness and fabulous defeats: on it we penetrate and are penetrated: on it we love (1988: 150).

The BwO is the outcome of material production, and material production (as well as the production of desire) is a consequence of the political BwO. So it is the location at which biology and the social collide. On the BwO are inscribed (as has been shown in the discussions in this book) the discourses of the social, alongside the sensations of the body – pleasurable and painful – and the positive desire of other BwOs. On its surface, intensities vie and intermingle: from this patterning of the BwO emerges the fabricated, political, ephemerality of identity – the human subject.

In this final chapter I want to explore a selection of fairly random musings on the politics of the BwO, and of a PSTH. Each is intended to illustrate the kinds of analysis which has become possible through a PSTH, and to open up new avenues for exploration. The first of these addresses an aspect of the politics of health-talk to which I have alluded at several points: the dual involvement of those who would theorize in this area not only as social theorists but also as human beings implicated in the pain and suffering of others, and involved with our own pain and suffering. I then consider a postmodern engagement with technology, and finally the use of fictional writing in exploring the politics of health-talk.

Pain and the Body-without-Organs

If one were to be cynical about the relationship between medicine and medical sociology, one might conclude that sociology is the branch of medicine in which pain has been rendered silent. Because it is 'a private sensation' (Baszanger 1992: 181), it has been declared an inappropriate topic for sociological analysis, to be left to the physiologists and psychologists. However, pain is not entirely absent from sociological discourse. It has been transformed, rendered into other forms more amenable to the model of the human fabricated by sociology. The *meaning* of pain becomes the focus, fleshing out the sociological subject, carrier of identity and biography produced out of the interplay between individual and society: agency and structure. So it becomes possible for Radley (1989: 232) to write that 'the body is not merely the location of disease but is that through which one continues to apprehend the world and oneself in it'. Pain impacts on the sense of self because of this duality.

This apparently banal insight is worthy of deconstruction to reveal the ideological positions it bears, and the discourse it makes possible. Firstly, it asserts a non-problematic character for 'disease' – a kind of epidemiological version to do with hosts and agents, as opposed to an ecologically informed analysis which would recognize 'disease' as itself socially constructed, the fabrication of values and norms. This opens the way for the sociological reading of disease: 'illness', in which the significance of 'biology' is reconstituted through the sociological concerns with experience and social determinations. (Incidentally, Radley's text moves in the next lines to discussion of 'illness', eliding any discontinuity between the concepts.)

Secondly, it asserts an essential human agent, interior to the body, its motivator but also ultimately its victim. Enter the sociologist, capable of interpreting the way the individual is affected by social forces. With this essentialist actor as the *creator* of meaning, pain – the physiological precursor – gains its significance from the opposition of the existential circumstances of embodiment with the socially constructed world (by which meaning becomes possible in the first place). It is this meaning which is of interest to the sociologist. This perspective is epitomized by the corpus of writing in the SHH on so-called 'biographical disruption' of the lived experience of those with chronic or terminal disease (Bury 1991). In Radley's text, this leads him to investigation of 'adjustment style' among these people (Radley 1989: 233). Once again, it is possible to see the model of prior agent, victim of both biology and culture.

Now, I am not questioning the logic that social theory looks at the social as its realm, and that, as such, the meanings ascribed to pain are worthy of exploration. But I do challenge the fabrication in the modernist SHH of a human agent constituted in Cartesian mind–body dualism, from which flows the interpretations which are then 'discovered' in people's accounts of pain and suffering. The positions which have been developed in this book supply a very different perspective, in which the essential, Cartesian individual is replaced by a postmodern self, constituted as an effect of intertextuality, inscribed yet capable of resistance. What I want to do is look at pain through this particular filter, if not to supplant the modernist analyses, to open up a 'politics of pain'.

The postmodern position questions the ontology of the human subject, and (as I hope to show) the character of the physical body as both creator of pain and mediator of lived experience. This view may be illustrated by the position which Charmaz (1983: 168) developed in her discussion of the effect of pain.

> Physical pain, psychological distress, and the deleterious effects of medical procedures all cause the chronically ill to suffer as they experience their illness. However, a narrow medicalized view of suffering ... ignores or minimizes the broader significance of the suffering ... the *loss of self* felt by many people with chronic illnesses. Chronically ill people frequently experience a crumbling away of their former self-images without simultaneous development of equally valued new ones (emphasis in original).

The self which Charmaz sees as crumbling is an active, controlling self: it is loss of agency which she equates to loss of self (1983: 171).

In the postmodern position, the anatomical body is not the carapace of the self, the self is not interior, buried somewhere in the cerebral cortex. If the self *does* inhabit such a location, it is as a consequence of discourse, of a territorialization into what Deleuze and Guattari (1988: 158) call the *organism* – a 'body-with-organs'. Needless to say, the organism is an effect, a pattern of intensities on the BwO. Classically the fabrication of the theologian and the philosopher, in the modern period, the principal discourse which created the organism has been a medical discourse.

Lived experience, be it as a prisoner of an organic body, as a paranoiac, a wage-slave or a magician, is the fabrication of a BwO, a political locus stratified by discourse, desire and physical sensation (including pain). Pain – as sensation – has no implicit meaning. But a territorialization of the BwO as organism (creature of biomedical and more recently human sciences discourses) provides the possibility for pain to signify. Once it signifies in relation to the organism, it contributes to the self, to subjectivity. In this reading, it is not the self which experiences pain or attributes meaning to it, the self *is* the pain, the self is an effect of the meaning.

Like any intensity on the political surface of the BwO, pain can be experimented with. For the masochist, pain is the medium by which s/he becomes other, deferring the re-territorialization of the BwO, creating a 'plane of consistency' of desire (Deleuze and Guattari 1988: 155). For the yogi, pain has been detached from the organism, it can no longer territorialize a subjectivity through its signification.

But for the patient, pain may have a major territorializing effect on the BwO. In de Swaan's study of a cancer ward (see Chapter 5), the meanings attached to pain and its significance as marker of finitude and dissolution, territorialize not only patients but also relatives and staff. Fear, anger, scorn, panic create a subjectivity which seems to dominate everything else. Subjectivities of a deeply discredited kind become attached to patients as they are constituted as demented or incapable of following codes of decorum (de Swaan 1990: 53–4). This territorialization of the BwO may in part be a consequence of the meanings not for the sufferer but for those around her/him, the visibility of obvious suffering causing friends and acquaintances discomfort, substituting a new less public or 'sociable' presentation of self (Charmaz 1983: 179).

This reading contributes a somewhat different version of the medicalization thesis which has become associated with discussions of stigma in the SHH. Discourses on health and illness, which have become dominated by medical and human sciences expertise, contribute to a particular territorialization of the pained BwO, organized in terms of the 'organism', a biomedical or biopsychosocial Body-with-Organs. An example of such territorialization, which incorporates both medical and psychological discourses, is supplied in Perakyla's (1989) study of terminal care of patients. Here, these discourses are used organizationally to constitute an 'experiencing subject' whose suffering can then be organized within the systems of care available in the setting. Within a 'psychological frame', motives are imputed to patients which explain their anger or resistance to treatment regimes. By adducing psychological suffering, it supplies an acceptable subjectivity to a patient whose non-compliance might otherwise be stigmatized as deviant (1989: 122–3).

The discursive construction of pain meanings is not really de-territorialized from the organism by the SHH discourses on biographic disruption. These merely serve to fabricate a subject who is effectively 'trapped' by her/his body and its sensations of pain or disability, and is required to 'adapt' to the limitations thus imposed. Fundamentally, they obscure the effects of the disciplines of the body (including sociology) in constituting this kind of subject.

I have attempted in this book to suggest how it is possible to de-territorialize the BwO, to enable becoming, or, to continue the discussion at the end of the last chapter, to facilitate arche-health. The experience of pain is often that which brings people into care settings in the first place, so for a PSTH, this most fundamental aspect of being healthy or being ill needs to be addressed. I have suggested that intertextual practices make resistance possible, and in the context of the meanings of pain and of illness, the postmodern position would emphasize the undecidability of such meanings, their continual deferral and slippage: differance. As an example of such slippage, and the potential for de-territorialization, this fragment of interview data from Lynam's (1990: 190) study of young people with cancer is illustrative.

> About the chemo, I swore I wasn't going to go back for it . . . I was scared and didn't want to go back. I talked to her [another woman who had had chemotherapy]. I changed the word to dread. That helped a lot, just how I spoke about it, from being scared of it, to just dreading it. It helped get it in perspective so I could get myself to go back.

The textuality of these associations is clear in this extract. Meanings are seen to be capable of transformation, with all sorts of possibilities for re-territorialization. Part of that process, I feel, is the deconstruction – in discourses on pain and the practice of care – of essentialism, the mind–body dualism and the interior–exterior conception of subjectivity. The individualizing of pain and suffering by medicine (often with the collaboration of the human sciences) territorializes an organism upon the political BwO: bodies-with-organs which are then the natural subjects for the expertise of medicine (for a discussion of the individualizing of care, see also May 1992).

Medical technology: a postmodern view

From what has just been said concerning the impact of discourses of medicine and the allied human sciences in territorializing the BwO into an 'organism', a body created in a biomedical or more recently biopsychosocial model, it might be expected that I would wish to take a particularly critical position concerning the technology which medicine has developed in this century.

Indeed, the Foucauldian perspective has interpreted the developments in modern medicine around such technologies as the gaze: the surveillance of bodies and populations both to identify disease and to construct normality (Foucault 1976; Armstrong 1983; Arney and Bergen 1983). In the wider sense of the term 'technology', as any technique which is rationalized as the means to a particular end, medicine has in the modern period become very heavily 'technologized', losing some of its previous character as art or craft. Daly (1989: 100) has set out this position particularly clearly, indicating the deterministic status of technical data.

Reductionist cause–effect thinking in medicine stems from the perception that medicine is a science striving for progressive control over disease by technically-based probing of the body. Where problems occur, for example, when it is found that diagnosis depends on who is doing the diagnosis, then these problems are attributed to the intrusion of social factors and attempts are made to remove them by increasing the technicality of the procedures.

In this section I want to tease out some of the implications of medical technology for the kinds of perspective on discourse and resistance outlined in this book. In so doing, I shall argue for a moderate position, which might best be called an *agnosticism* concerning the benefits of technology. While acknowledging the critiques which have identified the 'social' consequences of technology – for example, depersonalization, medicalization and the involvement of commercial interests (Zola 1972; Navarro 1976) – I shall contrast this agnosticism with the radical position of the 'strong programme' in the sociology of science and technology, which has argued that it is possible to understand scientific explanation as a consequence of socially constructed ideologies.

My agnosticism concerning medical technology leads away from such sociological determinism. Returning to a theme first developed in the introduction, I will argue that it is not possible simply to reduce the physical world to social epiphenomena. While, no doubt, the social is implicit in much science, and values are explicit in most technology, as a social theorist *I am simply not in a position to make judgements about natural science and the benefits of technology.* What I can do is look at how it is used discursively, to expose the ways technology is used for non-technical ends – for example, in bolstering 'expertise' among health professionals and disempowering those who are the subjects of medical technology.

To explore this position, I shall make much use of an article by Daly (1989), in which she reports the development in Australia of echocardiography as a diagnostic tool in the surveillance of people with possible cardiac murmurs or other abnormalities. Daly is critical of the technique, which, in the process of distinguishing between symptoms which may indicate heart disease and need treatment, and those which do not, and may – for instance – suggest a psychological cause of breathlessness or palpitations, creates a high level of anxiety among those who take the test, most of whom will turn out to be 'normal'.

> The medical discourse concerning tests emphasises technologically determined benefit for patients submitting to testing. Patients generally subscribe to the notion that the search for disease is beneficial. Technological rationality thus creates a social space in which doctors have discretion to diagnose in the interests of patients . . . medical technology plays an ideological role in the social relations of medicine. It allows doctors to mediate between patients and third parties and, within the medical system itself, it allows doctors to resolve differences over diagnosis and assert control over areas of patient care (1989: 113–14).

Technology has thus supplied an alternative discourse to the earlier one of clinical expertise which was used as their *logos*: their claim to speak the truth. It obscures, even further than did claims based in clinical expertise, the socially constructed character of the judgements which are subsequently made as a consequence of the test results. Patients in Daly's study were sometimes labelled as in need of psychological rather than cardiological therapy, when test results were negative. Nor are the negative effects confined to patients, argues Daly (1987: 114); eventually doctors become servants of the technology:

> They all know of patients, apparently very relieved by a normal test, who have nevertheless returned to the medical system with the same or related symptoms. When this happens, they have little option but to perform still another test on a more powerful machine hoping that the 'bigger gun' will be more effective.

Traditional re-evaluations of clinical expertise have been supplanted by a dependency on the technology with its apparent rationalization of the difficult business of diagnosis.

While accepting Daly's critique of the ideological character of this technology as it is currently used, I would raise the following in terms of a practical engagement with such innovation.

Firstly, I am unclear in what way the kinds of decision previously made by doctors over the treatment and disposal of patients are to be preferred.

Sure, the social processes can be deconstructed as based in claims to expertise and so on. But then, as Daly's article demonstrates, so can the technical discourse. The substitution, in part at least, with a technical discourse, may indeed weaken and challenge the claims based in clinical discourse to speak the truth about disease. In addition, admittedly echocardiography is a very *high-technology* procedure, but is it qualitatively different from other technology: for instance, the kinds of machinery used to test blood and other fluids for electrolytes, sugar, urea, and so on, upon which diagnoses are routinely made in a hospital and more frequently in a primary care setting? The output of an electrocardiograph is incomprehensible to many health professionals, let alone patients: yet important diagnostic judgements are made on the basis of such outputs by those capable of interpreting the traces during surgery or in intensive care. This 'academic encirclement' of medicine by science (Strong 1984) has been a continuing process: and the postmodern perspective on organization might usefully explore this, investigating the collusion and the rivalry between clinical and scientific/technological discourses.

Secondly, how are *we* to evaluate the benefits and disadvantages of the new technology? Doctors, as Daly says, have lost their Archimedean position, as a consequence of the claims made by a rival discourse of technical rationality. But are social theorists in a position to make the judgement? As I pointed out in Chapter 6, evaluation is based on a substantive rationality: determined by ideological commitments to certain ends. In the postmodern perspective, the social theorist can do no more than identify her/his own political commitments, and attempt to act within the kind of responsibility to otherness discussed in Chapter 6, in which resistance is encouraged and discourses which create identity and repetition are challenged.

Now this is precisely what Daly's analysis of echocardiography does by pointing up some of the 'social' disadvantages of the technology. Personally, I do not feel her deconstruction has touched on my first point, concerning the new relation of dependency which the machine has forced upon the professional, and I think that there could be some 'social' benefits which could flow from this. But in no way is it possible from this to evaluate – in any absolute sense – this kind of screening of the 'normal'. Other discourses – economic, epidemiological, ethical, managerial, and so on – would bring their own substantive rationalities to bear in different ways (Fox 1991a). What does seem reasonable, using the post-structuralist analyses which have been outlined in this book, is to show how the *intrinsically social* character of such enterprises can be used within the politics of health-talk. My agnosticism requires me to sustain a scepticism about technology, but does not supply me with any position from which to develop an overall evaluation of the costs and benefits in terms of care. I cannot weigh up anxiety against premature cardiac failure absolutely, any more than anyone else.

I will conclude this section by referring briefly to the discussion in the introduction in which I sought to distinguish between the postmodern position on scientific knowledge and the so-called strong programme (SP) in the sociology of science. It will be recalled that the fundamental tenet of the SP concerns the 'symmetry' between science and other discourses which try to explain the world, such as religion or astrology, in terms of their value-neutrality or freedom from social and political influences. As the introduction to one book on the sociology of science has it:

> the evidence presently available suggests that 'external' influences upon scientific judgment are neither unusual nor necessarily patho-logical, and that the barrier which such influences have to penetrate is not fundamentally different from the boundaries surrounding other sub-cultures (Barnes and Edge 1982: 8–9).

Consequently, when it comes to developing a particular theory, or of making claims as to the right way to do something based on scientific theory, it is to be expected that theory choice will be 'under-determined' by the substrate of the physical world, and socially constructed positions will contribute to a decision as to which theory or technical application is preferred (1982: 236). The SP has documented many examples of these social processes in historical and current science. (For a classic work in the SP, see Bloor 1976; for a discussion in relation to the SHH, see Bartley 1990.) It has found its way into the SHH literature under the title of 'social constructionism' (see, for example, King 1987; Nicolson and McLaughlin 1988), where it has been used to argue that illness labels and biomedical theorizing can be explained more by reference to social proc-esses such as status and closure, than by the natural world. My own argument (Fox 1988) that asepsis was preferred to antisepsis in surgery for reasons concerning the authority of the healer is just such an assessment.

The problem with this position, from a postmodern view, is that, while theory or technology may well be under-determined by the physical world, and be the consequence of social process or political theory, it is almost certainly the case that any SP 'explanation' will suffer from the difficulty that it is liable to be under-determined by the social world in just the same way. To give an example, no doubt I could demonstrate (fabricate) that the preference for infection explanations over susceptibility ones for a range of diseases from TB to AIDS during the twentieth century was due to the emphasis upon the nation-state. But no doubt you could rally 'facts' which would demonstrate that it was to do with the development of powered flight ('air-borne disease'), or a decrease in religious fatalism.

The agnosticism of a PSTH might (as has been seen throughout this book) concern itself with the *how* of the particular part of health-talk which is 'technology-talk', that is, how claims concerning the usefulness of tech-nological innovations come to be accepted or questioned, and the part which expertise, professionalism or control/repetition/possession play in these discourses and resistances. Such an interest is necessary if a PSTH is fully to explore the creation of the cared-for as subject. But it departs from the SP over efforts to explain the *why* of an innovation. It is, if you like, symmetrical as to its beliefs in science and the SP to be able to account satisfactorily for their claims concerning scientific knowledge and technological innovation.

This position of agnosticism concerning the truth claims of natural science (Derrida 1992) illustrates the confusion which has arisen in some SHH writing between the SP and post-structuralism. Whereas the SP privileges the social as the realm in which we can 'really' understand why the world is how it is, for Foucault (1970) at least, the epistemological grounding of the human sciences – when compared with that of the natural sciences – was both more questionable and more ephemeral.

On the other hand, a concern with intertextuality once again supplies a means to engage with technology. Returning to the example of echocardiography above, I suggested that there was indeed something to be said for the substitution of a professional discourse by a technical one. A machine is not, in itself, discursive. Meanings are read on to that machine, and a machine may be the focus for the contestation of discourses. As an example, I want to refer once again to an episode in my ethnography of the surgical ward round (Fox 1993). A very old woman had suffered a cardiac arrest during an operation. This extract documents the first post-operative ward round after this had occurred:

Mrs O was a very small woman virtually obscured by a mass of high technology equipment placed around her bed: monitors, a complicated three-way drip and ECG equipment, all of which had been erected post-operatively by the medical (as opposed to surgical) staff who had become involved following the arrest. Mr D stopped some way back from the end of the bed with his junior colleagues.

Mr D: That's a very impressive array of tackle. (The word tackle is emphasized and the others smile.)

He approaches the patient.

Mr D: You're doing fine.

Mrs O: Nnnnnnnnnnn . . .

Mr D holds her hand and tries to make eye contact beneath the oxygen mask. When there is no response, he turns to the equipment, and after looking it over starts to fiddle with one of the taps attached to the drip. After a few seconds he turns away.

Mr D: (to house-officer) Here's a bit of IT (intensive therapy) for you.

House-officer: I'm enjoying it.

The technology in this setting, it could be suggested, is a direct affront to Mr D's claims to expertise. Not only did the operation leave Mrs O worse off than before, but he has been forced to secede his authority for her care to the physicians, even though the patient remains on 'his' ward and under his care. But Mr D subtly rewrites the technology. He derides it as 'tackle' (as opposed to his sophisticated surgical hands?), he asserts (rather unconvincingly, it must be said) his knowledge of the machinery's workings, he concerns himself with the person beneath the machine, and finally he suggests that it is a useful experience for his house-officer to gain during his time in surgery.

This rewriting offers Mr D opportunities to sustain his subjectivity as surgeon against the physicianly challenge. Similarly, in other circumstances, one might conceive ways to subvert the meanings attached to machines which could serve other objectives. Discussions in the SHH of the 'new reproductive technology' have emphasized the potential further medicalization of women's bodies by these techniques. The existence of the technology might, on the other hand, be co-opted into feminist discourses on control over reproduction or independence from normalizing discourses on motherhood, maybe even capitalizing on the claimed 'neutrality' of scientific discourse.

The politics of technology-talk reiterates all the discussions of de-territorialization which have been outlined in this book: it is in the play of texts (and technology is just a text) that resistance becomes possible. The inscriptions of a technical innovation upon the BwO are rooted, not in some feature of the technology in itself, but in the expertise which it mediates, and the repetitions which it is capable of fabricating. Decoupling technology and expertise is feasible, with outcomes which the innovators cannot possibly predict.

Fictions of health and medicine

The scientific aspirations of sociology have assisted a separation between a 'legitimate' subject-matter of the 'real world' and an inappropriate one deriving from fiction and self-conscious story-telling. The development of cultural studies, and the kind of critical-cultural analyses which were heralded by Jameson (1984) have begun to dissolve this opposition, so that – for example – the 'Postmodernism' issue of the journal *Theory, Culture and Society*, subsequently published as a monograph (Featherstone 1988), and the edited collection *The Body* (Featherstone *et al.* 1991) took both 'real world' and 'cultural production' realms as appropriate objects of study.

Under the influence of post-structuralism it has become hard to delimit philosophy, literary criticism, cultural and media studies and some elements of social theory. This has been particularly noticeable in writing concerning gender studies (for example, Kroker and Kroker 1988). As these disciplinary boundaries fragment, new possibilities for study have become possible. Literary theorists and postmodern social theorists read each other's books and can discuss common approaches to study (Clifford 1986: 3), and indeed some of the perspectives in this book are a consequence of such interactions. Social anthropology has recently recognized the fictional character of the stories it tells about people in other cultures. Because of the problem of translation, and the much more apparent 'Otherness', the discovery that what field reports do is tell plausible stories about cultures, has come from this discipline rather than from sociology (Clifford 1986; Tyler 1986), although I mentioned in an earlier chapter the brilliant deconstruction of sociological ethnography by Paul Atkinson (1990), which demonstrates the ways in which such stories come to be seen as true. Some recent discussions of representations of reality in sociological discourse have begun to address this question more fully; see Aldridge (1993) for an incisive critique of how sociological research reports are fabricated. Throughout this book I have emphasized such ideas as reading, inscription, fabrication and fiction, trying to make the point that the representations of the world deriving from social theory are as fictional as novels or poems. Tyler (1986: 129) suggests that postmodern ethnography evokes a participatory and emergent 'reality', opening up possibilities to think about cultural forms.

In Chapter 5 I suggested that tale-telling could be used to resist discourse, to de-territorialize the BwO. Here I want to look at the ready-made fictions of health and medicine (here I mean the ones that do not pretend to be true), to think about how these stories constitute meanings, and whether they can also assist in de-territorialization: in short, to look at another element of the politics (and ethics) of health-talk.

I am indebted to two reviews of the interaction between the popular media and issues of health and medicine, and I will draw on these – a predominantly British review by Karpf (1988) and a US study by Signorielli (1990) – before briefly looking at the fictional writing of the author and doctor Colin Douglas. Both of these reviews suggest that health and medicine are significant themes in popular media drama (in addition to a wealth of factual and semi-factual output from television and film media). Medical dramas from *Emergency Ward 10* to *Marcus Welby MD* and the UK soap *Angels* have had huge audiences, while the darker *St Elsewhere* had a small but high-profile audience (Karpf 1988: 181). The US Cultural Indicators project found that over 17 years, 40% of drama shows depicted episodes of physical illness. Health professionals in TV drama are five times as frequent as their real-life counterparts, while only criminals and law enforcers outnumber TV health professionals as characters in drama (Signorielli 1990: 98–9).

The images of health on US television have similarly deviated from 'real life'. Industrial accidents and road traffic accidents are rare causes of death on TV, although they are the predominant causes of violent death in America. On the other hand, in prime-time programmes, only 11% of men and 2% of women smoke (below national averages). Alcohol is the most frequently consumed beverage on television, and the references to alcohol are increasing, with 70% of recent drama programmes representing or mentioning alcohol (Signorelli 1990: 103–6). In 1977, 42% of characters in daytime soaps had health problems, although few suffered from cancer. Behind homicide, heart disease accounted for two-fifths of soap illness, predominantly among men, while women regularly attempt suicide, get pregnant eight times more frequently than in 'real life', and have an alarming rate of miscarriage (Karpf 1988: 180–5).

The point I want to make here is not really concerned with this 'mismatch', which both Signorielli and Karpf discuss. What I want to suggest is that the concepts of health and of medicine have been constituted in these popular culture representations as 'floating signifiers', by which I mean, ideas which – rather than having any intrinsic or stable meaning – are available as mediators of all sorts of different meanings or associations. As such, 'health' and 'medicine' may come to have much less fixed significances as a consequence of popular culture representations. In this way, real life may come to resemble fiction, rather than vice versa. In fact, it no longer makes any sense to privilege 'reality' as the bedrock upon which such imagery has been grounded. This is, of course, a typically deconstructive manoeuvre, which I will suggest is more than just a game of words, but has implications for health care and for the PSTH.

I want to look in particular at the representations of medicine and health professionals, and the way in which these images are floating signifiers, capable of endless and unstable fabrication. The material which Karpf has drawn together is once again invaluable, and read as I shall read it, supplies the basis for a genealogy of media medicine, in which discontinuities mark the production of new discourses, rather than any kind of progression or rational development. Karpf documents the first six of the following associations in popular culture (films, TV dramas and soaps), while the seventh is my own contribution.

1 Doctor as paragon. The doctor, usually male and white, as hero figure, motivated by altruism, scientific zeal or modernist rationalism, mediated the progressive, humanistic values of rationalist scientific medicine – which in time would cure or prevent all disease. High-technology equipment and dangerous or heroic interventions (usually surgical) contribute further signifiers for this discourse.

2 Doctor as human figure. The doctor, usually male and white, is the focus for personal interactions with patients, in place of bureaucracy or impersonal caring. Often the doctor has endless time to spend with his patient of the week, and may be paying a friendly visit when the first signs of illness are manifested by symptom or dramatic seizure. House calls are much more frequent than in 'reality'.

3 Doctors/medicine as emotional broker. Doctors in popular culture deal with psychological, emotional and family problems in their patients, as

well as the somatic illness. They are great communicators, and while the medical problem may resist treatment, the emotional problem is always resolved. Illness entails a psychosocial transition, requiring patients to abandon old ways of thinking and adopting new ones, learn to communicate with others and with themselves: 'illness is more than just bodily hurt' (Karpf 1988: 190). Holistic care and a biopsychosocial model became the norm in TV soaps long before it became a 'real-life' discourse of medicine. Two recent (1993) episodes of the US show *Northern Exposure* featured a doctor failing to solve a medical problem, but serving as emotional broker. In the first, he was chained up and forced to listen to the arguments of a husband and wife for three days. In the second, he fails to discover the biochemical reason why a male friend is sexually attractive (against his wishes) to almost all women. The doctor's emotional investment pays off when his friend loses his attractiveness after he meets a woman who does not fancy him. In another US comedy soap, *Nurses*, the senior doctor is female and is portrayed as having an emotional as well as a clinical existence: often the two become intermingled as a medical problem illuminates the working through of feelings.

4 Health care as alienation. In a new breed of popular drama in the 1980s, the spotless operating theatre is replaced by the corridor as the recurring motif. Doctors become humans again, but with a negative edge: they have problems and illnesses themselves, they suffer mental disorders and may commit crimes or be guilty of malpractice. The high-technology hospital becomes the stuff of nightmares (for instance, in the films *Coma* and *Dead Ringers*).

5 Health care as bureaucratic or inefficient. The personalized care of the earlier soaps is substituted by a machinery in which patients are victims, on a conveyor belt governed by economic or bureaucratic interests. Incompetent doctors, or even impostors (in the film *Paper Mask*) kill their patients, while domineering and vindictive nurses terrorize the patients.

6 Health and medicine as comedy. The dependency of the patient is played out in comic situations, sometimes entailing role reversals with medical staff or between usually active men and passive women, or playing on the loss of privacy of the medical setting for humour involving embarrassment or unusual sexual licence. Staff's personal lives take precedence over the needs of the sick or dying, or they end up the victims of the health-care system, forced to taste their own medicine.

7 Health and the human condition. Replacing comedy by irony as the motif, doctors, nurses and patients are dissolved as separate agents into representatives of humanity, victims of the frailty and finitude of human existence. Illness and death are markers of the pointlessness of human aspiration, and the HCS processes these fading aspirations into oblivion. Even the grandeur of tragedy is unattainable: no value survives this ironic movement.

There are, no doubt, many variations on these themes, and in listing these I am not attempting any kind of categorization, but merely suggesting that health and medicine are not stable signifiers in popular culture, but may be used to generate all sorts of dramatic possibilities. Nor is any kind of progression implied. As I write, I can imagine any or all of these themes in contemporary drama.

Brody (1987) has argued that literary representations of health and medicine, such as Alexander Solzhenitsyn's *Cancer Ward* and Thomas Mann's *The Magic Mountain*, are appropriate data to be explored alongside the more traditional data deriving from social practices which have commonly been the subject-matter of social science. For Brody (1987: 65), these readings are useful in 'telling us about sickness'; in other words, we can read off from such fiction the cultural meanings attributed to health and illness. He states his intention in so doing (which is not dissimilar from the kinds of argument I entered into during my introductory chapter) as follows:

> When we give meaning to the experience of sick persons, let us take their suffering and their needs into account. Let us avoid giving meaning to illness that merely makes us feel better, and at the cost of increasing the suffering of the ill person (1987: 64–5).

The interest in a postmodern perspective is less to do with using these images from literature or popular fiction to somehow 'help make sense of reality', than it is strategic: to do with the dissolution of two realms – the cultural production and the real – which are opposed in modernism. Such a manoeuvre brings popular culture into the practical politics and ethics of health-talk: it is recognized as constitutive of 'health', 'illness' and 'medicine', not merely a reflection, parody or cultural manifestation. Popular representations are accorded the same weight as 'real' stories of health, whether they derive from professionals or patients' 'lived experience'.

The radical impact of this elision of the cultural and the real can be seen in an absurd form in the case of 'Jennifer's ear', during the 1992 British general election. The Labour party used an election broadcast to document the case of a child who had waited over a year for an ear operation because her parents could not afford private care. Professionally directed and packaged, using many emotive images, the broadcast led to immediate political arguments which focused on the ontological question of whether this was a real case or merely a dramatic representation of a wider problem. The Labour party found itself first challenged to prove the veracity of the case, and, when it had produced 'Jennifer', accused of the exploitation of a child for political ends. The efforts to discredit the broadcast might be taken as an indication of the impact which it was feared such a dramatic, popular culture presentation of health might have upon the electorate's anxieties over the continuity of the National Health Service.

Popular culture fabrications of health and medicine supply a further route for reading these concepts, to allow them to signify in different ways, to say 'it can be like this instead'. Faced with the discourses of the medical and its allies in the human sciences, popular culture offers a route to de-territorialize these inscriptions. Mass culture, with its consumerism and the substitution of the mimicry of parody by *pastiche* – an imitation which no longer recognizes that there is an original (Jameson 1988: 15; Kaite 1988; Butler 1990: 142ff.) – has the potential to dissolve such discourses, to allow the free play of desire upon the BwO, to refuse repetition, to celebrate difference. To conclude this section, I want to discuss briefly a reading of medicine which uses the strategy of pastiche, to look at the potential de-territorialization of the medical.

The British doctor and author, Colin Douglas, has written a series of fictional tales about young doctor David Campbell, the earliest of which, *The Houseman's Tale*, became a TV drama. In these tales, the predominant theme is death, and patients and doctors are equally victims, although the causes of death among the doctors are often bizarre or dramatic. Campbell himself, at the end of *The Houseman's Tale* survives hepatitis. When asked what he is going to do next, he replies 'I'm going to get better'. Medicine is depicted as a profession in which almost everyone except the hero is motivated by greed, lasciviousness, career prospects or incredibly distorted or insane perspectives deriving from scientific or clinical discourses. Research is incompetently and unethically conducted, is servant to commercial interests or the ambitions of academic medics, and is usually of no clinical value. Clinical work is occasionally beneficial, but is routine, often of little effect and regularly has damaging or fatal consequences as a result of error or chance.

Douglas's ironies can be read as a parody of an original. But instead of seeing them as some kind of critique of the health system, it is possible to use these texts to reread health and medicine. The humour and the irony come not in discovering the 'truth' about the original, but that there was no original, that the original was a copy, and a failed one at that, constructed in repetition and discourse, just as Campbell's (fictional) world is a fabrication. Campbell may doubt the values of his world, but he is at home in them, as he would be in any other. In Douglas's books, long passages are taken up with narrative sections of clinical interactions and medical detail, baldly reported and sometimes with no relevance to the 'plot'. Little happens 'plot-wise' anyway, and is often fairly trivial, revolving around minor details of work and personal life.

Read in this way, these particular fictions deprivilege 'real' health care. Health and medicine are revealed as floating signifiers, capable of transformation in the play of intertextuality. Other texts might offer different de-territorializations: which to choose comes down to politics. A PSTH may engage with this process, reading these fictions of 'health', not to demonstrate how things 'really are', but as a poetics of care, a new text, itself a pastiche of a copy which claimed to be an original.

The Body-without-Organs of medical sociology

At the end of a book it could be tempting to make some predictions or suggestions as to the way that a subject will develop theoretically or in terms of policy. Fortunately, the postmodern position enables me to hedge my bets, and predict only that we are unable to predict how social theory will articulate with health and healing in the future. Chance and discontinuity, the undecidability of meaning and the continuous slippage into new discourses or challenges to existing ones, mean that any developments are unlikely to follow a rational programme in the future any more than they have in the past. Having said that, of course, these words and the different readings of them will contribute to the intertextuality of social theory, and it is unimaginable that I would have devoted so much effort to a project which I did not intend to impact upon the sociology of health and healing.

I am interested in the influence of reflexivity in the fabrication of postmodern positions. It is this aspect of postmodernism, a self-referentiality which continually challenges the texts which are being produced as no more than attractive fictions, which I believe will limit any move into what could be seen as a postmodern metanarrative (Valverde 1991: 184). The organization of intellectual life may well generate elements of such a structure, while the imperatives of the publishing world may sustain a trend in postmodern social theory for reasons grounded in the market. Academic life as a postmodern social theorist within an organizationally modernist institution is a theme which deserves a novelistic format. See Bauman (1988) for a discussion of the opposite: a modernist social science in a postmodern era.

In terms of theory, for those who choose to develop some of the postmodern readings of health, I believe it is more probable that this will continue to fragment the subject area rather than constitute a new paradigm, to replace the old modernist one in a Kuhnian-style revolution or paradigm shift. It is also probable that the extent of the postmodern challenge to rationalism and modernist approaches to the social will supply a momentum for rereadings of theorists who do not share the postmodern position. This has happened in French philosophy, with a resurgence of interest in phenomenological approaches following the initial hiatus caused by deconstructionism. If there is one 'message' from this book, it is concerned with just such intertextualism as the opportunity for generating new positions and resisting existing discourse.

I have attempted to show in the last part of this book how it is feasible, if problematic, to engage with the world within the postmodern perspective. But as advocates, postmodern social theorists are compromised by the status which they accord to their own pronouncements. Robbed of claims to have access to a disinterested knowledge, and continually privileging difference and discontinuity, their credibility – at least within a scientific environment still wedded to the search for truth – is seriously weakened (Barnes and Edge 1982: 10). Particularly for those in the SHH who work very closely with natural scientists or health professions, the rise of postmodern perspectives may further marginalize this sub-discipline in one of two directions, either away from social theory, or away from medicine, depending on which way they choose to jump.

One of the things which I hope has become clear in this book is that, from a PSTH perspective, modernist sociology – with its unique capacity to fabricate a privileged realm of the 'social' – has been embraced by medicine in the past decades, in particular as the source of the theoretical basis for the new biopsychosocial model of health (Armstrong 1987: 1218). The investments which derive from this association make the medicine–sociology axis a productive and healthy relationship for both parties. While postmodern readings of 'health' make this association much more obvious, it seems unlikely that the mutual benefits for both parties will rapidly be abandoned in the face of this theoretical move.

While this challenge to modernist sociology has been a theme throughout, there may be a need for a more thoroughgoing analysis of the collusion between medicine and the SHH than has been possible in this book. In retrospect I am glad that I have devoted myself not to this but to the positive task of developing a PSTH. The many readings in the SHH upon which I have drawn, many of which derive from modern perspectives, illustrate the wealth of material which is available for the play of intertextuality which the postmodern position encourages, indeed requires. Postmodernism projects the disappearance of the author(ity), and the pleasure of the never-ending text.

One scenario which I have avoided discussing concerns the question of whether we are now in a 'postmodern era'. For this reason, readers will not have found reference to Lyotard, Baudrillard or their critics here, and they must seek discussion of this position elsewhere (see, for example, some of the contributions in the collection published by *Theory, Culture and Society* (Featherstone 1988)). At some point in the future, it will no doubt become possible to write a history in which the rise of post-structuralism and postmodern philosophical positions will be seen as an epiphenomenon of the last fling of high modernity, consumerism, the collapse of communism or whatever. Personally, I shall be less interested to read such a determinist perspective of intellectual ideas, than to see the publication of another history – one in which modern ideas of health and illness have come to seem quite strange.

Postscript: a postmodern prayer

Where there was identity
    may there be difference
Where there was truth
    may we celebrate ambiguity
Where there was control
    may we be generous
Where there was repetition
    may there be multiplicity
Where there was inscription
    may there be desire
                NJF 1993

GLOSSARY

This glossary is intended to provide readers with an indication of how some terms in post-structuralism and postmodern theory are used in this book. Concepts which have a wider circulation in sociology are not included, and readers should consult a dictionary of social science terminology. Where terms are discussed at length in the text, a page reference is given in place of a glossary definition.

arche-health A term coined by the author to describe a resistance to control or definition, a 'becoming-different' which is potentially emancipatory. See pp. 137–40.

becoming A process of transformation, counterposed to a fixity of being or identity, often used to indicate a becoming 'other' or different, with no specific end-point as a goal.

Body-without-Organs The term invented by Deleuze and Guattari (1984, 1988) to describe a non-anatomical, political body inscribed by power and desire. See pp. 35–8.

deconstruction A strategy to explore the authority by which a statement or claim to truth or knowledge has been made. See pp. 38–41.

desire Used either (in psychoanalysis) to describe the yearning to resolve a lack of some object (the object of desire), or (by Deleuze and Guattari 1984) to signify a positive investment in another person or thing. See pp. 72–9.

différance A word coined by Derrida to imply both the characteristic of language to give meaning to words in terms of their difference from other words, and the deferral of meaning as **signifiers** refer endlessly to others. See pp. 7–8.

discourse, discursive practice Written, spoken or enacted practices organized so as to supply a coherent claim to a position or perspective. Used in post-structuralism to indicate the association between 'knowledge' and power. See also **text**.

essentialism, essence A philosophical perspective on human identity which locates the self as internal and existing independently and prior to social structure and/or language. The capacity to act as an individual is a consequence of this essential self.

eternal return See pp. 130–3.

finitude The sense of limitation in human affairs consequent upon embodiment and mortality, and the inability to experience as another.

gaze Used to describe the exercise of power through surveillance. Knowledge gained by observation is used to control the person who is the object of surveillance, and to create that person as a **subject** constituted through that knowledge. See also **power/knowledge**. See pp. 28–9.

genealogy An analytical strategy which documents the ways in which a practice has been described discursively. Unlike a standard history, no effort is made to discover a rational progression of understanding of the practice, or to 'explain' why different perspectives were dominant at different points in time. Instead, discontinuities between discourses are highlighted.

Gift The feminine relation of generosity and trust, opposed to the **Proper**. See pp. 91–2.

governmentality See pp. 32–5.

Imaginary Term used in psychoanalysis to describe the relationship between the infant and the environment prior to the development of language, and the entry into the realm of the **Symbolic**. Feminist post-structuralists have suggested that the realm of the Imaginary is feminine and resistance entails a return to the Imaginary – a realm in which the Mother rather than the Father is the significant figure.

intertextuality See pp. 68–9; 103–5.

logocentrism The claim to authority, to be able to 'speak the truth' about something. Religion and science are logocentrisms which make particular claims to possess this authoritative knowledge. See pp. 8–11.

logos Truth, or knowledge of the world or some element of it.

metanarrative An overarching discourse or position which organizes other positions. Class and gender have been used in structuralist social theory to explain the organization of societies in terms of economics or patriarchy. Postmodernism is suspicious of any efforts to connect events or attributes within such frameworks of 'explanation', seeing metanarratives as fabrications rather than representations of social reality.

modernity, modernism An era generally taken to have begun with the Enlightenment (*c.*1800), characterized by a philosophical commitment to the rational and/or scientific elucidation of the world, and the progressive accumulation of knowledge. Modern disciplines in the human sciences use methodological strategies to represent 'reality' more and more accurately.

nomad subject A subjectivity freed (briefly) from discourse, able to 'become' different, free to explore the discourses of the **Body-without-Organs**, to discover new possibilities for being or for action. See p. 104.

the Other Literally, that which is not the self: a person, thing or idea.

phallocentrism, phallogocentrism See p. 11.

phonocentrism See p. 11.

postmodernism Used in this book to describe a philosophical position which rejects modernist efforts to discover knowledge about the world, and replaces this with a focus upon the strategies by which such modernist knowledge-claims are made. See pp. 6–9.

post-structuralism A position originally deriving from literary theory, which rejects structuralist efforts to discover systems of meaning or **metanarratives** constructed in cultural, social or political structures. The reader of a text is accorded privilege as the creator of meaning in place of the writer, whose intentions – it is concluded – can never be known decisively. In social theory, post-structuralism concerns itself with the indeterminacy in social interactions and the efforts which are made by human agents to control or define reality.

power/knowledge The linking by Foucault of power to knowledge abandons the view that power is unitary and coercive. For example, medical power is seen to be a consequence of expertise, a body of knowledge which is able to legitimate the rights of those who hold it to subject others to particular practices. Power is exercised in the micro-processes of interaction, in every encounter which is organized by a discourse on knowledge. It may be contested by rival discourses, based in alternative bodies of knowledge.

presence An unmediated knowledge of an aspect of the world, presence is the basis of a logocentric claim to 'know the truth'. Science claims presence – knowledge of its subject matter – through discourses on method. Presence of God is the basis of religious experience. **Essentialism** is sometimes used to make claims to presence concerning knowledge of the self, feelings or existence.

Proper The masculine relation of control and possession. See p. 91.

reflexivity Analysis which interrogates the process by which interpretation has been fabricated: reflexivity requires any effort to describe or represent to consider how that process of description was achieved, what claims to '**presence**' were made, what authority was used to claim knowledge.

signifier In semiotics, the written, spoken or otherwise inscribed symbol which stands for a concept or signified. In post-structuralism, signifiers are seen as incapable of ever defining a particular signified unquestionably. Because they are defined in relation to other signifiers (white is that which is not-coloured, etc.), they always defer meaning. See *différance*, **intertextuality**.

subject, subjectivity In postmodern theory, subjectivity is the outcome of power, and the subject is no more than an effect of power, constituted in discourses of **power/knowledge**. In this book it is argued that, in spite of this, the undecidability of meaning involved in any discursive practice enables subjectivities to be multivocal rather than fixed, and capable of '**becoming**' through resistance to **power/knowledge**.

Symbolic In psychoanalytic theory, the realm of representation which a child enters into with her/his acquisition of language. It is regarded as a realm dominated by the Father. Desire in the symbolic realm is always about possession and control, about filling a lack which was created when language intervened between self and the other. See also **Imaginary**.

text A set of **signifiers** – written, spoken or enacted – which can be read. Derrida's much misunderstood statement that 'there is nothing outside the **text**' is intended to indicate that everything constitutes a textual practice to the extent that it can be read for meaning (Derrida 1992).

will-to-power In this book, this term, which derives from Nietzsche, is used synonymously with the notion of desire as a positive investment in the **Other**, and with the notion of '**becoming**'.

BIBLIOGRAPHY

Aldridge, J. (1993) 'The textual disembodiment of knowledge in research account writing', *Sociology*, **27**, 53–66.

Anderson, M. (1980) *Sociology of the Family*. Harmondsworth: Penguin.

Anspach, R.R. (1988) 'Notes on the sociology of medical discourse: the language of case presentation', *Journal of Health and Social Behaviour*, **29**, 357–75.

Arluke, A., Kennedy, L. and Kessler, R.C. (1979) 'Re-examining the sick role concept', *Journal of Health and Social Behaviour*, **20**, 30–6.

Armstrong, D. (1979) 'Child development and medical ontology', *Social Science and Medicine*, **13A**, 9–10.

Armstrong, D. (1981) 'Pathological life and death: medical spatialisation and geriatrics', *Social Science and Medicine*, **15**, 253.

Armstrong, D. (1983) *The Political Anatomy of the Body*. Cambridge: Cambridge University Press.

Armstrong, D. (1987) 'Theoretical tensions in biopsychosocial medicine', *Social Science and Medicine*, **25**, 1213–18.

Armstrong, D. (1990) 'Use of the genealogical method in the exploration of chronic illness: a research note', *Social Science and Medicine*, **30**, 1225–7.

Arney, W.R. and Bergen, B.J. (1983) 'The anomaly, the chronic patient and the play of medical power', *Sociology of Health and Illness*, **5**, 1–24.

Arney, W.R. and Neill, J. (1982) 'The location of pain in childbirth, natural childbirth and the transformation of obstetrics', *Sociology of Health and Illness*, **4**, 1–24.

Asher, K. (1984) 'Deconstruction's use and abuse of Nietzsche', *Telos*, **17**, 169–78.

Ashmore, M., Mulkay, M. and Pinch, T. (1989) *Health and Efficiency*. Milton Keynes: Open University Press.

Atkinson, P. (1990) *The Ethnographic Imagination*. London: Routledge.

Atkinson, P. and Heath, C. (eds) (1976) *Medical Work: Realities and Routines*. London: Gower.

Barnes, B. and Edge, D. (eds) (1982) *Science in Context*. Milton Keynes: Open University Press.

Bartley, M. (1990) 'Do we need a strong programme in medical sociology?', *Sociology of Health and Illness*, 12, 371–90.

Baszanger, I. (1992) 'Deciphering chronic illness', *Sociology of Health and Illness*, 14, 181–215.

Baudrillard, J. (1988) *Selected Writings*. Cambridge: Polity.

Bauman, Z. (1988) 'Is there a postmodern sociology?', *Theory, Culture and Society*, 5, 217–37.

Bauman, Z. (1989) *Modernity and the Holocaust*. Cambridge: Polity.

Bauman, Z. (1992) 'Survival as a social construct', *Theory, Culture and Society*, 9, 1–36.

Bellaby, P. (1988) 'Sickness in the life-course: reflections on the implications for social theory of beginning to study some of the effects of closed-head injury'. Paper presented to BSA Medical Sociology Conference, York, September.

Bennet, G. (1987) *The Wound and the Doctor*. London: Secker & Warburg.

Benton, T. (1991) 'Biology and social science: why the return of the repressed should be given a (cautious) welcome', *Sociology*, 25, 1–29.

Bertholet, J.M. (1991) 'Sociological discourse and the body' in M. Featherstone, M. Hepworth and B.S. Turner (eds), *The Body*. London: Sage.

Bloor, D. (1976) *Knowledge and Social Imagery*. London: Routledge & Kegan Paul.

Bloor, M. (1977) 'Professional autonomy and client exclusion: a study in ENT clinics' in M. Wadsworth and D. Robinson *Studies in Everyday Medical Life*. London: Martin Robertson.

Bolton, G. (1993) 'Just a bobble-hat. The story of a "writing as therapy" training worshop', *Changes* 11, 37–42.

Bolton, G. (1994) 'Stories at work: fictional-critical writing as a means of professional development', *British Educational Research Journal* (in press).

Bogue, R. (1989) *Deleuze and Guattari*. London: Routledge.

Bond, J. (1991) 'The politics of care-giving: the professionalization of informal care'. Paper presented to the British Sociological Association Conference, Manchester, April.

Boston Women's Health Book Collective (1978) *Our Bodies Our Selves*. Harmondsworth: Penguin.

Boyne, R. (1991) 'The art of the body in the discourse of postmodernity' in M. Featherstone, M. Hepworth and B.S. Turner (eds), *The Body*. London: Sage.

Boyne, R. (1992) *Foucault and Derrida*. London: Unwin Hyman.

Boyne, R. and Lash, S. (1984) 'Communicative rationality and desire', *Telos*, 61, 152–8.

Bransen, E. (1992) 'Has menstruation been medicalised, or will it never happen?', *Sociology of Health and Illness*, 14, 98–110.

Brody, H. (1987) *Stories of Sickness*. New Haven, CT: Yale University Press.

Brooks, P. (1984) *Reading for the Plot: Design and Intention in Narrative*. New York: Random House.

Brownlea, A. (1987) 'Participation, myth, realities and prognosis', *Social Science and Medicine*, 25, 605–14.

Brubaker, R.S. (1984) *The Limits of Rationality*. London: Allen & Unwin.

Bury, M.R. (1986) 'Social constructionism and the development of medical sociology', *Sociology of Health and Illness*, 8, 137–69.

Bury, M.R. (1987) 'Social constructionism and medical sociology: a rejoinder to Nicolson and McLaughlin', *Sociology of Health and Illness*, 9, 439–41.

Bury, M.R. (1991) 'The sociology of chronic illness', *Sociology of Health and Illness*, **13**, 451–68.

Busfield, C. (1990) 'Sectoral divisions and consumption. The case of medical care', *Sociology*, **24**, 77–97.

Butler, J. (1990) *Gender Trouble*. London: Routledge.

Calnan, M. (1987) *Health and Illness: The Lay Perspective*. London: Tavistock.

Cant, S. and Calnan, M. (1992) 'Using private health insurance. A study of lay decisions to seek professional medical help', *Sociology of Health and Illness*, **14**, 39–56.

Canguilhem, G. (1989) *The Normal and the Pathological*. New York: Zone Books.

Charmaz, K. (1983) 'Loss of self: a fundamental form of suffering in the chronically ill', *Sociology of Health and Illnesss*, **5**, 168–95.

Clegg, S.R. (1990) *Modern Organizations*. London: Sage.

Cixous, H. (1986) 'Sorties' in H. Cixous and C. Clement, *The Newly Born Woman*. Manchester: Manchester University Press.

Cixous, H. (1990) 'The laugh of the medusa' in R. Walder (ed.), *Literature in the Modern World*. Oxford: Oxford University Press.

Clifford, J. (1986) 'Introduction: partial truths' in J. Clifford and G.E. Marcus *Writing Culture*. Berkeley: University of California Press.

Clode, D. (1991) 'Unravelling the conundrum', *Community Care*, 28 November, 12.

Collins, H.M. (1981) 'What is TRASP? The radical programme as methodological imperative', *Philosophy of the Social Sciences*, **11**, 215–24.

Cooper, R. (1989) 'Modernism, postmodernism and organisational analysis 3: the contribution of Jacques Derrida', *Organisation Studies*, **10**, 91–112.

Cooper, R. and Burrell, G. (1988) 'Modernism, postmodernism and organisational analysis: an introduction', *Organisation Studies*, **9**, 91–112.

Cox, D. (1991) 'Health service management – a sociological view: Griffiths and the non-negotiated order of the hospital' in J. Gabe, M. Calnan and M. Bury (eds), *Sociology of the Health Service*. London: Routledge.

Crawford, R. (1986) 'Individual responsibility and health' in P. Conrad and R. Kern (eds), *The Sociology of Health and Illness*. New York: St Martin's.

Currer, C. and Stacey, M. (eds) (1986) *Concepts of Health, Illness and Healing*. Leamington Spa: Berg.

Daly, J. (1989) 'Innocent murmurs: echocardiography and the diagnosis of cardiac normality', *Sociology of Health and Illness*, **11**, 99–116.

Danziger, S.K. (1986) 'The use of expertise in doctor–patient encounters during pregnancy' in P. Conrad and R. Kern (eds), *The Sociology of Health and Illness*. New York: St Martins.

Davis, A. and Horobin, G. (eds) (1977) *Medical Encounters: The Experience of Illness and Treatment*. London: Croom Helm.

Davey-Smith, G., Bartley, M. and Blane, D. (1991) 'The Black report on socio-economic inequalities in health 10 years on', *British Medical Journal*, **301**, 373–7.

Dean, M. (1991) *The Constitution of Poverty: Toward a Genealogy of Liberal Governance*. London: Routledge.

Deleuze, G. (1983) *Nietzsche and Philosophy*, tr. Hugh Tomlinson, Minneapolis: University of Minnesota Press.

Deleuze, G. and Guattari, F. (1984) *Anti-Oedipus: Capitalism and Schizophrenia*. London: Athlone.

Deleuze, G. and Guattari, F. (1988) *A Thousand Plateaux*. London: Athlone.

Derrida, J. (1976) *Of Grammatology*. Baltimore, MD: Johns Hopkins University Press.

Derrida, J. (1978) *Writing and Difference*. London: Routledge.

Derrida, J. (1992) Seminar, University of Cambridge, December.

Dews, P. (1987) *Logics of Disintegration*. London: Verso.

Department of Health (1991) *Care Management and Assessment: Managers' Guide*. London: Department of Health.

de Swaan, A. (1990) *The Management of Normality*. London: Routledge.

Dingwall, R. (1976) *Aspects of Illness*. Oxford: Martin Robertson.

Douglas, M. (1970) *Natural Symbols*. Harmondsworth: Penguin.

Douglas, M. (1984) *Purity and Danger*. London, Routledge & Kegan Paul.

Douglas, M. and Isherwood, B. (1979) *The World of Goods*. London: Allen Lane.

Doyal, L. (1981) 'A matter of life and death: medicine, health and statistics' in J. Irvine, I. Miles and J. Evans (eds), *Demystifying Social Statistics*. London: Pluto.

Dworkin, A. (1981) *Pornography: Men Possessing Women*. London: Women's Press.

Eagleton, T. (1983) *Literary Theory*. Oxford: Blackwell.

Eco, U. (1988) *Foucault's Pendulum*. London: Picador.

Ehrenreich, B. and English, D. (1979) *For Her Own Good: 150 Years of the Experts' Advice to Women*. London: Pluto.

Elston, M.-A. (1991) 'The politics of professional power: medicine in a changing health service' in J. Gabe, M. Calnan and M. Bury (eds), *Sociology of the Health Service*. London: Routledge.

Emerson, J. (1970) 'Behaviour in private places: sustaining definitions of reality in gynecological examinations' in H.P. Dreitzel (ed.), *Recent Sociology 2*. New York: Macmillan.

Engel, G.L. (1977) 'The need for a new medical model: a challenge for biomedicine', *Science*, **196**, 129–36.

Eysenck, H. and Kamin, L. (1981) *Intelligence: The Battle for the Mind*. London: Pan.

Featherstone, M. (ed.) (1988) *Postmodernism*. London: Sage.

Featherstone, M., Hepworth, M. and Turner, B.S. (eds) (1991) *The Body*. London: Sage.

Finlay, M. (1989) 'Postmodernizing psychoanalysis', *Free Associations*, **16**, 43–80.

Fisher, S. (1991) 'A discourse of the social: medical talk/power talk/oppositional talk?', *Discourse and Society*, **2**, 157–82.

Fitzpatrick, R. (1991) 'Society and changing patterns of disease' in G. Scambler (ed.), *Sociology as Applied to Medicine*. London: Baillière Tindall.

Flax, J. (1990) *Thinking Fragments*. Berkeley: University of California Press.

Forrester, J. (1990) *The Seductions of Psychoanalysis*. Cambridge: Cambridge University Press.

Foucault, M. (1967) *Madness and Civilisation*. London: Tavistock.

Foucault, M. (1970) *The Order of Things*. London: Tavistock.

Foucault, M. (1976) *Birth of the Clinic*. London: Tavistock.

Foucault, M. (1979) *Discipline and Punish*. Harmondsworth: Penguin.

Foucault, M. (1980) 'The eye of power' in C. Gordon (ed.), *Power/Knowledge*. Brighton: Harvester.

Foucault, M. (1984) *The History of Sexuality Part 1*. Harmondworth: Penguin.

Foucault, M. (1986) *The Care of the Self*. New York: Random House.

Foucault, M. (1988) 'Technologies of the self' in L.H. Martin, H. Gutman and P.H. Hutton (eds), *Technologies of the Self*. London: Tavistock.

Fox, N.J. (1988) 'Scientific theory choice and social structure: the case of Lister's antisepsis, humoral theory and asepsis', *History of Science*, 26, 367–97.

Fox, N.J. (1991a) 'Postmodernism, rationality and the evaluation of health care', *Sociological Review*, 39, 709–44.

Fox, N.J. (1991b) 'Green Sociology', *Network*, 50, 23–4.

Fox, N.J. (1992) *The Social Meaning of Surgery*. Buckingham: Open University Press.

Fox, N.J. (1993) 'Discourse, organisation and the surgical ward round', *Sociology of Health and Illness*, 15, 16–42.

Fox, N.J. (forthcoming) 'Self-directed approaches in multidisciplinary health studies', *Journal of Interprofessional Care*.

Frankenberg, R. (1980) 'Medical anthropology and development', *Social Science and Medicine*, 14, 197–207.

Fraser, N. (1989) 'Talking about needs: interpretive contests as political conflicts in welfare-state societies', *Ethics*, 99, 291–313.

Fraser, N. (1992) 'The uses and abuses of French discourse theories for feminist politics', *Theory, Culture and Society*, 9, 51–71.

Freidson, E. (1983) 'Theory of the professions: the state of the art' in R. Dingwall and P. Lewis, *The Sociology of the Professions*. London: Macmillan.

French, S. (1988) 'Experiences of disabled health and caring professionals', *Sociology of Health and Illness*, 10, 170–88.

Gabe, J., Calnan, M. and Bury, M. (1991) *Sociology of the Health Service*. London: Routledge.

Gallop, J. (1982) *Feminism and Psychoanalysis: The Daughter's Seduction*. London: Macmillan.

Game, A. (1991) *Undoing the Social*. Milton Keynes: Open University Press.

Gerhardt, U. (1979) 'The Parsonian paradigm and the identity of medical sociology', *Sociological Review*, 27, 229–51.

Gerhardt, U. (1987) 'Parsons, role theory and health interaction' in G. Scambler (ed.), *Sociological Theory and Medical Sociology*. London: Tavistock.

Gerson, E.M. (1976) 'The social character of illness: deviance or politics', *Social Science and Medicine*, 10, 219–24.

Giddens, A. (1971) *Capitalism and Modern Social Theory*. Cambridge: Cambridge University Press.

Giddens, A. (1984) *The Constitution of Society*. Cambridge: Cambridge University Press.

Giddens, A. (1987) *Social Theory and Modern Sociology*. Cambridge: Polity.

Giddens, A. (1991) *Modernity and Self-identity*. Cambridge: Polity.

Glassner, B. (1989) 'Fitness and the postmodern self', *Journal of Health and Social Behaviour*, 30, 180–91.

Goffman, E. (1968) *Asylums*. Harmondsworth: Penguin.

Goffman, E. (1970) *Stigma*. Harmondsworth: Penguin.

Goldstein, J. (1984) 'Foucault among the sociologists', *History and Theory*, 15, 170–92.

Gonos, G. (1977) '"Situation" versus "frame": the "interactionist" and the "structuralist" analyses of everyday life', *American Sociological Review*, 42, 854–67.

Gouldner, A. (1970) *The Coming Crisis of Western Sociology*. London: Heinemann.

Graham, H. (1979) 'Prevention and health: every mother's business' in C. Harris,

The Sociology of the Family (Sociological Review Monograph). Keele: University of Keele.

Graham, H. (1991) 'The concept of caring in feminist research', *Sociology*, 25, 61–78.

Graham, H. and Oakley, A. (1986) 'Competing ideologies of reproduction: medical and maternal perspectives on pregnancy' in C. Currer and M. Stacey (eds), *Concepts of Health, Illness and Disease*. Leamington Spa: Berg.

Grim, P. (1982) 'Scientific and other values' in P. Grim (ed.), *Philosophy of Science and the Occult*. Albany: State University of New York Press.

Grosz, E. (1990) *Jacques Lacan: A Feminist Introduction*. London: Routledge.

Gubrium, J. (1989) 'Local cultures and service policy?', in J. Gubrium and D. Silverman (eds), *The Politics of Field Research*. London: Sage.

Hamilton, P. (1992) 'The Enlightenment and the birth of social science' in S. Hall and B. Gieben, *Formations of Modernity*. Cambridge: Polity.

Hanmer, J. (1990) 'Men, power and the exploitation of women' in J. Hearn and D. Morgan (eds), *Men, Masculinities and Social Theory*. London: Unwin Hyman.

Hannay, D. (1980) 'The iceberg of illness and trivial consultations', *Journal of the Royal College of General Practitioners*, 30, 551–4.

Hart, N. (1985) *The Sociology of Health and Medicine*. Ormskirk: Causeway.

Haug, M. (1973) 'Deprofessionalisation: an alternative hypothesis for the future' in P. Halmos (ed.), *Professionalisation and Social Change*. Keele: University of Keele.

Heart of Our City (no date) *Report*. Sheffield: Heart of our City.

Heart of Our City (1992) *Heart Health Promotion in General Practice*. Sheffield: Heart of Our City.

Hekman, S. (1990) *Gender and Knowledge: Elements of a Postmodern Feminism*. Cambridge: Polity.

Helman, C. (1986) 'Feed a cold, starve a fever' in C. Currer and M. Stacey (eds), *Concepts of Health, Illness and Healing*. Leamington Spa: Berg.

Herzlich, C. and Pierret, J. (1986) 'Illness: from causes to meaning' in C. Currer and M. Stacey (eds), *Concepts of Health, Illness and Healing*. Leamington Spa: Berg.

Hoyes, L. and Means, R. (no date) 'Implementing the White Paper on community care'. Bristol: School for Advanced Urban Studies, University of Bristol.

Hugman, R. (1991) *Power in Caring Professions*. Basingstoke: Macmillan.

Hunt, M. (1991) 'The identification and provision of care for the terminally ill at home by "family" members', *Sociology of Health and Illness*, 13, 375–95.

Hutcheon, L. (1989) *The Politics of Postmodernism*. London: Routledge.

Hutton, P.H. (1988) 'Foucault, Freud and the technologies of the self' in L. Martin, H. Gutman and P.H. Hutton (eds), *Technologies of the Self*. London: Tavistock.

Jameson, F. (1984) 'Post-modernism and the cultural logic of late capitalism', *New Left Review*, 146, 53–92.

Jameson, F. (1988) 'Post-modernism and consumer society' in E.A. Kaplan (ed.), *Postmodernism and its Discontents*. London: Verso.

Jeffrey, R. (1979) 'Normal rubbish: deviant patients in casualty departments', *Sociology of Health and Illness*, 1, 90–108.

Jolley, M. and Brykczynska, G. (1992) *Nursing Care: The Challenge to Change*. London: Edward Arnold.

Kaite, B. (1988) 'The pornographer's body double: transgression is the law' in A. Kroker and M. Kroker (eds), *Body Invaders*. Basingstoke: Macmillan.

Kamin, L. (1981) 'Some historical facts about IQ testing' in H. Eysenck and L. Kamin *Intelligence: The Battle for the Mind*. London: Pan.

Karpf, A. (1988) *Doctoring the Media*. London: Routledge.

Katz, P. (1984) 'Ritual in the operating room', *Ethnology*, 20, 335–50.

Kellner, B. (1988) 'Postmodernism as social theory: some challenges and problems', *Theory, Culture and Society*, 5, 239–70.

King, D. (1987) 'Social constructionism and medical knowledge: the case of transsexualism', *Sociology of Health & Illness*, 9, 351–77.

Kleinman, A. (1980) *Patients and Healers in the Context of Culture*. Berkeley: University of California Press.

Kleinman, A. (1988) *The Illness Narratives*. New York: Basic Books.

Kristeva, J. (1986) *The Kristeva Reader* (edited by T. Moi). New York: Columbia University Press.

Kroker, A. and Kroker, M. (1988) 'Theses on the disappearing body in the hypermodern condition' in A. Kroker and M. Kroker (eds), *Body Invaders*. Basingstoke: Macmillan.

Kumar, K. (1978) *Prophesy and Progress*. Harmondsworth: Penguin.

Lacan, J. (1977) *The Four Fundamental Concepts of Psychoanalysis*. London: Hogarth Press.

Lash, S. (1991) Genealogy and the body: Foucault/Deleuze/Neitzsche' in M. Featherstone, M. Hepworth and B.S. Turner (eds), *The Body*. London: Sage.

Laslett, P. (1992) 'Europe's happy families', *History Today*, 42, March, 8–11.

Laudan, L. (1977) *Progress and Its Problems: Towards a Theory of Scientific Growth*. London: Routledge and Kegan Paul.

Lemert, C. (1992) 'General social theory, irony, postmodernism' in S. Seidman and D. Wagner (eds), *Postmodernism and Social Theory*. Oxford: Blackwell.

Leiderman, D.B. and Grisso, J. (1985) 'The Gomer Phenomenon', *Journal of Health and Social Behaviour*, 26, 222–32.

Letwin, O. (1987) *Ethics, Emotion and the Unity of the Self*. London: Croom Helm.

Levin, D.M. and Solomon, G.F. (1990) 'The discursive formation of the body in the history of medicine', *Journal of Medical Philosophy*, 15, 515–37.

Levi-Strauss, C. (1963) *Structural Anthropology*. Harmondsworth: Penguin.

Lorber, J. (1975) 'Good patients and problem patients: conformity and deviance in a general hospital', *Journal of Health and Social Behaviour*, 16, 213–25.

Lynam, M.J. (1990) 'Examining support in context: a re-definition from the cancer patient's perspective', *Sociology of Health and Illness*, 12, 169–91.

Manier, E. (1980) 'History, philosophy and the sociology of biology', *Studies in the History and Philosophy of Science*, 11, 1–24.

Martin, R. (1988) 'Truth, power, self: an interview with Michel Foucault' in L. Martin, H. Gutman and P.H. Hutton (eds), *Technologies of the Self*. London: Tavistock.

Marsh, P. (1981) 'Life and careers on the soccer terraces' in D. Potter *et al* (eds), *Society and the Social Sciences*: London: Routledge & Kegan Paul.

Maseide, P. (1991) 'Possible abusive, often benign, and always necessary. On power and domination in medical practice', *Sociology of Health and Illness*, 13, 545–61.

Massumi, B. (1992) *A User's Guide to Capitalism and Schizophrenia*. Cambridge, Mass: MIT Press.

May, C. (1992) 'Individual care? Power and subjectivity in therapeutic relationships', *Sociology*, 26, 589–602.

McKeganey, N. (1989) 'On the analysis of medical work: general practitioners, opiate abusing patients and medical sociology' *Sociology of Health and Illness*, 11, 24–40.

Meyer, P. (1990) 'News media responsiveness to public health' in C. Atkin and L. Wallack (eds), *Mass Communication and Public Health*. Newbury Park, CA: Sage.

Miles, A. (1991) *Women, Health and Medicine*. Milton Keynes: Open University Press.

Millman, M. (1977) *The Unkindest Cut: Life in the Backrooms of Medicine*. New York: William Morrow.

Moi, T. (1985) *Sexual Textual Politics*. London: Methuen.

Morgan, G. (1986) *Images of Organization*. London: Sage.

Mumby, D.K. and Stohl, C. (1991) 'Power and discourse in organization studies: absence and the dialectic of control', *Discourse and Society*, 2, 313–32.

Nathanson, C. (1975) 'Illness and the feminine role: a theoretical review', *Social Science and Medicine*, 9, 57–62.

Navarro, V. (1976) *Medicine under Capitalism*. New York: Prodist.

Nead, L. (1992) *The Female Nude: Art, Obscenity and Sexuality*. London: Routledge.

Nettleton, S. (1988) 'Protecting a vulnerable margin: towards an analysis of how the mouth came to be separated from the body', *Sociology of Health and Illness*, 10, 156–69.

Nettleton, S. (1991) 'Wisdom, diligence and teeth: discursive practices and the creation of mothers', *Sociology of Health and Illness*, 13, 98–111.

Nettleton, S. (1992) *Power, Pain and Dentistry*. Milton Keynes: Open University Press.

New, C. (1991) 'Being healthy'. Paper presented to the British Sociological Association Conference, Manchester, April.

Nicolson, P. (1993) 'Public values and private beliefs. Why do women refer themselves for sex therapy?' in J.M. Ussher and C.D. Baker (eds), *Psychological Perspectives on Sexual Problems*. London: Routledge.

Nicolson, M. and McLaughlin, C. (1987) 'Social constructionism and medical sociology: a reply to MR Bury', *Sociology of Health and Illness*, 9, 107–26.

Nicolson, M. and McLaughlin, C. (1988) 'Social constructionism and medical sociology: a study of the vascular theory of multiple sclerosis', *Sociology of Health and Illness*, 10, 234–61.

Oakley, A. (1980) *Women Confined*. Oxford: Martin Robertson.

Oleson, V.L. (1989) 'Caregiving, ethical and informal: emerging challenges in the sociology of health and illness', *Journal of Health and Social Behaviour*, 30, 1–10.

Ostrander, G. (1988) 'Foucault's disappearing body' in A. Kroker and M. Kroker (eds), *Body Invaders*. Basingstoke: Macmillan.

Parker, M. (1990) 'Postmodernism and organisational analysis: a contradiction in terms?' Paper presented at the British Sociological Association Conference, Guildford, April.

Parsons, T. (1951) *The Social System*. New York: Free Press.

Parsons, T. and Fox, R. (1952) 'Illness, therapy and the modern American family', *Journal of Social Issues*, 8, 31–44.

Paul, J.A. (1978) 'Medicine and imperialism' in J. Ehrenreich (ed.), *The Cultural Crisis of Modern Medicine*. New York: Monthly Review Press.

Perakyla, A. (1989) 'Appeals to the experience of the patient in the case of the dying', *Sociology of Health and Illness*, 11, 117–34.

Pinder, R. (1992) 'Coherence and incoherence: doctors' and patients' perspectives on the diagnosis of Parkinson's disease', *Sociology of Health and Illness*, **14**, 1–22.

Pope, C. (1991) 'Trouble in store: some thoughts on the management of waiting lists', *Sociology of Health and Illness*, **13**, 193–212.

Prior, L. (1987) 'Policing the dead: a sociology of the mortuary', *Sociology*, **21**, 355–76.

Radley, A. (1989) 'Style, discourse and constraints in adjustment to chronic illness', *Sociology of Health and Illness*, **11**, 230–52.

Roberts, H. (1985) *The Patient Patients*. London: Routledge & Kegan Paul.

Rose, N. (1989) *Governing the Soul*. London: Routledge.

Rosenau, P.M. (1992) *Post-modernism and the social sciences*. Princeton, NJ: Princeton University Press.

Roth, J. (1977) 'A Yank in the NHS' in A. Davis and G. Horobin (eds), *Medical Encounters*. London: Croom Helm.

Sarup, M. (1988) *An Introduction to Post-structuralism and Postmodernism*. Hemel Hempstead: Harvester Wheatsheaf.

Sawicki, J. (1991) *Disciplining Foucault*. London: Routledge.

Sayers, J. (1986) *Sexual Contradiction: Psychology, Psychoanalysis and Feminism*. London: Tavistock.

Seidman, S. (1992) 'Postmodern social theory as narrative with a moral intent' in S. Seidman and D. Wagner (eds), *Postmodernism and Social Theory*. Oxford: Blackwell.

Sedgewick, P. (1982) *Psychopolitics*. London: Pluto.

Sennett, R. (1980) 'Destructive Gemeinschaft' in R. Bocock *et al.* (eds), *An Introduction to Sociology*. London: Fontana.

Sewell, G. and Wilkinson, B. (1992) '"Someone to watch over me": surveillance, discipline and the just-in-time labour process', *Sociology*, **26**, 271–90.

Signorielli, N. (1990) 'Television and health: images and impact' in C. Atkin and L. Wallack (eds), *Mass Communication and Public Health*. Newbury Park, CA: Sage.

Silverman, D. (1970) *The Theory of Organisations*. London: Heinemann.

Silverman, D. (1983) 'The clinical subject: adolescents in a cleft palate clinic', *Sociology of Health and Illness*, **5**, 253–74.

Silverman, D. (1985) *Qualitative Methodology and Sociology*. Aldershot: Gower.

Silverman, D. (1989) 'The impossible dream of reformism and romanticism' in J. Gubrium and D. Silverman (eds), *The Politics of Field Research*. London: Sage.

Silverman, D. and Perakyla, A. (1990) 'AIDS counselling: the interactional organisation of talk about "delicate" issues', *Sociology of Health and Illness*, **12**, 293–318.

Silverman, H. (1987) *Inscriptions*. London: Routledge & Kegan Paul.

Stacey, M. (1986) 'Concepts of health and illness and the division of labour in health care' in C. Currer and M. Stacey (eds), *Concepts of Health, Illness and Healing*. Leamington Spa: Berg.

Sontag, S. (1978) *Illness as Metaphor*. New York: Farrar, Straus & Giroux.

Strickler, J. (1992) 'Reproductive technology: problem or solution?', *Sociology of Health and Illness*, **14**, 111–32.

Strong, P. (1978) *The Ceremonial Order of the Clinic*. London: Routledge & Kegan Paul.

Strong, P. (1984) 'Viewpoint: the academic encirclement of medicine?', *Sociology of Health and Illness*, 6, 339–58.

Strong, P. (1990) 'Epidemic psychology: a model', *Sociology of Health and Illness*, 12, 249–59.

Strong, P. and Dingwall, R. (1989) 'Romantics and stoics' in J. Gubrium and D. Silverman (eds), *The Politics of Field Research*. London: Sage.

Szasz, T. and Hollender, M. (1956) 'A contribution to the philosophy of medicine: the basic models of the doctor–patient relationship', *Archives of Internal Medicine*, 97, 585–92.

Tattersall, R. (1992) 'Towards an understanding of power in the medical'. Unpublished thesis, Department of General Practice, University of Sheffield.

Townsend, P. and Davidson, N. (1982) *The Black Report: Inequalities in Health*. Harmondsworth: Penguin.

Tuckett, D., Boulton, M., Olson, C. and Williams, A. (1985) *Meetings between Experts*. London: Tavistock.

Turner, B.S. (1984) *The Body and Society*. Oxford: Blackwell.

Turner, B.S. (1987) *Medical Power and Social Knowledge*. London: Sage.

Turner, B.S. (1992) *Regulating Bodies*. London: Routledge.

Twaddle, A.G. (1969) 'Health decisions and sick role variations: an exploration', *Journal of Health and Social Behaviour*, 10, 105–15.

Tyler, S.A. (1986) 'Postmodern ethnography' in J. Clifford and G.E. Marans (eds), *Writing Culture: the Poetics and Politics of Ethnography*. Berkeley: University of California Press.

Ungerson, C. (1983) 'Why do women care?' in J. Finch and D. Grove (eds), *A Labour of Love: Women, Work and Caring*. London: Routledge & Kegan Paul.

Valverde, M. (1991) 'As if subjects existed: analysing social discourses', *Canadian Review of Anthropology and Sociology*, 28, 173–87.

Vaughan, M. (1991) *Curing their Ills*. Cambridge: Polity.

Waissman, R. (1990) 'An analysis of doctor–patient interactions in the case of paediatric renal failure: the choice of home dialysis', *Sociology of Health and Illness*, 12, 432–51.

Waitzkin, H. (1989) 'A critical theory of medical discourse: ideology, social control and the processing of social context in medical encounters', *Journal of Health and Social Behaviour*, 30, 220–39.

Wallack, L. (1990) 'Mass media and health promotion: promise, problem and challenge' in C. Atkin and L. Wallack (eds), *Mass Communication and Public Health*. Newbury Park, CA: Sage.

Weber, M. (1930) *The Protestant Ethic and the Spirit of Capitalism*. London: Unwin University Books.

Westwood, S. (1990) 'Racism, black masculinity and the politics of space' in J. Hearn and D. Morgan, *Men, Masculinities and Social Theory*. London: Unwin Hyman.

White, A. (1990) *Within Neitzsche's Labyrinth*. London: Routledge.

White, S. (1991) *Political Theory and Postmodernism*. Cambridge: Cambridge University Press.

WHO (1985) *Targets for Health for All*. Geneva: World Health Organization.

Wilensky, A. (1964) 'The professionalization of everyone?', *American Journal of Sociology*, 70, 137–58.

Wiles, R. (1993) 'Women and private medicine', *Sociology of Health and Illness*, 15, 68–85.

Williams, G.H. (1989) 'Hope for the humblest?', *Sociology of Health and Illness*, 11, 135–59.

Wright, W. (1982) *The Social Logic of Health*. New Brunswick, NJ: Rutgers University Press.

Zerubavel, E. (1981) *Patterns of Time in Hospital*. Chicago: University of Chicago Press.

Zola, I.K. (1972) 'Medicine as an institution of social control', *Sociological Review*, 20, 487–504.

AUTHOR INDEX

SUBJECT INDEX